A Touchstone Book

the Irish

REVISED EDITION

Donald S. Connery

A Touchstone Book Published by
SIMON AND SCHUSTER   New York

For my father,
Alder F. Connery

All photographs in this book by Brian Seed

CONTENTS

INTRODUCTION TO THE
REVISED EDITION

When this book was first published in the spring of 1968 the people of Ireland, that ancient land of sorrows, were enjoying a prolonged period of peace, progress and well-being. There had been nothing like it in living memory.

The Irish, of course, still had their troubles. In many ways, they were years behind the times. Their living standards were well below those of most other Western nations. Life was hard for most people even though they had a knack for making it look easy. The island was still tragically partitioned between the independent 26-county Republic and the six counties of Northern Ireland where the British flag flies. Individual Irishmen still managed to take sides against each other for reasons of history or religion or language, and sometimes for no reason at all.

Nevertheless, a new generation of Irishmen preferred living in the present to squabbling interminably over the wrongs of the past, and there were clear signs of a thaw in the cold war between the predominantly Roman Catholic south and Protestant-ruled north. Above all, in a crowded, explosive world which seemed to be coming apart at the seams, Ireland looked to outsiders like a serene oasis where the grass is greener, where life is more relaxed than strained, and where people have time for each other. A fair number of foreigners, like the Dutch artist in County Kilkenny who told me that "Ireland is the most civilized country in the world," had already decided that it was a nice place to visit but they would rather live there.

The dramatic improvement in the fortunes of the Irish people in the course of a single decade was the reason for this book. It was a pleasure writing it: good news is hard to come by these days.

A year after the book appeared, however, the image of Ireland as a calm retreat on a troubled planet was shattered by the news of civil rights demonstrations in Ulster, of street warfare between Protestants and Catholics in Belfast and Londonderry, and of British troops flying in to save the Irish from slaughtering each other.

Although the violence, the worst in many decades, seemed to be confined to Northern Ireland, it was possible to believe that the trouble had spread to the rest of the island. Could it be that this eruption of hatred and terror had turned back the Irish clock to the bad old days?

Quite apart from my personal concern for the Irish as a people who deserved happier times, I had an author's reason to fear that events had rendered many of my observations of the Irish scene obsolete. It was only when I set about preparing this new edition of *The Irish* that I realized how little the uproar in Ulster had changed the shape of things in Ireland as a whole. It could almost be said that the greatest unwritten story of the trouble in Northern Ireland was the way the three million people in the Irish Republic quietly went on about their business. They did not react recklessly. They kept their emotions in check. Apart from a few bellicose gestures by their government, it was a hands-off response which would have been hard to imagine ten years ago. Even the I.R.A., the outlawed remnant of the old Irish Republican Army, played no important role. Overall, there was a most mature awareness that interference would only make matters worse and that, anyway, the tide of history was on the side of those who were demanding a more genuine democracy in Ulster.

The explosive events in the North served to emphasize the serenity and stability of the greater part of Ireland. As I read over the seven chapters of this book devoted to the Irish Republic I found little that needed to be changed and little that I wished to add. The general election in 1969, which amounted to a vote of confidence in the existing administration, was notable mainly for giving Irish politics a badly needed infusion of fresh talent, particularly the controversial scholar-diplomat, Dr. Conor Cruise O'Brien. But the new men scarcely made up for the death, some time earlier, of the admirable Donogh O'Malley, whose activities as a modern-minded Minister for Education are described in these pages.

It seemed to me sensible to let my description of life in Eire, the Irish Republic, stand as it is, adding only—in this space—a note about the one area where the process of change is too rapid to hold still on the printed page. I speak of the accelerating liberality of thought and artistic expression in a country which has been notorious for stifling its original thinkers and creators.

The censorship apparatus described in the opening pages of Chapter Seven as an intriguing anachronism still functions but it becomes more irrelevant with each passing day. ("After a half year's absence from Dublin," wrote a Galway priest to the *Irish Times*, in November 1969, "I went with some eagerness into one of its fine bookshops, and it took me a few minutes before I recognized what was different: it was the uniform colour of nudeness on the covers of the paperbacks, nudity and an insistent erotic intent.") The reader might as well read my account of Irish censorship as an early epitaph for a venerable institution which, like the village matchmaker and the boisterous wake, is not long for this world. As the censors fade from the scene, so also do the aggressively philistine politicians and the sin-shouting bishops. Today, the Irish state actually encourages its exiled writers, artists and composers to come home, and the rest to stay home, by freeing them from paying taxes on their earnings from creative works. Finance Minister Charles Haughey, when introducing the new legislation in 1969, said that the purpose was "to create a sympathetic environment here in which the arts can flourish."

As for Northern Ireland, I thought it best to let my Chapter Eight description of "The Neurotic North" remain unchanged as well so that it could set the stage for a new chapter on the civil rights struggle.

The reader will note that I had come to a cautiously optimistic conclusion about the trend of events in Northern Ireland in the 1960s. Although recognizing Ulster's "foundations of cleavage, hatred and intolerance," I had become convinced that these foundations were being eroded, and with increasing rapidity. Not only was the province being exposed to liberalizing forces from the outside, but there was a growing sentiment within Ulster for an end to the historic and brutalizing hostility between Protestants and Catholics. Militant Catholics who were clamoring for an end to discrimination in jobs, housing and politics were beginning to attract significant Protestant support, especially from educated youth. A fair-minded prime minister was attempting to drain away the poisons of history. Reform was not only being demanded but reform was under way—slowly but surely.

As in the American civil rights crusade, however, the pace of change proved to be too slow for those who wanted their freedom now. The arousing of expectations led to a more acute sense of frustration and then to confrontation. It seems inevitable now that demonstrators would take to the streets and that there would be an appalling backlash. Yet the violence led to a political crisis and British intervention, and the outcome is a more earnest effort by men of good will to pull Ulster into the twentieth century. These events have reinforced the central conviction of this book: that life in Ireland—in both parts of Ireland—is changing more swiftly than ever, and changing on the whole for the better.

INTRODUCTION

The quickest way to silence a crowd in a Dublin pub is to say, by way of explaining your presence, that you are writing a book about Ireland. You have been appraised and indulged as an innocent visitor fresh in from Britain or America, with nothing more on your mind than the Blarney Stone and the Ring of Kerry. Now, as the glasses of Guinness and whiskey neats pause in mid-air, the atmosphere changes dramatically, and the Irish eyes are no longer smiling. They reveal scorn, suspicion, incredulity and compassion.

"Is it a travel book you're doing?" asks the little man in the grimy coat who has already stood you to a pint. An affirmative answer will be welcomed, for there is not much harm seen in writing about Killarney or restored castles so long as hordes of tourists are not directed to places where Irishmen go.

No, you are not doing a travel guide. "Is it another history, then?" your companion asks. The word "another" is well chosen. The bookshops in Ireland are groaning under the weight of works by authors, Irish and foreign, dissecting Irish history with toothpicks.

When you protest that nothing is further from your mind, an elderly citizen wants to know which Irish author or playwright is being written about this time. Joyce? Yeats? O'Casey? Swift? Synge? Surely not Brendan Behan? You reveal that you are writing about something quite different: about modern Ireland, the Irish today, the present and future. This too is a silencer, until the man at your other elbow says resentfully, "If you're looking for shamrocks and shillelaghs and pigs in the parlor you'll have a hard time finding them." Knowing how deeply sensitive the Irish are about "stage Irishmen" and the quaint-Ireland image, you protest that it is the reality of Irish life to-day that you are after: economic improvement, social progress, the flight from the land, emigration, the state of the Church, the quality of education, the impact of television, the ambitions of the younger generation.

Your audience groans at the folly of it all. If writing about Irish clichés is abhorrent, writing about "modern" Ireland is absurd. "There's no such place," you are quickly informed. "It's a contradiction in terms." The bewhiskered man at the end of the bar asks, "What do you want to be writing about this bloody country for? It's the sinkhole of Europe." You beg to differ by noting the signs of prosperity all about. Now they know that you are a proper fool, well and truly brainwashed by the Department of External Affairs. "Prosperity, is it? Who's been coddin' ya? It's prosperity for the politicians driving about in luxurious Mercedes, and it's high prices and murderous taxes for the rest of us!" You are loudly informed that the government is composed entirely of scoundrels. You are told lurid tales of their private lives. When you put in a good word for the man who led the country through its economic upsurge of the past decade, the retort is crushing: "That bloody fellow! He couldn't find his way across O'Connell Bridge!"

Now under assault for harboring too naïve and rosy a view of the country's condition, you allow that plenty of things are wrong all right. Inefficient agriculture and poor social services, for example, and the peculiar marriage rate: the dismal prospect that a third of the girls in Dublin will never marry. To which someone cries, "If you saw a third of the girls in Dublin you'd know why!" But now the climate has changed again. Your reference to Ireland's shortcomings is unwelcome. Only the Irish are allowed to criticize the Irish. It is the great national sport, all but sanctified by the Gaelic Athletic Association, and not

open to outsiders. Besides, you learn, no one can possibly understand the Irish except the Irish, who are still working on the
problem. ("I'll tell you the truth, sir, God bless you," said a
Dublin down-and-outer to a visiting journalist, "I've lived in
Ireland every minute of my life, and the more I see of the place,
the less I understand its intentions.") Your friends in the pub
advise you against writing the book at all, and to have another
drink. "After all, what's the point in it, anyway?"

A good question. During the past few years I have often asked
myself why I was spending so much time in a damp, peculiar
island of no particular consequence which lies fretfully beyond
the fringe of Europe. A place, moreover, which tens of thousands of Irish people have been abandoning every year for well
over a century. The novelist George Moore once described Ireland as "a fatal disease" from which "it is the plain duty of
every Irishman to disassociate himself." George Bernard Shaw,
who made his escape early, wrote that "every Irishman who felt
that his business in life was on the higher planes of the cultural
professions . . . felt that his first business was to get out of
Ireland."

Ireland is a seductive, infectious, intoxicating land. I was first
exposed to it twenty years ago and then, like one of those
notorious Irish bachelors fleeing frantically from matrimony,
managed to resist further involvement for fifteen years. When
I finally returned I found that the once sad and grimy beauty
had undergone a striking recovery of spirit. I have made re-
peated journeys since then, but always resisted the temptation
actually to live in the country, the most fatal step of all. When
I asked an American friend in Dublin why she had, despite
great misgivings, chosen to make her life there, she quoted a
neighbor's observation that "once you have lived in Ireland
you're afraid to live anywhere else." The Irish, she had found,
were exasperating and enervating, yet who could deny the richness and variability of their deeply human qualities?

It is this triumph of the Irish personality, even more than the splendors of the Irish landscape, which makes the country unforgettable. But it is a personality so dominating that everyone knows, or thinks he knows, all about the Irish while knowing nothing at all about Ireland as it is today. The radiance of the performers blinds the audience to the stage and its furniture. Moreover, it is the Irish abroad—the millions of emigrants and descendants of emigrants, who outnumber the Irish in Ireland by at least ten to one—who are far better known than the present-day inhabitants of the home country. The popular image of the natives is a kind of gummy Irish stew of comedians, colleens, characters out of *The Quiet Man*, drunk poets, I.R.A. gunmen, censorious priests, and cantankerous old farmers who sleep with their boots on. It is as if time had stood still in the Ould Sod while other nations had moved on, and the infrequent press accounts of Irish affairs which reach the outside world tend to confirm every last stereotype. In a world which is changing with ruthless speed it has been comforting to believe that at least Ireland remains the same. But Ireland is moving on, too, and that is what this book is about.

I am writing in particular about the independent Irish Republic—"Catholic Ireland"—which occupies twenty-six of the thirty-two counties of the island. Predominantly Protestant Northern Ireland, or Ulster, which accounts for the remaining six counties, has half the population of the Republic and a way of life which has become more British than Irish. It has been a more or less self-governing appendage of Great Britain since partition in 1921, but Irish Republicans still dream of seeing it reunited with the rest of the island. For the sake of convenience, at least until I get to the final chapter on Ulster, I mean the Irish Republic and its nearly three million citizens when I speak in generalities about "Ireland" and "the Irish."

Because this is not an anatomy of Irish institutions or a political history, I have relied less on library research than on much personal observation. And while I have interviewed most of the

leaders and many of the primary personalities of the nation, I
have spent more time with farmers, housewives, parish priests,
schoolmasters, journalists and other representative Irishmen.

No writer about the Irish can pretend to absolute objectivity,
however much he may struggle for the fair and balanced view.
One would have to be a mental eunuch not to become emotionally involved in Irish affairs, particularly when the Irish
seem so determined to be their own worst enemies. Though life
has enormously improved since the days when Ireland wallowed
in its misery, there is still meaning in the words of James Connolly, the most radical-minded hero of the Irish uprising of half
a century ago: "The man who is bubbling over with love and
enthusiasm for 'Ireland,' and can yet pass through our streets
and witness all the wrong and suffering, the shame and degradation wrought upon the people of Ireland, aye, wrought by Irishmen upon Irish men and Irish women, without burning to end
it, is, in my opinion, a fraud and a liar in his heart."

One can love Ireland, of course, and enjoy the Irish as a
unique and delightful people, while casting a cold eye on their
proceedings. One must, in fact, because taking the Irish seriously
is a soul-searing experience. "Once a writer's eye gets chilly
about their beautiful souls," wrote Sean O'Faolain, "he becomes
like the only sober man at a drunken party, and the only decent
thing for him to do then is either to get blind drunk with the
rest of the boys (all singing in chorus, 'I'll take you home again,
Kathlee-een') or else go home and scrub himself clean in a raging satire on the whole boiling lot of them."

Satire probably would be more decent, but a straightforward
description of the Irish as they are—not as they pretend to be,
or are supposed to be—may be more useful. Such is the purpose
of this book. It is how the Irish, at this moment in history, seem
to me.

Chapter 1

THE AWAKENING

*Its shapes and contours make of it a paradise that is
unhappy. And so it must forever remain, far away from
the stream of life and with the sadness of all things that
are a little remote from reality. . . . This green country
on the edge of the world, with nothing beyond it.*

—SACHEVERELL SITWELL, 1936

*The years ahead will be a great time to be alive and to
be young—and to be Irish.*

—SEAN LEMASS, 1966

Ireland is not the place it used to be. The sweet, slow, sorrowful
land of cheerful indolence and doleful memory is being over-
taken by something called progress. Ireland is changing. It is
changing today more profoundly than at any time since the
Great Hunger of more than a century ago.

In the wild west of Ireland, where they say the next parish is
Boston, old people sitting by turf fires in primitive cottages watch
television and shake their heads at the sight of young people
arguing with a priest. At Shannon Airport, where a new industrial town of Scandinavian modernity has risen beyond the
runways, made-in-Ireland Dutch pianos and South African industrial diamonds fly out to customers in Europe and America.
In the Bay of Bantry the peacefulness of Whiddy Island is shat-

tered by the construction of one of the world's greatest depots for oil brought in by the world's largest ships. In Dublin, as rush-hour traffic jams form in the shadow of stately Georgian town houses, dignitaries as well as plain Irishmen in search of a free drink converge at a reception for the Bolshoi Ballet. Bookshops openly display copies of *Ulysses* and some of the more shocking American paperbacks. A physician reports on TV that the use of the birth-control pill is widespread in Ireland despite the ban on contraceptives.

Irish farmers who used to count themselves lucky to own a horse protest against national agricultural policy by blocking country roads with battalions of farm machinery. City people complain about the shortage of maids. A headline announces: "PROTESTANT PRESIDES AT CATHOLIC CEREMONY." Advertisements promote sauna baths and Mediterranean holidays. In sleek lounge bars which threaten the existence of the aromatic Irish pubs the Irish talk as only the Irish can talk, about the weather and scandal and government foolishness, about the politician who talked back to the bishop, and about beat clubs; freeze-dried vegetables, comprehensive schools, the Language Freedom Movement, the Censorship Reform Society, and the leftward trend of Irish politics.

In a popular Irish magazine a marriage counselor writes of the exhausted condition of countless Irish mothers and wives and declares, "The pace of life has increased almost beyond bearing." In Cork, a leading citizen, disturbed about the state of the nation, tells a foreign visitor that "the fast-buck people are taking over."

Profound Change

In 1916, as the heart of Dublin lay in smoking ruins after an abortive one-week attempt at revolution by a small band of patriots, William Butler Yeats wrote:

All changed, changed utterly;
A terrible beauty is born.

But Ireland did not change utterly. The uprising after more than seven hundred years of British rule led to the winning of independence, to partition and the civil war in the early 1920s, and then to the supernationalism and search for self-sufficiency in the decades following, but these were all slowly drawn-out political changes which scarcely affected the resigned and often desperate way of life of ordinary Irishmen. The dreamed-of social and economic upheaval never happened.

"In the history of Europe," writes a Catholic sociologist, "Ireland's revolution surely is among the most un-revolutionary . . . self-government, once achieved, led to no radical or violent uprooting of established institutions." Ireland, for all of its newfound liberty and sound democratic machinery, remained one of the most backward, conservative, dispirited and moribund nations in the Western world. Less than fifteen years ago *The Vanishing Irish* and other alarming reports warned that the Irish nation, with multitudes emigrating and multitudes more resisting marriage, was committing racial suicide.

The malaise was expressed by Sean O'Casey:

> I'm afraid we're withering. Even the shadow of what we once were is fading. . . . Someone or something is ruining us. . . . What do we send out to the world now but woeful things —young lads and lassies, porther, greyhounds, sweep tickets, and the shamrock green. We've scatthered ourselves about too much. We've spread ourselves over the wide world, and left our own sweet land thin. We're just standing on our knees now.

The phenomenon of today's Ireland is that it has come up from its knees, and that the Irish people, for the first time in centuries, have begun to believe in themselves and in their possibilities. Obsessive concentration on a tragic past has given way to a restless anticipation of a brighter future. The glum fatalism of a rigorously religious people has been superseded by the consideration that the fault is not in the stars but in themselves. The psychological change in Ireland is the most important of all, but it is less visible than the evidence that Ireland is now experiencing a delayed social and economic revolution.

A once unique community has begun to take on the trappings of the affluent society and the welfare state. It is experiencing, decades after most other European states, the growing pains of industrialization and urbanization. No longer remote from the main currents of world affairs, it is moving into modern times, but as warily as a farmer's daughter anxious for sophistication yet fearful of losing her virtue in the wicked big city.

"This has been a mummified society," said a professor's wife in Galway. "Now the wraps are coming off." The easygoing tempo of Irish life has suddenly quickened, and, while much in Ireland still looks the same as always, things will never be the same again. There are simply too many impatient young people who would agree with the writer in *Hibernia* magazine who said that "we must cease being a nation of unskilled workers, public-house orators and back-garden gossips." For generations the Irish have had the world's lowest marriage rate as well as the latest marriages. Today the Irish are marrying more willingly, and they are marrying much earlier. Despite the continuing national disgrace of high emigration, the Irish population for the first time in well over a century is actually increasing. In a generation's time the Irish will look back to the slow-motion Ireland of picturesque poverty and wonder where it all went.

Bitter History

Most Irishmen are unaware of the magnitude of the changes now taking place. They know, of course, that much is happening today that would have been inconceivable only a few years ago, but they would question whether things are *really* changing. They are natural skeptics, conservative to the core, distrustful of change, and always ready to demonstrate that Ireland is indeed "the land of derision." The attitude is expressed in one handy Irish line: "Ireland has a great future, but then she always has had."

There is little in Irish history to give reason for optimism. The past sits mockingly on the shoulder of every Irishman who seeks improvement or thinks things will change for the better. To feel a genuine glow of pride in their native accomplishments, as distinct from those of their invaders, the Gaelic Irish must root far back in history.

The Celts came to Ireland from the Continent about 350 B.C. and prevailed over the more primitive tribes already inhabiting the island. They were quarrelsome, high-spirited, pleasure-loving men of quick emotions. Looking back over the panorama of Irish history since those early times, G. K. Chesterton was moved to write:

> For the great Gaels of Ireland
> Are the men that God made mad,
> For all their wars are merry
> And all their songs are sad.

The Celts built a Gaelic civilization which flourished in splendid isolation from the Roman Empire. After Saint Patrick brought Christianity to Ireland in the fifth century, thus becoming the national saint of the Irish, the country developed into one of the great intellectual centers of Europe. During the Dark Ages it was "the island of saints and scholars" which kept the light of Christian learning bright when it was being extinguished elsewhere. The astonishingly beautiful Book of Kells in the Trinity College library is the best surviving example of the high Irish art of illuminating Latin manuscripts. Gaelic literature flowered at the same time, and it is this memory which helps inspire those present-day Irishmen who persist in the dream of restoring the ancient language as the common tongue of contemporary Ireland.

(Irish Gaelic belongs to the Goidelic branch of Celtic, one of the original languages of Western Europe. It is almost identical to the Gaelic, or Erse, of the Scottish Highlands, and related to the Welsh language. In Ireland today it is customarily called "Irish" instead of Gaelic, and I have done so in this book.)

As the Irish went from strength to strength in their native culture, they weakened as a military power and became sorely divided internally. Whereas in the pre-Christian years the Irish were dreaded marauders who repeatedly raided Britain, now it was they who came under attack. In the ninth and tenth centuries the Vikings stormed into Ireland. Their galleys, as Joyce wrote in *Ulysses*, "ran here to beach, in quest of prey, their bloodbeaked prows riding low on a molten pewter surf." They conquered much of the island and founded such trading towns as Dublin, Cork, Limerick, Waterford and Wexford. King Brian Boru, Ireland's greatest hero of ancient times, drove out the Vikings after a struggle which reached its climax at the Battle of Clontarf in 1014. He and his sons lost their lives in the fight and left an Ireland full of feuding lesser kings. But the Irish had another 150 years of self-rule before, with the Norman invasion late in the twelfth century, they succumbed to seven centuries of foreign domination. It was not until 1536–41, however, that the whole of Ireland was brought under the English Crown. Henry VIII was the first English monarch to assume the title of King of Ireland.

The story of occupied Ireland is far less a history of glorious deeds than a melancholy tale of humiliation and frustration. Over and over again, the native Catholic Irish rebelled, and the discontented Anglo-Irish rebelled, but they were beaten down. The Irish masses were deprived of the most elementary human rights, driven from their land and forced to flee the country. It is a wonder that the spirit of the nation survived at all, for the Irish, as Jonathan Swift saw them, became "A servile race

in folly nursed / Who truckle most when treated worst." The
Statutes of Kilkenny, enacted in 1366, were designed to halt
the weakening of the English colony through too intimate association with the native Irish. They forbade the settlers to marry
the Irish, speak their language, use their laws, maintain Irish
poets, bards or minstrels, wear Irish costumes, or otherwise
adopt local customs.

Harsh anti-Irish measures taken in the cause of racial purity,
and to safeguard the imperial rule, were given a religious justification with the coming of the Reformation in the sixteenth
century. The Act of Supremacy was imposed on Ireland by
Henry VIII. Under Edward VI the saying of Mass was made
illegal and the Book of Common Prayer was introduced. Per-
secution of the Catholics became wholesale under Elizabeth I.
She had to contend with widespread rebellion after she was
excommunicated by Pius V. A major revolt in 1579, led by one
of the Munster earls, James Fitzmaurice Fitzgerald, was crushed.
The herds of the pastoral Irish in Munster, the southwest
territory, were then slaughtered, and such an effective scorched-
earth policy was carried out that large-scale famine resulted.
Great portions of land were "planted" with English Protestants.
Sir Walter Raleigh was but one of many English adventurers
who were richly rewarded in Irish estates for their work in
suppressing the Irish insurgents. After the Catholic nobles of
northern Ireland fled to the Continent in 1607 in the famous
"Flight of the Earls," Ulster too underwent a massive plantation
of English and Scottish settlers. It completely altered the character of the area and paved the way for the partition of Ireland
in this century.

When the Irish fought back against their oppressors, Oliver
Cromwell's forces massacred thousands of rebels and innocents
in Drogheda and Wexford in 1649. They herded a multitude of
Irishmen into exile and uprooted so many Catholics from their
land (driving them "to hell or Connaught") that three quarters
of Ireland came into the possession of Protestant landlords.

Inevitably, many of the new owners did not work the property themselves, but remained in England and lived well on the rents provided by their Irish tenants. Such large-scale absentee landlordism was the cause of much of the wretchedness of the Irish peasant.

The notorious Penal Laws of 1695 and onward virtually made slaves of the Irish Catholics. It was even said by a Lord Chancellor that "the law does not suppose any such person to exist as an Irish Roman Catholic." Edmund Burke denounced the Penal Laws as "well fitted for the oppression, impoverishment and degradation of a people, and the debasement in them of human nature itself." Catholics were deprived of the right to vote or hold office. They were forbidden to bear arms. They were barred from teaching, trading and entering the professions. Catholic estates, because of new restrictions on ownership and inheritance, were broken into ever smaller portions. A Catholic owning a horse worth more than five pounds could have it taken from him at that price by any Protestant. Catholic schools were forbidden and the Catholic clergy outlawed. Any bishop found in the country was liable to be hanged, drawn and quartered. The Catholic Church went underground. Priests said Mass in the fields while lookouts kept watch for the authorities, and children were taught clandestinely in the "hedge schools." More than ever, the Irish became dodgers of the law, ingratiating talkers and masters of deception. Such character traits linger on. V. S. Pritchett tells of asking an Irishman the whereabouts of an old friend and receiving as an answer, "I have no treasonable information."

It was during this anguished period that Jonathan Swift, dean of St. Patrick's Cathedral in Dublin, drew attention to the hordes of emaciated children roaming the country by suggesting in *A Modest Proposal* that they be fattened and eaten. ("I have been assured by a very knowing American of my acquaintance in London that a young healthy child, well nourished, is at a year old a most delicious, nourishing, and wholesome food, stewed, roasted, or boiled . . .") For the Anglo-Irish Ascendancy, however, eighteenth-century Dublin was a place to be proud of as one of the most elegant and sophisticated cities of Europe. The Anglo-Irish, moreover, were prospering commercially, and they had succeeded in winning a large measure of self-rule for Ireland. The worst abuses of the Penal Laws were eventually removed. Catholics were permitted to acquire property and to worship more freely. Then in 1798 the Society of United Irishmen, led by a Protestant lawyer, Theobald Wolfe Tone, and inspired by the French Revolution, staged a rebellion, but it was a fiasco and the captured Tone committed suicide in prison. Another Anglo-Irish Protestant, Robert Emmet, led another rising five years later. It too was a failure, amounting to little more than a street riot, but his speech from the dock helped put him in the front rank of Irish martyrs. "When my country takes her place among the nations of the earth," he said, "then, and not till then, let my epitaph be written."

In the meantime, the Act of Union of 1800, the handiwork of Prime Minister William Pitt, had dissolved the Irish Parliament and brought Ireland under the direct rule of London. Dublin lost its importance overnight and became a mere provincial city. Many of its most distinguished citizens packed up and left for good. Ireland lay motionless during most of the first half of the nineteenth century, but the period was marked by the emergence of Daniel O'Connell, an Irish-speaking Catholic lawyer from Kerry, as the dynamic champion of Catholic civil rights. Gladstone called him "the greatest popular leader the world has ever seen." His personal magnetism and demagogic skill brought about the Catholic emancipation of 1829 which admitted Catholics to Parliament and to most public offices. Nonetheless, the Ascendancy remained in control of Irish affairs, and O'Connell's fight for Home Rule, for the repeal of the Act of Union, failed. He died in 1847, a broken man, in the midst of the greatest disaster in Irish history.

The island's population had risen to well over eight million persons. Vast numbers existed on little more than potatoes grown on stony patches of land owned by absentee landlords. Beginning in 1845, Ireland was struck by the potato blight. During the several years of the Great Famine, which was made worse by cruel evictions of families from their cottages, some one and a half million people died of hunger and disease, while a million more fled on the "coffin ships" to North America. Emigration continued at such a pace that by the end of the century Ireland's pre-Famine population had been cut nearly in half. Much of the distress was relieved, but very slowly relieved, by a succession of land reforms which established fair rents and made it possible for tenants to acquire ownership of the farms they worked. Despite everything, most Irishmen seemed content to remain British subjects—or else they had no stomach for drastic political changes. There was no mass sentiment for rebellion and no large support for the revolts of the Fenians and other secret and semi-secret societies. There was, however, a popular desire for Home Rule and an awakening pride in the Irish language and culture, thanks largely to the Gaelic League, founded in 1893 by a Protestant scholar, Douglas Hyde.

The Irish champion of Home Rule was Charles Stewart Parnell, the "uncrowned king of Ireland," but the cause was gravely damaged by the revelations of Parnell's affair with Mrs. Kitty O'Shea and their marriage after a sensational divorce case. Home Rule was finally voted by Parliament in 1914, despite the objections of the Ulster Protestants, who feared Catholic domination, but its operation was suspended for the duration of World War I. There were Irish rebels, however, who wanted nothing less than an independent Irish republic. They struck in Dublin on Easter Monday, 1916, and held out for a week before surrendering. It was yet another fiasco, and one which was particularly resented by the Irish public because of the tens of thousands of Irishmen fighting in the British forces on the Continent. One of the principal revolutionaries, Thomas

MacDonagh, explained in his speech to the court, "We do not profess to represent the mass of the people of Ireland. We stand for the intellect and the soul of Ireland. To Ireland's soul and intellect the inert mass, drugged and degenerate by ages of servitude, must, in the distant day of resurrection, render homage and free service, receiving in return the vivifying impress of a free people."

The mindless execution of MacDonagh, Patrick Pearse, Thomas Clarke, James Connolly and eleven other leaders of the uprising changed the public mood. The Sinn Fein ("Ourselves Alone") movement, founded by Arthur Griffith in 1900, set up an Irish national assembly—the original Dail Eireann—in 1919. The nation became ever more defiant. Martial law was imposed, and for two and a half years the island was convulsed by the acts of terror against the authorities by the Irish Republican Army (the celebrated I.R.A.) and other armed rebels, and by the savage reprisals of the Auxiliaries and the "Black and Tans," the special security forces which had been recruited in England to reinforce the regular constabulary. Sinn Fein rejected the Home Rule Act of 1920, which split off the six most Protestant Ulster counties from the rest of the island, but a truce was arranged in June 1921 and the Anglo-Irish Treaty was signed the following December. Although partition was a high price to pay, the creation of the 26-county Irish Free State meant that independence had been won at last. The achievement was soured, however, by the civil war between the new government under William T. Cosgrave and the anti-Treaty dissidents, led by Eamon de Valera, who were finally crushed in 1923. The Free State had a status within the British Empire similar to that of the Dominion of Canada. As the years passed the southern Irish cut most of their formal links with Britain but they remained within the Commonwealth until the establishment of the Republic of Ireland soon after World War II.

Political freedom brought no relief from the day-to-day difficulties of life in Ireland. The Irish were too poor and dispirited to forge on in a spirit of optimism. Even today, when the Irish are better off than at any other time in history, there is much that they find depressing. More than 15,000 men and women, mostly young and pitifully ill-prepared for life in the outside world, flee the country every year for better opportunities abroad. "Ireland is like a life raft," said Dr. Noel Browne, an outspoken physician-politician. "The surplus people are pushed off. The ones who are left are all right." The flight from the land has so denuded the poorer regions of the island of everyone but the very old and the very young that "Save the West" committees are crying for action. The so-called industrial boom is flagging. Prices are high, and taxes on higher incomes are severe enough to discourage enterprise. Anti-intellectualism and the "censorship mentality" have had a debilitating effect on the Irish arts. The educational system is backward by modern European standards, and social-welfare concepts are decades behind the times. In the teeth of the Vatican Council's historic liberalization of Catholicism, the Church in Ireland remains reactionary: the crotchety mother-in-law of the Church in Rome.

And yet, for all that, the ferment in Irish life today is so pronounced when compared to the national inertia of only a decade ago that even an Irish optimist, that rare figure, can hold his ground in an argument. When I first went to Ireland soon after World War II it seemed to me a most despondent place, but it was actually faring well when compared to those European lands which had suffered grievously during the war. By the late 1950s, however, Ireland was little improved and its economy was even going backward. During the dramatic years of Western Europe's economic recovery, Ireland's rate of growth was less than two per cent a year, and then it actually declined between 1955 and 1958. As many as sixty thousand people voted with their feet each year by emigrating to Britain, America and elsewhere in the world—the greatest numbers since the era of the Famine. As if in frustration about Ireland's immovability and the failure to have achieved so many of the aims of the Irish martyrs, extremists of the outlawed Irish Republican Army stepped up their useless hit-and-run attacks along the Northern Ireland border.

Revival of Confidence

The Irish yearned for something, anything, to breathe life again into a sinking society. The times produced the men, and the men turned out to be hardheaded and almost un-Irish economic activists who thought more about the Gross National Product than the glories of Gaelic culture. A well-meaning but ineffectual coalition government was swept aside in 1957 to bring back to power the Fianna Fail Party of the indestructible Eamon de Valera, one of independent Ireland's founding fathers. This by itself was hardly a good omen. It was de Valera who, as prime minister during most of independent Ireland's existence, had championed the notion of an ascetic, isolated nation living in "frugal comfort." But now he gave his blessing to a blueprint for national growth prepared by Dr. Kenneth Whitaker, the brilliant Secretary of the Department of Finance. In 1958 it became Ireland's First Programme for Economic Expansion, a five-year plan to propel the nation into modern times. When de Valera moved on the following year to become President of Ireland, a largely ceremonial job, he was succeeded by Sean Lemass, the most industrious and pragmatic of his ministers, a man who had longed for a free hand to force the pace of development.

Because Ireland catches cold whenever Britain sneezes, it was the new government's good fortune that the drive for foreign investment and new industry coincided with the ebullient years when the British, along with most Western Europeans, surged on to mass prosperity. Instead of being left out of things, the Irish too "never had it so good." Under the First Programme, now succeeded by a more ambitious Second Programme (too ambitious, as it turns out), the growth rate was twice as high as the cautious planners had predicted. Within only a few bracing years, two hundred new factories were opened, thirty thousand new jobs were created, and emigration was cut by more than half. Psychologically, it was a powerful tonic, almost a magic elixir, which did wonders for Ireland's deep-seated inferiority complex. Legions of reformers and men of action had tried and failed to rouse a people who had become accustomed to servility and passivity. Lemass now had the supporting fire of prosperity as he called for new efforts. He said in his speeches, "Our hopes in the future rest on our confidence in ourselves, and on the final dying out of the old slave spirit which, in the past, bedevilled our efforts to get the nation reorganized for progress, and which still influences the behaviour of some individuals."

When I went to Ireland early in 1963 to see what was going on, it was impossible not to feel the atmospheric change or notice the many signs of modernization. There was an unaccustomed briskness about the way Dubliners moved and a freshness of complexion which I had not seen before. Even the grumbles were indicative: there were too many Germans and other foreigners moving into the country to suit some people; there were complaints about all the money being spent on jet airliners and luxury hotels; and it was annoying that the upsurge in car ownership meant that the Irish would now have to take examinations for driving licenses.

I asked a young newspaperman, Cathal O'Shannon, who has since become a leading TV reporter, what the Irish were like these days. "More aware of world events than they were," he said. "Rather proud of their soldiers in the Congo. Working harder, living on hire purchase, glued to television sets, better dressed, spending money. The pace is slower than in England, the country isn't crowded, housing is improving though prices are rising. They are a different race altogether from the Famine Irish of one hundred twenty years ago." Another friend, Martin

Sheridan, added something I have never forgotten: "Now we are seeing the first *free* Irishmen."

The new freedom was being expressed, though often with timidity, in a variety of ways. Increased economic and social security meant that the individual Irishman had more choices to make: in the duration of his schooling, in the work he would do, in the manner of his existence. It was no longer a simple matter of scraping by or getting out. The opening up of Ireland's windows to winds of change meant that he was exposed to new, and foreign, and "dangerous" ideas. He was more willing to consider taboo subjects, to resist the pressures for conformity which can be brutal in Ireland, and to question orthodox opinion.

Though the Irishman is reputed to be the supreme individualist and a natural rebel, he has been cowed by authority during most of Irish history. Even in today's Ireland, for all of its democratic content, and for all the talk against the autocratic manners of Church and state, the Irishman is more submissive than many other Europeans. He suppresses any truly radical thoughts with all the vigor of an old-style parish priest thundering against sin. Nonetheless, the dying out and waning influence of the older generation of Irish patriots has emboldened younger Irishmen to question old beliefs and demand more contemporary solutions to social and economic disorders. It has even become possible for the members of Ireland's small and timorous Labour Party to identify themselves as socialists.

The essential business of creating and sustaining Irish self-confidence was given an historic boost in the summer of 1963 when John F. Kennedy flew into Ireland for a brief but significant "homecoming." His presence gave a kind of presidential seal of approval to the nation's new look. I listened in the gallery of the Irish Parliament when he said, "The Ireland of 1963, one of the youngest of nations and the oldest of civilizations, has discovered that the achievement of nationhood is not an end, but a beginning." He spoke glowingly of Irish progress and rising living standards. "Other nations in the world in whom Ireland has long invested her people and her children are now investing their capital as well as their vacations in Ireland. . . . This revolution is not yet over."

The visit of the extravagantly admired young President was a time of high emotion for the Irish. It was the first time that all Irishmen agreed on the same thing at the same time. As the great-grandson of an Irish emigrant of Famine times his occupancy of the most powerful office on earth was as much an inspiration as his vitality was a rebuke to Irish lethargy. A women's-magazine editor in Dublin wistfully described Kennedy to me as "the Irishman of the year 2000." His assassination just half a year later was a blow to the Irish. They still place his portrait next to that of the Pope in homes throughout the country. There are, as well, mounted bits of poetry, maudlin but heartfelt, tacked and taped to many an Irish mantlepiece. This one, for example, which I found in a little house on one of the Aran Islands:

> If tears, Dear Jack,
> Could bring you back,
>   'Tis live you'd surely be.
>
> But none have left
> Their tears unshed
>   For John F. Kennedy.

Garret FitzGerald, a noted Irish commentator, has written of Kennedy's "immediate rapport" with the Irish people:

He and the crowds understood each other. It was a relationship that no one who is not Irish can ever fully understand. The Irish, contrary to common belief, are not a sentimental people, and they have no time at all for those third- or fourthgeneration Irish-Americans who return to Ireland believing it to be full of leprechauns. John Kennedy was unsentimental too. He was tough, loved a laugh, and treated us as we really are. That's why he was different, and that's why we worship the Kennedy family.

Three years after the Kennedy visit, the Irish celebrated the fiftieth anniversary of the Easter Rising which had sparked the independence struggle. The momentum of change by 1966 was undeniable despite a disillusioning tumble in the economic-growth rate. It could be seen in the way that the tourists were pouring into Ireland and in the cascade of reports by commissions and study groups calling for the improvement of everything from higher education to the fishing industry. As economic planning came to be taken for granted, reformers were concentrating more on social justice. The political parties, all of them essentially conservative, were shifting en masse to the left, though not so far left as to cause undue concern in a deeply Catholic country. There is a dedication to the idea of *laissez-faire* economics which would warm the heart of a Goldwater, but what the Irish do in practice is something else. The lack of private capital and the limitations of Irish private enterprise have compelled a degree of state intervention in industry which is greater than that of any other nation in Western Europe.

To a casual observer of the Irish scene, the Easter Rising ceremonies would have seemed a likely occasion for a great amount of national self-congratulation on the achievement of better times in a free and independent Ireland. On the contrary, the ceremonies themselves and the whole pattern of events in 1966 and afterward revealed a discontent and impatience of notable proportions. Disappointment in the past and eagerness to move on into the future were there in equal proportions.

To older patriots and the dwindling ranks of ultranationalists, the trouble was that Ireland was still a partitioned island and the Irish language had not been restored as the common tongue. The Union Jack still flew in Ulster, and the great mass of Irishmen spoke English to each other. Noting that 1969 would be the eight-hundredth anniversary of the landing of the Normans in Ireland, one nationalist publication demanded: "ENGLAND NOW IN IRELAND 797 YEARS. MUST GET THEM OUT BY 1969!"

A few weeks before the Easter events the foremost landmark in Dublin, Nelson's Pillar, which had stood in the middle of O'Connell Street for 158 years, was blown up, or down, early one morning. The stone head of Admiral Nelson turned up at a London antique shop a short while later, but the dynamiters, presumably nationalist extremists, were not apprehended. It was widely believed that the authorities were at no pains to find the parties who had done it. Though most Irishmen regretted the action, if only because it destroyed the best sight-seeing perch in the capital, they would not have enjoyed the sight of their countrymen going to jail for disposing of an English admiral. A ballad was soon going the rounds about "The Man Who Blew Oul' Nelson Down":

> Now some countries like to sing
> All about their noble king,
> And praise the head that wears the royal crown.
> Ah! but we'll remember long
> And immortalise in song
> The man who blew oul' Nelson down.

Irishmen could not help but admire the efficiency of the Nelson operation, which damaged little on O'Connell Street but the column and the statue. When the military experts moved in afterward to explode what remained of the column for easier removal they managed to shatter office and shop windows. It was one of those Irish mishaps which are so lovingly discussed in the Dublin pubs. The toppling of Nelson led to fears that the Easter ceremonies would be marred by a renewal of I.R.A. violence. (The Irish Republican Army, a secret volunteer force, is banned in all parts of Ireland, but its remaining zealots still meet and carry on training exercises.) Along with other foreign journalists in Dublin I was given many a hint of violence to come. Though it is an old Irish sport to put gullible foreign reporters on false scents, the warnings could not be discounted. It had not been long since extremists, waving their "Smash Partition" banners, called for the use of force to recover Ulster.

As it turned out, the anniversary ceremonies were as decorous and as nonviolent as they could be. It looked as if the days of the nationalist hotheads were gone for good. A number of ordinary Dubliners I met could not be bothered to attend the parades. They were sick of the sight of "the old fossils" going on and on about "the martyred dead" and the sacrifices of a half century ago. "What's all that got to do with me?" asked a taxi driver. "There was only one great man in the lot of 'em, and that was James Connolly. He was for the workingman, but you won't find his statue on the streets of Dublin."

Those Irishmen who are more concerned with social realities than Gaelic nostalgia find much that is disappointing in present-day Ireland. "Maybe," said Sean O'Faolain, "all we old Republicans idealized too much." At the time of the anniversary he wrote:

What we have got is a modern version of the kind of society that James Joyce described so contemptuously, as he saw it, in the Dublin of 1902, a society from which this modern thing differs only in that Irish names have been plastered over English names . . . We have set up a society of urbanised peasants, whose whole mentality, whose whole image of life is, like that antiquated society, based on privilege; a society run by a similar minority of ambitious businessmen, "rugged individualists" looking down at, fearing, even hating "the men and women of no property," thriving on the same theory of God-made inequality, welcoming and abetting, by the same self-interested silence, the repression of every sign of individual criticism or reconsideration of the social and moral results of history.

In the early summer of 1966, Eamon de Valera ran for a second seven-year term as president of Ireland. Though in his eighties and nearly blind, he was still a commanding figure, as statuesque and majestically aloof as his junior in France, General de Gaulle. He had been the dominant personality in Irish life since the days of Lenin, Lloyd George and Woodrow Wilson. As Chief of State he was supposed to be above party politics and everyday government, but his influence was still important, and he symbolized old-fashioned Ireland.

De Valera's opponent for the presidency was a relatively young and little-known lawyer named T. F. O'Higgins. As expected, de Valera won, but his margin of victory—less than one per cent of the more than a million votes cast—was so slight that it was virtually a repudiation. It was widely interpreted as a cry for new men and new ideas. Half a year later, Sean Lemass, at sixty-seven the most pragmatic and modern-minded of the Old Guard, stepped down as prime minister in favor of a younger man, Jack Lynch. As the architect and manager of Ireland's economic recovery, Lemass had been the most progressive Irish leader since independence, but he too was a "1916 man" and he felt it was time to make room for the next generation.

Only a year earlier a French film producer visiting Ireland had commented, "This seems to be a country led by old people in all spheres. Your young people know this and feel they cannot fight against it." It was suddenly realized that this kind of observation, while true enough in the Irish countryside and in many walks of life, was becoming out of date. Indeed, in some quarters, youth (which in Ireland stretches from the twenties through the forties) was clearly in the ascendancy. The Irish Cabinet, thanks to the appointments made by Lemass in the years just before his retirement, was said to be the youngest in Europe. Young men of ability and enterprise were commanding key government departments and the semi-state industries. Though the hierarchy of the Irish Catholic Church had an antediluvian image, a number of young priests, sometimes behind their bishops' backs, were calling for social changes and saner attitudes about sex and popular culture. Television was largely in the hands of young Irishmen who had become national personalities. The chances for youth to make itself heard were greater than ever. A Trinity College student named Brian Trevaskis, who achieved a certain notoriety for describing a well-known bishop on television as a moron, typified new attitudes when he wrote to a newspaper: "My father and his generation have accepted poverty as being the Will of God. They have equally accepted slums as being inevitable. What we poor, passionate, immature members of the younger generation do not accept and do not believe is that either slums or poverty *are* inevitable, but have more to do with the will of man than the Will of God."

Liberalization

There have been at least five principal events during the past decade which have converged to revitalize Ireland: the economic improvement which has created both confidence and new demands; the shift from isolationism to outward-looking national policies; the sweeping in of all manner of foreign influences; the advent of television; and the liberalization of the Roman Catholic Church initiated by Pope John XXIII.

Nineteen fifty-eight was both the year that Ireland conceived its Programme for Economic Expansion and the first year of Pope John. Lemass was soon justifying his ventures in state-financed industry and economic planning by referring to the Pope's encyclical *Pacem in Terris*, which took the view that no political system is undesirable if it benefits the people. The Prime Minister became known as a "Pope John socialist."

Because the new economics called for a relaxation of the nation's extreme protectionism and for a campaign to lure foreign investors to Ireland, it followed that Ireland must play a more active role on the international stage. After independence the country had closed into itself. Tariff walls were raised high.

Ireland moved away from Britain and finally withdrew from the Commonwealth. It remained stubbornly neutral through World War II even as tens of thousands of Irish volunteers served in the British forces. Membership in the North Atlantic Treaty Organization was rejected after the war on the grounds that Britain still occupied Ulster; to join an alliance with Britain would, it was argued, amount to recognition of Northern Ireland's separate existence.

A new attitude began to take hold after Ireland entered the United Nations in 1955. As Cold War neutrals the Irish enjoyed a certain popularity among the Afro-Asian representatives. Ireland was, after all, a veteran among the world's ex-colonies. It thus acquired a disproportionate influence in UN circles, at least for a time, despite an almost total lack of military and economic strength and a population smaller than that of Chicago. Ireland had an outstanding UN ambassador, Frederick Boland, who was president of the General Assembly when Nikita Khrushchev staged his famous shoe-banging tantrum. Thousands of Irish troops served, and twenty-six died, on peace-keeping missions in the Congo. The Congo experience had interesting side effects. Irish soldiers used Irish as a means of keeping their commands and messages secret. (An opponent of "compulsory" Irish in the schools told me it was the only time the old language ever came in useful.) Irishmen took to saying, by way of insult, "You bloody Baluba!," having in mind the tribe that ambushed an Irish contingent in 1960 and killed ten soldiers. The Irish have since soldiered elsewhere in the world for the United Nations, particularly in Cyprus, and one consequence is a new consciousness that many another small nation is far worse off than Ireland. A fair amount of room has been made at Dublin's universities for African and Asian students.

Ireland's outward look is also demonstrated in its eagerness to enter the European Common Market, once the British are accepted, and in its more relaxed attitude to the Communist world. For all the nation's dedication to nonalignment, it is as anti-Communist as the United States and, in some respects, even more so. Ireland has no diplomatic relations with any Communist country. The easing of the Cold War, however, and the shock of seeing Soviet officials calling at the Vatican have paved the way for new trade relationships with Communist nations. The average Irishman has a surprisingly tolerant and levelheaded view of the Communist world.

The Irish are seeing more kinds of foreigners today than ever before in history. The establishment of foreign-owned enterprises has brought in Germans, Danes, Finns, Dutchmen, Frenchmen, South Africans, Italians and others, though not in large numbers. It is the British and the Americans who are the most numerous, but they are not "foreign" to the Irish. It is tourism, however, which is saturating the country, at least during the summer months, with unfamiliar faces and accents. Tourism is Ireland's greatest growth industry and the biggest export industry after agriculture. It has become as vital to the nation's well-being as the tourist business is to the Swiss and the Spaniards. Nearly one and a half million travelers from abroad (not counting Ulster) enter the Irish Republic each year and spend over £80 million. The number of tourist cars has quadrupled in just six years. Although many of the travelers are Irish emigrants home for a visit, the impact of the foreigners on the traditional Irish way of life and on Irish thought is immense. Tourist spending spreads through the whole society, from the operators of hotels, restaurants and car-hire firms to chambermaids, shopkeepers and guest-house owners. The Irish Tourist Board (known as Bord Failte, or "Welcome Board") emphasizes in its propaganda that one of the pleasures of the country is talking to the Irish. Thanks to the English language and the Irish readiness to converse, the actual amount of communication between visitors and natives is possibly greater than in any other country. The Irish have become considerably more worldly in the process.

The waning of parochialism and the gaining of sophistication can also be seen in the loosening grip of the censors and in the more professional tone of Irish journalism. The newspapers, with few exceptions, were passive and conservative until recent times. They could not be counted on to probe deeply into Ireland's ills or to report fairly on affairs in Northern Ireland. They were all too susceptible to official and ecclesiastical pressure, and the worst of them were stridently nationalistic. They reflected the average Irishman's tendency to magnify Ireland's problems and Ireland's place in the world. Even now there are still examples of provincialism carried to laughable extremes. The *Evening Press* of September 29, 1966, for example, had "IRISHMAN IN AFRICAN JAIL" as its front-page banner headline. And on an inside page: "IRISH DOG STOLEN IN LONDON." But the Irish press as a whole has acquired both perspective and sharper reporting skills. One press critic has written that "Irish journalism is passing from the defensive to the aggressive" in its treatment of the nation's internal problems. The demands for social justice are becoming more insistent and there seems to be less fear of making the bishops angry. It is significant that the *Irish Times*, which has long been the most intelligent newspaper but which was handicapped by its outdated image as the organ of the Anglo-Irish Protestants, has had a rapid growth in circulation in recent years. It is even being read by priests who would not have been caught dead with it a few years back.

There has been a growth, too, in Irish periodicals, which reflects both economic improvement and a desire for the facts of life, sexual and otherwise. Before the recent era of industrialization there would have been little point to a publication like *Business & Finance*. The women's-magazine field used to be dominated by imported English publications, but a new Irish magazine, *Woman's Way*, now outsells them all. Its advertisements—for carpets, refrigerators, spin dryers, bathing suits, vacations in Italy—eloquently reveal that Irish housewives, those classic drudges, are coming into their own as consumers. The magazine is so candid about sexual matters, whether frigidity or family planning, that it might well have been hounded out of business in the less permissive climate of a few years ago.

Television

But perhaps the greatest Irish discovery of the past decade is that it is possible to think the unthinkable and speak the unspeakable. The Irish are beginning to say in public what they think in private. It is television, above all other instruments of change, which has opened up the Irish mind by exposing it to things unfamiliar and thoughts taboo.

Of all the peoples of Europe, the Irish have been "the most insulated and isolated," to quote the headmaster of a Dublin school. Television was bound to have an impact greater than anything seen in other nations. Until recent times the life of the typical Irish family centered almost entirely on the local parish. People seldom went anywhere or heard opinions which conflicted with the orthodox views of the priest, the schoolmaster and the elders of the community. It was a pattern of life which had scarcely changed for centuries. For the country as a whole, the most rigorous censorship system of any democratic nation was in force to protect young and old from improper thoughts in books, publications and films. Ireland was infamous for banning the works of great authors and castigating many of its brightest talents as blasphemous pornographers.

In 1962, when the Irish Republic began its own television service (state-owned but with revenue from commercials as well as license fees), there already were sixty thousand TV sets operating. Irishmen in the right parts of the country could, by erecting outsized aerials on their rooftops, get British or Northern Irish television programs. There was no intervening censor. "Telefis Eireann" came on almost in self-defense. Some saw it as an instrument for spreading the Irish language and propagating the traditional culture and values of rural Ireland. For many practical reasons, however, Irish TV was soon behaving much

like television services elsewhere in the world. Foreign programs, especially canned American comedies, Westerns and
thrillers, occupied two thirds of the air time. Now they occupy
about half. The fact that only a fraction of the Irish nation
could follow a program in the Irish language dictated that most
broadcasts be done in English. Irish comes on every so often,
but it is widely considered an invitation to switch off or switch
over to BBC.

The absence of Irishmen with television experience meant
that the key job of controller of programs was given to a
foreign TV veteran, a Scandinavian-Canadian named Gunnar
Rugheimer. Despite the "tremendous pressures in a small community like this where everybody knows everybody else," he
was able to develop a modern, professional service. When he left
Ireland for a new post in Sweden, Rugheimer told me that it
probably was just as well that an outsider like himself had been
brought in for Irish TV's early years. "There is a great cult of
the amateur here, you know: the idea that anyone can play
Shakespeare and the view that it is good enough to do things
in an offhand way. And then there is a great tendency to avoid
imaginary trouble. You have people creating their own taboos
because they imagine there will be objections from bishops or
old revolutionaries. We wanted to carry the Winston Churchill
funeral at length like almost every other television country in
the world, but the official line was that it would be controversial
and might cause disturbances. Yet for three years now we've
been putting on the Orangemen's parade from Belfast without
trouble." Rugheimer told another interviewer that "the greatest
danger in broadcasting is the danger of underestimating the
Irish public's capacity to take new and different ideas."

That capacity has been amply demonstrated by the acceptance
today of subject matter which caused shock and controversy
only a few years ago. Such programs as *The Late Late Show*,
Person in Question and *Home Truths* have taken on everything
from narcotics and premarital sex to the question "Are We a

Nation of Liars?" A few years ago there was an uproar when an interviewer asked members of an audience what they wore on their wedding night and someone answered, "Nothing!" A more recent program went into a spirited discussion of the pros and cons of pornography. The parish priest at Sallynoggin in County Dublin complained at morning Mass the next day that no one on the program had expressed "the proper view."

The bulk of Irish television, of course, is far more bland and inoffensive than these items suggest, but virtually every program, even those meant solely to entertain, has the effect of introducing ideas into what was virtually a vacuum. For better or worse, there has been a creation of dissatisfaction and a desire for more goods, comforts and amusements. Education programs have been invaluable in supplementing instruction in schools that have small staffs and few facilities. A series of excellent shows on new agricultural methods has had an impact on Irish farming. Documentaries have hit hard at the country's educational and social deficiencies. The spectacle of the clergy having to justify and defend, in open and often heated discussion, the doctrines and practices of the Roman Catholic Church, has been an eye-opener to worshipers long accustomed to rigid ecclesiastical authority.

The great majority of the Irish people continue to be good Catholics. They are possibly more truly Christian in their behavior today than ever before, even if they are less pious. But they are no longer so submissive to the clergy or so uncritical of the Church. The breakdown of traditions, the intrusion of outside ideas, and the renovation of the Church of Rome itself, are changing the nature of Irish Catholicism. Archbishops, bishops and priests are respectfully listened to these days but not necessarily obeyed in matters which are not directly religious. The Church's control of the greater part of Irish education is being undermined by government policies which show a clear movement toward state direction of the schools. The laity is less inclined these days to equate sex with sin or to believe that all Protestants are going straight to hell. But then the clergy is less inclined to present such simplicities to a more knowing laity. The individual parish priest may still be the most important man in his community, but he can no longer be the autocrat he used to be—and he may not wish to be. The more progressive priests have decided that something is wrong if all the leadership and organizational chores are heaped on their backs.

The reports from abroad of controversy within the Church about social welfare, contraception, divorce, mixed marriages and even married priests and nuns have raised doubts and questions in an Irish Church which has been mighty in its certainties. It is a bewildering time for ordinary Irishmen who have held to a simple faith, and it is an agonizing time for the clergy.

It is, on the other hand, an exciting time for those who have dreamed of the day when all Irishmen would live together without religious bitterness and bigotry. The worldwide ecumenical movement is already producing a more intimate relationship between Catholics and Protestants in an Ireland which is geographically divided largely on religious grounds. Within the Irish Republic, the Protestant minority, "the five per cent," has been exceedingly, even remarkably, well treated. The Protestants continue to have, on the whole, a higher living standard than the Catholics. The new departures are making it possible for individual Catholics and Protestants to behave more naturally toward each other. In Northern Ireland, which is two-thirds Protestant, religious differences are far more acute and difficult to resolve. Here, to a considerable degree, Catholics are second-class citizens in a territory controlled by tough-minded politicians of the other faith who fear the "Romeward trend" of the ecumenical movement. But new men of greater tolerance are coming to power, and economic advances in both parts of the island are making cooperation easier. There has been a heartening thaw in the Irish cold war during the past few years.

Nearly twenty years ago, in *The Face and Mind of Ireland,*

the distinguished Irish scholar Arland Ussher wrote: "Before 1916, Ireland was regarded as a mad country in a civilised world; today she may be considered a relatively healthy and hopeful country in an increasingly mad world, a state . . . free from social, radical or ideological strife." It is an observation which I believe can be made more forcefully today, when an awakened social conscience and a fresh liberality of thought make Ireland a nation at once attractive and aglow with promise.

Chapter 2

THE IRISH SCENE

Ireland, Sir, for good or evil, is like no other place under heaven; and no man can touch its sod or breathe its air without becoming better or worse.

—GEORGE BERNARD SHAW

The wonder and miracle of Dublin is its compactness. Within a radius of eight miles a man can have every experience he would ever wish to enjoy. It is complete in itself. Indeed it could be said that Dublin is not a city; it is a lazy man's continent.

—ANTHONY BUTLER

In a radio broadcast in 1943, Eamon de Valera, then prime minister of Ireland, described his vision of the nation that ought to be. "The Ireland which we have dreamed of," he said, "would be the home of a people who valued material wealth only as a basis of a right living, of a people who were satisfied with frugal comfort and devoted their leisure to the things of the spirit; a land whose countryside would be bright with cozy homesteads, whose fields and villages would be joyous with the sounds of industry, with the romping of sturdy children, the contests of athletic youths, the laughter of comely maidens; whose firesides would be forums for the wisdom of old age. It would, in a word be the home of a people living the life that God desires men should live."

It is a sign of the times that most Irishmen today would find this idyllic picture touching but old-fashioned, and not for them. They have become more material-minded than they like to admit. They want comfort but not frugality. Their leisure time is seldom devoted to things of the spirit. The comely maidens are running off to Dublin and England. There are more forums on television than by firesides. The wisdom of the old seems irrelevant to the young.

Quiet Beauty

The new mood of the Irish has not, however, drastically changed the physical face of Ireland. Nor is it soon likely to. Ireland's premier actor, Micheal MacLiammoir, has said that "nations are people in slow motion," and the motion of the Irish is still slow enough. Irish crowds and factories are so far confined to a few cities and the new industrial estates. The sweetness of Ireland, the wild green of its magic places and the stillness of the landscape make it one of the world's last refuges for poets and lovers of solitude. John Millington Synge wrote long ago:

> Still south I went and west and south again,
> Through Wicklow from the morning till the night,
> And far from cities, and the sights of men,
> Lived with the sunshine, and the moon's delight.
>
> I knew the stars, the flowers, and the birds,
> The grey and wintry sides of many glens,
> And did but half remember human words,
> In converse with the mountains, moors and fens.

Synge's Ireland may still be found along the western coast and in stretches of countryside which time seems to have abandoned. Whitewashed stone cottages with thatch against the rain huddle like hermits in the folds and valleys. Oarsmen in

the fragile tar-black currachs which defy the pounding ocean
have the look and speech of men from another century. Almost
too good to be true, there are red-haired boys driving donkey
carts loaded with turf for the family fire and covered wagons
of tinkers creaking down country lanes. In quiet gray towns
the musty, cluttered shops do more conversation than business.
The Victorian signs, primly hand-painted, announce, "DALY:
UNDERTAKER, PAINTS & OILS" and "JAMES CORK: VICTUALLER." There
are dark sweaty pubs, all brass and mahogany, their counters
"glowing with the love of a million elbows," and little one-
teacher schoolhouses with a scattering of muddy boots at the
door. Silent men with cloth caps and the smell of sheep lean
like ladders against walls of weathered brick. (An Englishman
writing of Ireland at the turn of the century described a priest,
anxious to put some life into his parish, who was "appalled
by the Oriental languor of the Kilronan men, who will stand
long hours together propped like posts against a wall, their
hands in their pockets, scarcely opening their mouths to spit,
much less to speak.") An old lady wrapped in a black shawl
tells you it is a great class of a morning—and so it is, with
the sun painting away the dew and the breeze soft.

On a July Sunday at the highest point of Inishmore, the
largest of the Aran Islands, I heard an Irish girl say in delight,
"To think that foreigners pay thousands of pounds for a house
with a view like this and we have it free in Ireland!" At a dance
hall in Carrick I asked Tommy Drennan, one of the most popular
"showband" singers, what he thought of America now that he
had been there on a tour. "I like Ireland better," he said. "We
don't have much, but it's more agreeable." In a hotel lobby
in Glengarriff on the shore of Bantry Bay an insurance executive,
home again after years in England, declared, "This is the best
place in the world to live."

He could be right. Ireland is a great national park, open to
all. No wonder the Irish raise such a fuss when foreign property
owners put up barbed-wire fences and block the pathways to

empty golden beaches. Things are on a human scale. The tallest building (in Cork) is only fifteen stories high. The mountains are softly rounded and easy to climb; thousands of pilgrims struggle to the heights of Croagh Patrick, the holiest of the mountains, on Garland Sunday each July. There are awesome cliffs facing the Atlantic, but you may find an Irishman or two sitting on the edge, dangling a fishing line to the boiling sea hundreds of feet below. Only a few castles and great mansions remain intact. The moss-covered ruins of the rest and the tumbled-down cottages of emigrant families may be seen from Bloody Foreland and Malin Head on the ragged edge of Donegal to Skibbereen and Mizen Head on the southern knobs of Cork.

The day may be past when the greatest danger one might meet on a country road would be the postman on his bicycle, but the automobile has not taken over completely. Ireland offers the most enjoyable driving experience in Europe. It is possible to motor for dozens of miles in Kerry and Clare and Mayo without meeting another car or having to slow down for anything more than a flock of sheep, a wandering cow or a donkey. It is a country which was probably made more for horses than for people. They have a paradise of their own in the Curragh, to the west of Dublin, where a lush, rolling carpet of grass covers thousands of lightly fenced acres. I have saved this item from a noted country newspaper, *The Kerryman*:

> What must have been the largest horse fair in living memory was held in Listowel on Thursday of last week. From early morning till late at night the streets were crowded with animals and pedestrians. Prices were high and the trade was brisk. The number of horses on show in this age of tractor and motor car was amazing and is a reliable indication of the fact that whatever mechanisation and automation may do the horse in Ireland still holds its own.

Driving about MacGillicuddy's Reeks and the shores of Dingle Bay one October day, I asked my wife to jot down the creatures encountered: horses, donkeys, cows, bulls, pigs, grey-hounds, ordinary dogs, dogs sitting on gateposts, cats scurrying under hedges, goats, stoats, sheep, ducks, geese, hens, seagulls, butterflies—and not forgetting the seal we had seen by Garnish Island, that semitropical garden in Bantry Bay. No snakes, however; Saint Patrick drove them out.

MacLiammoir has spoken of Saint Patrick as "probably the very first of that band of quixotic enthusiasts from the world outside Ireland who for some inexplicable reason find the country and its people absolutely irresistible." The enthusiasm of the outsider for Ireland is understandable enough. Those who come in from overcrowded, mechanized countries with their nerves all ajangle discover a priceless serenity and all the flowing natural juices of life which they thought had disappeared from the so-called civilized world. They find it an "easy" country to live in and wonder what its secret is, not noticing that it is easy because people take it easy.

The attitude of the foreigners who have settled down in the Irish countryside in the postwar years was summed by the man who said, "It's a great country to visit, but I'd rather live here." Film director John Huston, who has an estate in the west of Ireland and serves as joint master of the Galway Blazers, a century-old hunt club, told an interviewer, "I love Ireland. I love living there. It's rich and amusing. There's a wonderful way of life there, way behind the times, thank Christ. It's kind of pre–Civil War. People stay in each other's houses, and hunting takes precedence over everything else."

A proper Irishman will angrily protest that hunting is for those who can afford it. He looks with a certain puzzled disdain at the foreigners who go into ecstasies about the charm of old Ireland when he is concerned about an up-to-date Ireland which puts more money in his pocket. Quite a few outsiders, on the other hand, are convinced that the Irishman will be the ruination of Ireland yet. Historically he has not made, or been allowed to make, the best use of the country. It was Bismarck who is supposed to have suggested as a solution to the Irish problem that the population of Holland and Ireland change places; within a short space of time the diligent Dutch would make Ireland blossom, while the feckless Irish would let the dikes of Holland fall into disrepair and soon drown themselves.

Today, when "the test of whether a thing is worthwhile in Ireland is whether it can make a profit" (according to Senator Owen Sheehy Skeffington), it is feared that the Irish will follow other nations in destroying many of their natural and man-made assets. Some of the handsome Georgian houses in central Dublin have been torn down to make way for modern office blocks. Lady Gregory's great house in the west, famous for its association with the Irish literary revival, has been broken up. H. V. Morton in 1930 described the Claddagh at Galway as "one of the most remarkable sights in Europe. . . . Nothing is more picturesque than this astonishing fishing village of neat, white-washed, thatched cottages planted at haphazard angles with no regular roads running to them. . . . It is a triumph of unconscious beauty." The Claddagh has been destroyed. There is a danger that the unspoiled beaches and other coastal beauty spots will be turned into tawdry small-scale Brightons and Blackpools. "Is any nation an island in the mid-twentieth century," asks the travel writer Elizabeth Nicholas, "with no responsibility to anything or anyone but itself? Should the Irish be allowed to ruin, without a word said, a heritage more precious than any gold, a coast that remains today as it was at the time of the Creation?"

Ironically, it will probably be tourism more than Irish sensibilities about their heritage which will save the situation. It is being realized that, apart from the Irish personality, the country's distinctive attraction to visitors is its unsullied scenery and pre-industrial atmosphere. A strenuous campaign is under way to safeguard the coasts, save the best of Georgian Dublin, build folk parks for the preservation of ancient dwellings, and renovate the remaining castles and mansions. Lissadell, for example, is the distinguished (though gloomily gray) late-Georgian mansion of the Gore-Booth family which faces the sea as the centerpiece of an estate just twenty minutes by car from Sligo. It has historic importance as the home of both Constance Gore-Booth, the heroine (as Countess de Markievicz) of the 1916 uprising, and her sister Eva, the poetess. Yeats, who lies buried in a churchyard at nearby Drumcliffe, used to stay and write in the house.

> The light of evening, Lissadell,
> Great windows open to the south,
> Two girls in silk kimonos, both
> Beautiful, one a gazelle.

The house has a magnificent gallery–music room, all oval and yellow, a dining room with extraordinary life-sized figures painted by Count de Markievicz, and a bizarre collection of relics, trophies, Arctic birds and works of art. Nonetheless, Lissadell was ignored by the nation and allowed to fall into disrepair despite the efforts of the Gore-Booths to keep the house going. When I took my family there early in 1967 the mansion was still musty and leaking and the gardens were choked with weeds, but some money was coming in at last from the Irish Tourist Board. A few months later Lissadell was opened to the public for the first time.

Such recoveries as this go almost unnoticed in Ireland amid the greater excitement of the rehabilitation of the old castles. American millionaire Bernard McDonough, who made his fortune manufacturing shovels, has turned Dromoland Castle near Ennis into an opulent resort hotel for wealthier visitors to Ireland— Americans mostly, but the President of Pakistan and the Beatles as well. The fifteenth-century Knappogue Castle near Shannon Airport has been renovated by another wealthy American, Mark E. Andrews, a former United States assistant secretary of the Navy, and his architect wife. Like Dunguaire Castle, which specializes in drama and literary evenings, Knappogue is a stop on the "mediaeval tours" which the Irish tourist authorities began a few years ago with much imagination and undreamed-of success.

Tourists who fly into Shannon Airport and are booked for a tour are whisked away into an Ireland which has little to do with the contemporary life of the Irish. The afternoon program, for instance: "Depart for leisurely coach drive through the Irish countryside featuring: visit to Bunratty Folk Park for tea in an Irish thatched cottage; drink in a local pub in the typical Irish village of Sixmilebridge; tour of 12th century Quin Abbey; Irish coffee reception and a display of step dancing by children in an old world hotel; reception in the great hall of Bunratty Castle followed by a Mediaeval Banquet."

A good many of my Irish friends are appalled by all this. They speak of "bogus Bunratty" and deplore the false image of the country which is given to the innocent traveler. It is my observation, however, that most tourists are willfully innocent and rarely interested in true images. The Taj Mahal and the Golden Temple in India still attract more visitors than the slums of Calcutta or the flyblown villages of Maharashtra. Ireland's "mediaeval tours" are no more sinister than Colonial Williamsburg or the *son et lumière* productions in England and on the Continent. Middle-aged American businessmen and their blue-rinsed wives wear great bibs and get the full treatment as "guests of the Great Earl of Thomond, savouring the victuals of those robust days, quaffing mead and listening entranced to the lovely voices of the Bunratty Castle singers."

It is all most skillfully and tastefully done, and the tourists get their money's worth. "I still think with deep feeling of my wonderful two days in Ireland," writes an aunt in New York. "I really loved it. So different from England, so much in the past and so little in the present—the fire on the hearth that has not gone out for two hundred years (or so they said), the thatched roofs and the wonderful old castles with their stories of battle, love and hate." Each year more than sixty thousand travelers flying between North America and Europe arrive for a quick taste of storybook Ireland. They may see little of modern Ireland, but they make jobs, leave money and contribute substantially to the economic recovery of the depressed Irish west.

Most other tourists, of course, stay longer and do the country properly. The effort to make things interesting for them has been a key factor in the festival boom. There are festivals now for everything from drama and light opera to films and oysters. They have done much to enliven things on an island which has suffered from a shortage of both cultural outlets and amusements.

Honor Tracy once spoke of "this boggy little piece of land with its few inhabitants; lying forlorn in the ocean, washed by rain and curtained by mist, in grave danger of being overlooked by the outer world were it not for its frequent and lively toots on the horn."

Ireland is certainly boggy enough; the marshlands account for a seventh of the island's surface. It is little: only about the size of Austria or Portugal, yet larger than Belgium, Denmark, Holland, Switzerland and many another small country. Its compact size makes it possible to drive almost anywhere in a few hours. I once had a leisurely lunch in Captain Boycott's old mansion (now a hotel) near the end of Achill Island, on the westernmost fringe of Ireland, and then drove the full width of the country to Dublin Airport to catch an evening flight. Within the course of a day a motorist can experience all the violent contrasts of scenery that Ireland has to offer, and inside of an hour's drive he can go from the most primitive landscape in Europe to the most up-to-date comforts of a luxury hotel.

Ireland is certainly washed by rain and curtained by mist, but not so often as all the talk about the weather suggests. An Irishman once told me, "There is nothing wrong with our climate except the weather." Someone else in Galway said, "If you stand on the shore here looking out to the Aran Islands and you can't see them, then it is raining. If you *can* see them, then it is *going* to rain." In all of my journeys about Ireland in all seasons I have never been particularly put off by the dampness; it only makes the sunshine more glorious. While the west of Ireland is wetter than Dublin and other parts of the east, the country as a whole is not worse off than most of Britain, and better off than parts of Scotland and Wales and England's Lake District. The real difference is that Ireland gets the rain first. It is, as one geographer put it, "Britain's anteroom, having a preview of the weather on the way to the larger island."

It is the unpredictable character of the weather that makes Ireland as much an ephemeral isle as "the emerald isle." But the climate is fairly uniform and seldom goes to extremes: the year-round temperature ranges from about forty to sixty degrees Fahrenheit. The winters in the north are raw and windy, but in the southwest the Gulf Stream has such a warming effect that palm trees and some other exotic vegetation manage to survive in certain sheltered places.

On a wet day in a lonely spot, with only the company of mournful fields and somber skies, it does seem that Ireland is forlorn and forgotten. There are some threadbare villages, half ruins and half tacky shops, which look as dreary and lifeless as ghost towns. Yet, overall, Ireland in the past decade has become a more cheerful-looking and spruced-up country. Irishmen returning home have noticed that roofs have been repaired, fences straightened out, churches restored and houses brightly painted, and that little factories and new school buildings have a way of popping up in remote places. Years ago a travel book about Ireland was able to dismiss Galway as "a rank country town spreading out and out, hither and thither like spilt drink." It had a bombed-out look. Today, like Limerick, Sligo, Ennis and other Irish small cities, Galway is smart and lively with new shops full of goods and streets busy with cars instead of fragrant with animals. Kinsale, a Spanish-flavored little port to the south of Cork City (and close to the site of the *Lusitania* sinking) was lapsing into oblivion only a short while ago. An enterprising Irishman named Peter Barry, who had had some experience running pubs in Wales and on the isle of Jersey, decided the time had come to make something out of Kinsale's historic associations with Spain and its look of a bedraggled Mediterranean hill town. The promotional effort which he launched sparked a revival which, in just a few years, has turned Kinsale into a bustling resort town with new hotels and restaurants, a shark-fishing fleet and several new factories.

Although a port like Kinsale depends heavily on free-spending foreign tourists, such seaside resorts as Salthill and Tramore are prospering because of the increasing numbers of Irish families which have acquired cars and go traveling about their own country. This has created a new social problem for farmers and their wives: looking forward to a quiet Sunday of rest, they find themselves inundated by relatives and friends from the city. The poet Patrick Kavanagh, returning to the place of his youth, found that "the people haven't changed much," but "the parish as a socially-centred world has been exploded a bit. Men now go outside the parish boundaries when looking for a wife. This was considered awful in my day. 'Had to go to Donaghmoyne for a woman. Native girl not good enough for him.' "

It is obviously dangerous to generalize about the look of Ireland. The flush of prosperity which can be found, for example, in Waterford, where the glass business is booming, is absent in a community like Portmagee in South Kerry. A thriving fishing village forty years ago, Portmagee is now visibly crumbling away as the Atlantic eats into the sea wall and empty houses fall into ruin. Emigration in recent years has been double that of the country as a whole. A local man named Brendan O'Keeffe, attempting to eke out a living in the town after returning from ten years in England, told a reporter, "All of us had to emigrate. There was nothing here for us. The whole thirteen of us had to go away. Do you think I am looking forward to the day when I might have to say goodbye to my children like my parents had to say goodbye to me and the rest of us?"

What I have observed in Ireland is a tilting effect, as if powerful economic and social forces had raised up the western side of the island and forced the population to slide east to the towns and into Dublin and over to England. Studies of population densities and movements reveal the western regions as the most empty and the ones suffering the heaviest losses of native sons and daughters, while Dublin (like Belfast in the North) fills up to bursting and succumbs to urban sprawl. A quarter of the population of the Irish Republic now lives in and around Dublin. More than half the telephones listed in the single national directory are Dublin phones. And it is primarily from Dublin Airport and the east-coast ports that the Irish go across the sea to work in Liverpool, London and other English cities.

So instead of looking at the country as a whole, it is probably a more useful exercise to examine, in turn, the dwindling western areas, the rest of rural Ireland and its towns, and, finally, Dublin. The phenomenon of emigration should be considered first, however, because it hangs like an accusing cloud over the whole island.

Emigration

For generations, Ireland's greatest export has been people. Not just any people, but usually the best people: the youngest, the brightest, the most able and ambitious. They are still leaving the Irish Republic at the rate of a thousand every two or three weeks. A decade ago it was a thousand a week.

Before the Great Famine, Ireland's more than eight million people made it one of the most densely populated countries in Europe. If the Irish had been able to expand at the pace of the British there would now be over 25 million persons on the island, making it (undivided) the fifth largest nation in Western Europe. As it is, there are less than four and a half million in the whole of Ireland and not quite three million in the Republic. In *The Vanishing Irish* (1954), Father John A. O'Brien spoke of "the wild and frantic exodus which has continued to the present day."

The Famine had the catastrophic proportions of a continuing earthquake that shook the inhabitants from their ancient moorings in the green island and set them scurrying in headlong haste to America, Canada, Australia, Great Britain, New Zealand, and all the countries of the world. Its terror and horror have gnawed their way into the inner marrow of the race's memory and would seem to have left upon the Gaelic soul a wound so deep that even the passage of a century has failed to heal it.

In a world booming with population explosions, only Ireland (the Republic, not Northern Ireland) offered the phenomenon of declining members. No other nation has read its annual population estimates with so much concern, like a dying patient with a constant eye on his own fever chart. Now, at long last, there is a small upward movement as the Irish become less afraid to marry and more willing to stay home. But the continuing problem is that emigration has become a way of life. The Irishman goes as readily to another country for a job as an American moves to another state. In the more depressed parts of Ireland it seems as if every family has sons or daughters in Britain or America. If there are children in their late teens it is almost taken for granted that they will soon be off across the water. It sometimes happens that an elderly lady who has never stirred from her own small community, who has never seen Cork or Dublin, will be taken on her first car ride to Shannon Airport, where she will fly off in a jet airliner to visit a son or daughter in Boston or Montreal. There are many Irishmen, home after years of exile, who are more familiar with London or New York than they are with any Irish city. The "returned Yanks" from America tend to make themselves unpopular by criticizing the inefficiency and lack of initiative of the local folks.

In some Irish towns one comes across "emigrant bureaus" which give advice to youngsters preparing to go abroad. Most of the graduating dentists, nurses and others who have gone the whole route in Irish education, at considerable cost to the country, go off to England to work. This Irish brain drain to Britain (which in turn has a brain drain to the United States) is a classic case of a foreign-aid program in reverse, with the backward society shipping its skilled young people to the wealthier country. Most emigrants, however, are unskilled and unequipped to take on anything but the heavy work, "the navvy jobs," in construction, roadmaking and other fields. The laboring Irish in Britain have been called "blacks with a brogue." They work hard, too, at least until they are told by British workers to take it easy, and the remittances they send home to their families amount to more than £15 million a year.

A leading government minister told me, "The Irish always seem to be going away to work. The trouble is that we are too close to Britain, and the British find us too acceptable. There ought to be a quota there, as for the Italians or the Chinese, or else we should build a wall around Ireland." This was said in private, however, and I doubt that he really meant it. The political stability of Ireland is largely due to the ease with which jobless and frustrated citizens can leave the country to make their living elsewhere. If they were forced to remain at home the unemployment problem would be seen for what it really is and strong measures or revolution would not be far behind. If it had not been for Britain's willingness and ability to absorb a million Irish citizens since the Free State was founded, Ireland might well be a socialist nation today, or at least a very different country.

The realists in Ireland say that the high emigration rate is nothing startling. The country is part of a single great labor pool. Economically, it is an offshoot of Great Britain, and there has been a natural gravitation to English industrial centers from Scotland, Wales, Northern Ireland and rural England as well as the Irish Republic. "Working-class" Irishmen, while reluctant to admit the country's dependency, understand the economic realities well enough; they know there are more jobs and higher wages in Britain than they will ever see in Ireland. On the other hand, Irish wages are not *that* low. Competition between Ireland and Britain for labor has put Irish industrial pay close to the British level even though Ireland's per-capita income is only about half that of Britain's.

The Irish go abroad more casually than ever before. In pre–World War II times when most emigrants went to America, it was a major, well-thought-out step for a young man or woman to leave home, perhaps forever. Today, with Britain offering plenty of work and the U.S.A. putting up unprecedented barriers to anyone without the guarantee of a job, the great weight of the movement is toward England. The ferry takes only a few hours, and the Dublin–London flight is just eighty-five minutes. Visits home are easy. There are no passport or visa problems. Ireland may be out of the Commonwealth, but the British give special privileges to the Irish, almost as if independence had never happened. Work permits are not required and the Irish who settle in Britain are immediately given the vote. Thousands of men who live in Ireland go to England each year for seasonal work, and university students work frantically in English factories during the summer holidays in order to pay the next term's fees. Although some emigrants who have acquired technical skills have been lured home by the new factories in Ireland, a survey a few years ago revealed that three quarters of the Irish-born residents in Britain meant to stay abroad permanently.

President de Valera has described Irish emigration as a push-and-pull business: people are pushed out by economic problems at home and pulled out by relatives and friends who have already established themselves abroad. A schoolmaster in Connemara said, "Our young people used to go to older relatives who would look after them. Now they more often go to friends of their own age who are as susceptible as they are to the wrong temptations."

Irish boys and girls are going to England at an earlier age than ever. A fifth of them are under eighteen. In many cases they do not have to leave; it is just a reflex action. They do not bother looking for jobs in Ireland. It is a startling fact of Irish life today that farmers are unable to get the workers they need ("Nobody wants to be a farmer any more") and many women cannot find a local girl willing to help out in the house ("They know they can make more money in Liverpool").

For a long time it has been a fact of considerable embarrassment to the Church in Ireland that so many "good Catholics" who go over to England soon stop going to Mass regularly and otherwise drift from the faith. It suggests that social pressures more than devotion account for the famous piety of the Irish in Ireland. Worse still, it is well known that many convent-educated girls "get into trouble" soon after reaching England, and that all too many Irish boys are confirming the English belief that the Irish are a fighting, drinking, irresponsible lot.

On the Sligo–Dublin train I talked to an Irish-born priest who has worked in England for some years. He was deeply critical of Catholic leaders in Ireland for virtually writing off the emigrants—for having paid so little attention for so long to the fate of the young Irish in Britain. He said, however, that there had been more concern recently and that the Church was sending more priests to Irish neighborhoods in Britain. The Irish Centre in London has been a particularly useful force in providing guidance to bewildered country Irish fresh off the boat train.

On his return to Ireland after running the Irish Centre for several years, Father Owen Sweeney said that "the English borstals are crammed with Irish boys and girls." He spoke of the "obvious danger to faith in a country in which illicit sexual indulgence is glorified as a normal way of life through all the media of communication." He urged action to keep youngsters under eighteen from leaving Ireland. "They see nothing and think of nothing but the bright lights of London."

The West

The flight of Ireland's young is seen most poignantly in the west, where the youth say, "There's nothing for us here." This is Ireland at its most picturesque and at its most melancholic. But as the boys and girls leave the clean air and the unsullied beauty of the offshore islands and rocky peninsulas for the grime and tenements of industrial England, the west becomes more attractive than ever to city Irish and world-weary foreigners who stream in to spend some days, and sometimes weeks and months, being rejuvenated in "the real Ireland." They exult in the bygone way of life and the natural use of the ancient language, and behave as if they had discovered the fountain of youth. I put myself into this category. Every time I go to Ireland I am drawn to the west by some powerful magnetic force. The best times I have had in the country have been spent in the nooks and crannies of the western perimeter, where the physical challenge and primeval silence evoke memories of northern Scotland and Lapland and the rock islands of the Scandinavian archipelagos. The totally natural surroundings demand that you grow a beard or build a fireplace or gather driftwood, which is just what the strangers do. "You can identify the visitors," said one observer, "by the fact that they alone wear native jerseys and Irish homespun."

It is remarkable how much of the mood and look of the Irish west has remained unchanged over the years. "This place is a geographic narcotic," wrote James Cameron of his visit to West Cork. "It is easy to understand why the southwest Irish have made such a wonderfully relaxed mess of progress, why they have totally failed to exploit any advantage that required an ounce of energy or will-power, why they are so slack and futile and charming and evasive and sympathetic. It is hopeless to resist the pressures of non-pressure."

"The west" means all of those rugged and ravaged areas "back of the beyond" where life is lived on a mere subsistence level, where the farms are too small, the soil too stubborn and the conditions altogether too defeating to hold out much hope of improvement. In parts of Connemara, to choose one place, it seems as if half the rocks in the world had been hurled onto this single knob of Ireland and that a race of men had been condemned to piling them up as walls to enclose an occasional cow or a patch of potatoes. Oliver St. John Gogarty once declared that the whole damned place should be evacuated and covered with forest.

The west is most particularly thought of as the Gaeltacht—those treeless islands and coastal enclaves from the brow of Donegal down to the land fingers of Kerry and West Cork, where Irish is spoken as the first language. It amounts to only a small fraction of Ireland's total area, and the native Irish-speakers, including a few in the southeast, now number fewer than eighty thousand. According to the Reverend James McDyer, who is famous in Ireland as the tireless champion of the co-operative movement, the Gaeltacht people "are a remnant of the Irish of history. Conquest, followed by plantation, dispossessed them of their better lands. Too poor to emigrate, they fled to the hillsides and the fastnesses and there carved out little homesteads that endure to the present day."

The traditional home is a whitewashed stone cottage with thatch on the roof and a curl of smoke from the turf fire coming out of the chimney. Such cottages can still be found all over the Gaeltacht—at the edge of a bog or by the sea or clinging to a hillside—but there are many more modern and well-appointed houses as well. Turf bricks for fuel are stacked just outside the doors, sheep wander about the labyrinth of stone walls, and youngsters play along the shore, where the rocks bear a peculiar orange coating of sea vegetation. What is left in Ireland of the old stories and dances and the mournful songs about shipwreck and dowries will be found in the Gaeltacht. Many older persons, at least, follow the customs of the ancient Irish and there is a survival of forms of speech of the Ireland of centuries ago.

It is because of this that the Gaeltacht weighs heavily on the conscience of the Irish. Their attitude toward it is much like that of a young couple in a city apartment who know they should be doing something for the old folks withering away on the broken-down family farm, but who are too busy to do much more than send off a little money now and then. The Gaeltacht has been receiving special but fitful attention ever since the last years of the nineteenth century, when language revival became the key-stone of the nationalist movement. The number of persons who could speak Irish had been halved in just half a century. The area hardest hit by the Famine was the Irish-speaking west. English had become the national tongue and the only useful language for getting anywhere in the world. To speak Irish was to identify oneself as inferior.

The enthusiasts for language revival sought to turn the tables and make Irish the badge of patriotism and, eventually, the universally spoken language of the land. Students and revolutionaries went to the Gaeltacht to learn Irish from the "native speakers." After independence, Irish was declared to be the first national language, even though only a small percentage of the Irish could use it, and the people in the Gaeltacht were given special help so that they would stay put and keep the wellsprings of the language flowing. A special government department was set up to look after the Gaeltacht; grants were provided for housing and home improvements; and an annual bonus was given for each child in an Irish-speaking family. Many Gaeltacht households survive today without anyone doing much actual work, through combinations of child bonuses, the dole, money sent home by emigrants and the boarding of language students. Ever since the 1930s a state organization called Gaeltarra Eireann has operated small factories making tweed, toys, knitted goods and other products. More recently, the imaginative language-revival organization, Gael Linn, has been running fishing and other enterprises in the Gaeltacht. A traveler has no feeling of being in a poverty-stricken region even if he does sense the pervading sadness.

It is probably true to say that those who remain are living more comfortably and securely than ever despite being only on the fringe of Ireland's new prosperity. And while some communities are clearly dying on their feet, others are enjoying a new lease on life. Killybegs in Donegal, for example, although well known for its hand-tufted carpets, was almost a ghost of a port a few years ago. It has come alive with a number of big new trawlers for herring fishing, a cooperative fish-processing plant, and new shops and restaurants. While some islands like the Blaskets have been abandoned altogether and others like Tory are steadily losing population, the Aran Islands are actually gaining in numbers and discovering new means of survival. Tourist spending is becoming more important, and a new fleet of trawlers, plus more enterprising fishing by men in smaller boats, is producing unexpectedly large earnings. The islanders have television now, and a few cars can be seen on the main island. Nonetheless, the outward appearance of the Arans is still as timeless as it was in the days when Synge set down the rhythms of its speech. ("A man who is not afraid of the sea will soon be drownded, for he will be going out on a day he shouldn't. But we do be afraid of the sea, and we do only be drownded now and again.") When the steamer from Galway calls at the two smaller islands, the canoelike currachs come out from the beaches to meet it. They look as though they would tip over if a man shrugged his shoulders or parted his hair the wrong way. They take on mail, beer and other mainland goods—most importantly the tanks of gas which provide heat and light in the chill island darkness.

And yet, "the west is dying." The farmers give up, factories fail, villages close, young people disappear, the old customs fade away, and fewer and fewer people speak Irish with real devotion or see the use of the language. (It is one of the many contradictions in Ireland that the youth in the Gaeltacht are anxious to learn English in order to get work in the outside world, while English-speaking Irishmen come in to learn Irish in order to meet the requirements for becoming a teacher or civil servant in Ireland.) A schoolmaster in a Connemara town told me that his handsome new building now has seventy-nine pupils; there were a hundred when it opened only a few years ago. Economically, the west has become more and more redundant in the age of large, mechanized farms and industrial concentrations. Those who decry the continuing hemorrhage of population and the shrinkage of the Irish-speaking areas call for strong government action but get only piecemeal response. They become convinced that "Dublin has written off the west."

"What is at issue," wrote Peadar O'Donnell, a fiery old Irish radical, "is people, Irish people, who are being shut out from accommodation within the wage economy of the nation, otherwise unprovided for, and marked for dispersal. The West of today, in its most neglected areas, is a version of the 'Irish towns' outside the walls of garrison cities in the darkest days of the conquest. Squalor is lacking, for the disowned people today are free to fly the country and they know where to go."

Father McDyer

In Galway I attended a "Save the West" meeting which put Peadar O'Donnell on the same platform with Bishop Michael Browne, one of the most conservative of Irish Catholic leaders. This by itself was seen as a sign that the danger to the west was at last being taken seriously by important people. Father McDyer, as the principal speaker, warned of the "creeping paralysis" that was taking place in western Ireland: "Now we have only the very old and the very young people left. The next stage will be the very old and older. Then wilderness." Unless, of course, people start doing something about it. "This is a war of enemies from within. Scratch many an Irishman and you may find greed and individualism. We must get together! Unity! Unity! Unity! Let us combat indolence, emigration, cynicism, greed and individualism."

Had I heard this before somewhere? I remembered a book called *My New Curate* which appeared at the turn of the century. The elderly narrator, Father Dan, tells how, as a young man, he had arrived at his new post in an Irish-speaking parish, full of resolution to put new life into the people, pave the streets, build factories, establish a fishing station and really make something out of the place.

I might as well have tried to remove yonder mountain with a pitchfork or stop the roll of the Atlantic with a rope of sand. Nothing on earth can cure the inertia of Ireland. It weighs down like the weeping clouds on this damp heavy earth, and there's no lifting it nor disburthening the souls of men of this intolerable weight. I was met on every side with a stare of curiosity as if I were propounding something immoral or heretical.

Father McDyer has had the same experience of trying to move a mountain with a pitchfork. He told me that he was "fearfully disappointed" about the slowness of the progress of the cooperative movement which he has been urging, and yet he is acknowledged to be the most effective and forceful leader to have tackled the problems of the west in decades. His work has been described as "a great human experiment conducted by a most exceptional man."

Father McDyer is a tall, husky man of commanding appearance: a rectangular head roughly hewn, dark hair brushed straight back, beetling black eyebrows and a long thin mouth. He can look as ominous as any old-style priest chasing courting couples out of the bushes with a stick, but he has an engaging, cheerful personality, and his views are so progressive (for Ireland) that he used to be labeled, or libeled, "the Communist priest." I say "used to" because his views are now receiving widespread endorsement. He has become a familiar face on Irish television, and even the bishops in his own Church who used to regard his work with intense misgivings are now giving him their blessing. He has recently been freed of many of his parochial duties in order to range more widely through the west as a spokesman for the cooperative idea. His basic message is that the people of a depressed community should help themselves by working together and pooling their resources.

Himself the son of a small farmer, Father McDyer, who is now in his early fifties, spent ten formative years in England before beginning his work in the Irish west more than fifteen years ago. Nothing distressed him so much as the sight of Irish youth flowing out of the country and the way that this phenomenon had come to be accepted as inevitable. He became the curate at Glencolumbkille, a bleak community wedged between sea and stubby mountains at the westernmost point of Donegal. It was then a woebegone place where fishing had all but died out and the sheep farmers, as he says, were "pathetically relying on old and antiquated methods, content to allow the hillsides, which scarcely feed more than one sheep to the five acres, to do their own work."

Father McDyer put new life into Glencolumbkille. He managed to bring such basics as electricity, piped water and paved roads into the area, and he struggled against "apathy, envy and suspicion" to get the locals involved in community projects. A community hall was built, and it soon became the social and cultural center of the area. A small weaving industry was created. With the help of money raised abroad and, eventually, some state assistance, a vegetable-growing cooperative was formed and a canning plant built. More recently, a "folk park" was opened. When I last saw Father McDyer he was working on other plans to lure tourists to Glencolumbkille.

He said it all amounts to a "holding action" to keep the community from disintegrating and give it time to revive. Emigration has been cut impressively, and the new communal spirit is evident. But the catch is that such an endeavor depends heavily on the bulldozing personality of one man, and a priest at that. "A priest has an advantage," he said. "If a layman tries to start something like this, people want to know what he's getting out of it. At least they know that a priest isn't doing it for money or politics." His ambition is to turn over direction of the projects to laymen, but it is difficult to do because of the reluctance of people to "put themselves forward" and the fact that so many of those who remain after the toll of emigration "are too old or too young or too conservative to alter their mode of life."

The story is the same throughout the west, and there have been few other Father McDyers appearing on the landscape. Despite the efforts of the national groups which are being formed to promote cooperatives, there is little likelihood of any dramatic reversal of conditions in the west, and certainly not of the ornery habits of western farmers. Nor is industry likely to be induced into the area on any large scale. Only tourism holds out much hope for the future, even though the season lasts only half the year. It has been a commonplace to say that "you can't eat the scenery," but an intelligent development of the west to attract the kind of travelers who want to get away from it all could make it possible.

The Country

Far back in history Ireland was covered with forest. Today the greater part of the Irish Republic is covered by a great green quilt of family farms—more than 200,000 of them. A few are lush estates with manor houses overlooking a countryside as perfect as any in the world. Some are stud farms where the horse is king and the grass is soft as Irish mist. Some are broad-shouldered, efficiently managed cattle ranches, and some are big dairy farms where the cows know only the cold touch of the milking machine. But most are just plain small farms: as shabby, homely and well broken in as old shoes that no one can bear to throw away. Two out of every three farms are less than fifty acres. Nearly a quarter are less than twenty acres.

The typical farm, if there is such a thing, is worked by the family, though there may be a hired hand as well. The families in rural Ireland are closely knit, with the farmer something of a tyrant, the mother powerful in her own right, and the eldest son anxiously awaiting his chance—at age forty or fifty or sixty —to take over the farm. Until then he doesn't feel he can "bring a girl into the place," so the countryside fills up with aging bachelors and spinsters. At the same time, it loses both the young men who cannot stand the plodding pace or the lack of money and the girls who know their chances of finding a husband are better in the city.

The farmhouse, either a sagging stone cottage or a vacant-looking gray stucco bungalow, is too ill-defined and tasteless to be called charming. It has the heavy coziness of wet mackintoshes, hard wooden chairs in the kitchen, stuffed armchairs in the parlor, religious pictures on the walls, fading flowery curtains, and cramped bedrooms with never enough room to put things away. The parlor is a kind of household museum for storing souvenirs and mounting the old family photographs, and for having tea with the priest when he calls for the dues. The kitchen is the center of life on the farm, the all-purpose room where something is always on the stove, where the family comes together and the neighbors are put at their ease. If there is a television set it may well be kept in the kitchen. The very existence of TV has cut down the amount of neighborly visiting which used to go on in the Irish countryside. Children try to do their homework in the kitchen—perhaps the only warm room in the house—but the light may be bad. There are still many small farms without electricity or running water, and many more without indoor toilets. (Official figures show that more than a third of the nation's households are without "special sanitary facilities.")

The farm itself has none of the neatness and little of the air of purposefulness of, say, a Danish farm where the most is put into the land in order to get the most out of it. There is the ramshackle look of a Balkan farm, with the soil all but played out (and not a bag of fertilizer in sight) and the farmer spending his time trying to keep things from getting worse. He has a few cows, several pigs, potatoes here, a dozen hens there, an acre of oats, some acres of hay, a barn with a leaking roof and fences badly in need of repair. He is afraid to specialize, fearful of getting into debt, suspicious of new ideas, and full of excuses for not doing better at the business to which he was born and bred. Of course, it might be said that the farmer simply enjoys the simple life and his small pleasures, and is smart enough not to kill himself with overwork. The sculptor Edward Delaney, the son of a County Mayo farmer, told me his father's philosophy: "If it's a great day for working, then it's a great day for fishing." But Delaney himself, who speaks with sadness of the diminishing life of rural Ireland, wishes that the farmers were "doing something more constructive. When I go to the west and talk to a farmer and we talk for five or six hours I become restless. I wonder why he doesn't have something to do. Like cut the hay or something."

It almost seems as if the farmer does not take farming seriously. He keeps few records or accounts, manages more by rule of thumb than by anything else, resists the advice of outside experts, and derides neighbors who take the risk of doing something new. He holds the view that the boys in the family who need the least amount of education are those who will stay in farming. Because his tendency is to take from the land what it will give him, without investing something in it, he behaves like a transient on his own property. In the deepest recesses of his mind there is the ancestral memory of the days when it was futile for a farmer to improve his land, because it would benefit only the landlord.

In *Hibernia* magazine, Nicholas Furlong, himself a successful dairy farmer as well as an agricultural journalist, has said of the Irish farmer:

The legacy and tradition he inherits is one of conservative, cautious, almost frightened insecurity, and in the case of the poor farmer in the subsistence bracket, this is allied to an abyss of destructive ignorance which affects everyone in the nation. In some cases, the pride and snobbery of the small farmer is both pathetic and alarming. This nightmare inheritance is certainly the fault of no education, and the Da's directive to a delighted 13 years old child, "You're man enough now to handle a fork, to hell with school." You may think I'm talking about an age long gone by. I do not. I speak of your Ireland of the mid-sixties.

Furlong adds, "I have seen a total resistance to progress or innovation of any kind, even artificial insemination, water, electricity and lime, which is almost beyond belief." One of Ireland's best-known farm authorities told me during a meal in Dublin, "It is necessary for me to go into the country every so often to remind myself what an ignorant, benighted lot they are: a lot of bloody fellows who just don't want to be efficient. This could be a great farming country. We have some of the finest grassland in the world and we aren't anywhere close to realizing our potential in dairy farming or cattle. But the average farmer isn't really interested in doing better. He grumbles all the time, but what he really cares about is the amount of time he can spend drinking with the lads. He doesn't mind his house being cold. But things are happening anyway. His wife and daughters are watching television and reading the women's magazines, and they have their wants now. They won't settle for the old way of life any more."

The kind of farmer so far described will no longer be typical a decade from now. He will be a relic. The more representative farmer of the Irish future is already emerging everywhere in the land. I have met at least a dozen farmers who are as ambitious and modern-minded as men can be; they lack only enough acres or enough capital to be really successful. In the flat central plains of Ireland where the tourists seldom go there are thousands of efficient, prosperous farms, and a number of thriving towns attest to the readiness of the farmers to borrow money, spend money, enter cooperative arrangements and make maximum use of fertilizers and machinery. Even in the far west there are farmers here and there who have broken the chains of despair. At Castlegregory on Dingle peninsula there is, for example, John Joe Kelliher, a relatively young farmer who has only thirty-five acres, of which just twenty are arable, but whose sheds are full of equipment and whose house is brimming with modern appliances, including a large freezer. He may have had more capital than most to start with, but there are countless farmers who hoard money instead of spending it on improvements. Kelliher was the first local man to buy a tractor, the first to lay down his own plastic pipeline to tap a public water supply, the first to take in tourists for "farmhouse holidays." He has developed a truck-garden business as a sideline. When my wife and I stayed at his house he was about to install a telephone and was preparing to buy a combine. According to Mrs. Kelliher, he went to the pub only once or twice a week, "to catch up on the news." She proudly described him as "a real go-getter."

The go-getters will survive as the marginal farmers are squeezed off the land by the same economic pressures which are reducing the farm population of nations everywhere in the Western world. Irish agriculture today is at a stage reached by more advanced countries several decades ago. According to Charles Haughey, the Minister for Finance, "There is no other country in Western Europe where agriculture occupies so important a place in the national economy." A third of the national work force is engaged in farming, and sixty per cent of Ireland's exports, especially live cattle, are agricultural products. Ireland still has a rural look and a rural mentality, but things are changing with brutal speed. "The uneconomic small farmer," said the *Irish Times*," must recognise that in terms of modern technology he is a has-been." Many people are bewildered by what is happening, and large groups of farmers have all but declared war on the government. Economist Christopher Dodd wrote: "We are used to thinking of ourselves as a predominantly agricultural community . . . So many generations have learnt at their father's knees that the wealth of Ireland lies in its soil, and that the family farm is the basic unit of Irish society." But times have changed. Now it seems that "our planners no longer consider agriculture as our way of life."

So far as the planners are concerned, Ireland in the early 1970s will see more people at work in factories than on the farms. The flight from the land is already going on at a faster rate than anticipated. Some fifteen thousand persons leave farming every year, but fewer than half that number of new industrial jobs are created to absorb them. Government policy on one hand seeks to help people stay on their farms ("to stabilize the rural communities as they exist today") while on the other hand it fosters the consolidation of uneconomic small units into productive larger farms.

The official emphasis has been on industrial development. From the earliest days of independent Ireland, the agricultural community has been taken for granted and treated like a poor relation. The farmer may have been "the backbone of the country," but he was given little encouragement to break out of his conservative old habits and make his work as productive and as personally enriching as it could be. There has been a land redistribution program, however, which put good but neglected or underused land into the hands of farmers who had been scratching away at rocks.

When the nation as a whole began to prosper, the farmer's lot improved more slowly than anyone else's. Only very recently did other Irishmen begin to realize just how badly off and insecure farm families were and how little chance they had to improve their conditions. In some years the prices for agricultural products have dropped disastrously. The cost of equipment and everyday needs go up and up as farm incomes fall further and further behind the rising wages of industrial workers. Many farmers earn only a few hundred pounds a year. Almost all farmers, big and small, enterprising and lethargic, have become convinced that the authorities pay only lip service to their problems and are willing to let them be victimized by the free play of market forces. The result has been an unprecedented amount of unrest and agitation. Beginning in 1966 and going on into 1967, thousands of farmers took part in protest marches and mass meetings. Nine leaders of the National Farmers' Association staged a three-week sit-down strike in front of the Agriculture Department. Farmers blocked roads with tractors and other machines, withheld their produce from the markets, went to jail for refusing to pay their rates, and otherwise made it known that they were tired of being the low men on the economic totem pole. They wanted protection, subsidies, better marketing systems, and help in raising capital for improvements and expansion.

The protesting farmers won themselves a lot of sympathy, but I found it striking that many city people viewed them with ill-concealed contempt. A visiting journalist was told by a Dublin taxi driver, "The trouble with them is that they don't work their land. I know for a fact that one of the ringleaders has two hundred fifty acres of weeds."

Noteworthy too was the fact that the more successful farmers were in the forefront of the agitation. Irish farming has come out of the dark ages when low living standards were taken for granted. Farmers who have acquired the taste for a better life now want more. In *The Affluent Society* John Kenneth Galbraith wrote, "It is not the poor but the well-to-do farmers who find onerous the uncertainties of the market." They have more to lose. During the American depression in the 1930s it was comparatively rich farmers of Iowa rather than the subsistence farmers of Kentucky and Tennessee who cried the loudest for farm relief.

Irish farming is becoming more of a speeded-up business than a static way of life. In some eastern parts of the country the old-style cattle markets are giving way to modern buying and selling methods. Payments are made by check. Similarly, supermarkets are threatening the little shops, and the automobile is breaking down the parish boundaries. Dancing at the crossroads has become a thing of the past as young people drive off to the new dance halls which have sprouted everywhere in the country. The old sport of road bowling is disappearing as traffic makes it impractical. And yet, for all the signs of change, it is astonishing how much survives of the intimacy and warmth and gentle customs of old Ireland. In western regions there is no difficulty in finding towns where colorful fair days fill the streets with cattle and sheep and the bargaining sounds of farmers, buyers, go-betweens, hawkers, pitchmen and tinkers, all doing business in the time-honored way. The streets slimy with mud and dung make a stage for the elaborate acting out of sales. A farmer may spend the better part of the day just trying to get an extra ten shillings for his single cow, and when he has finally slapped a buyer's hand to complete the deal, off he goes with his cronies into the nearest pub to drink it away.

Although young people profess to find country life boring, and the more studious call it a cultural desert, it has its diversions and amusements. There are dances, song contests, bingo sessions, meetings of patriotic associations, entertainments in the parish hall and occasional carnivals. Sunday-morning Mass is as much a social as a religious occasion, and the pubs are open afterward so that people can catch up on the gossip. Above all, there is sport and talk of sport in one of the most sports-loving of all nations. If he is not playing in one thing or another himself, or at least going fishing, the country Irishman in his leisure time will be at the greyhound track cheering on the dogs or else yelling himself hoarse at the hurling or football matches. Except, of course, when the horses are running. It is at such major sporting events as the Irish Grand National at Fairyhouse and the Irish Sweepstakes Derby at the Curragh that country and city people come together, Irishmen all, for the serious business of placing bets and watching the great horses thundering by.

Dublin

When the country Irish are tilted into the urban catchbasin of Dublin they do more than enter the nation's premier city: they go into what is almost another culture, another way of life. It is like stepping from Flanagan's grocery-pub into the vastness of the Guinness Brewery, which happens to be one of the largest in the world. Compared to London, Dublin is still a modest-sized, easygoing, easy-to-know city, but to a rural youngster it is an overpowering, all-devouring metropolis which is far removed from his tight little farming community. Here the O'Connell Street crowds hurry into the big stores and pack into double-decked buses, the priests are unknown faces reading the *Independent* in Chinese restaurants, and the hospitals are as large as whole towns.

Even to an urban Irishman from Cork, Limerick, Waterford or Galway, Dublin may seem, at first exposure, to be much too big, busy and impersonal for comfort. These are small cities with a small-town atmosphere, however grandly they may think of themselves. Cork, which is the second city of the Republic, has hardly a fifth of the population of Greater Dublin—though to hear the natives talk you would think it has five times the importance. The intense civic pride is understandable. Cork is famous as "the rebel city," a proud, shrewd, aggressive and self-assured place which takes no nonsense from visiting Dubliners. It has been described as a town with a sting to it. Most of its ancient structures are gone and a large part of the city was destroyed during the terrorism of 1920, but no matter: there is great dignity in the stately buildings which lie close to the River Lee and mystery in the narrow streets and dim alleys. A prominent statue honors Father Mathew, the great nineteenth-century Apostle of Temperance, but Cork is a hard-drinking city nonetheless. There are green hills within easy reach, and Blarney Castle with its undeservedly celebrated Blarney Stone is only a short drive to the west. Cork is a remarkably complete city. It has a university college, a new opera house, industries making everything from automobiles to ships, more cathedrals and churches than I have been able to count, and an annual international film festival. Cork has produced far more than its share of writers, public figures (including the present Prime Minister, Jack Lynch) and, of course, revolutionists.

The other cities are more compact but just as agreeable. Limerick, for example, is like an old dowager who drowsed away for years but has somehow been rejuvenated. The aviation, industrial and tourist activities at nearby Shannon have helped. The River Shannon, described as the watery backbone of the country, flows serenely through the city and on to the ocean. Galway is still more of a sea city. It somehow manages to retain some of the exotic flavor of the days when a vigorous trade with

Spain was carried on and merchants lived Spanish style in villas with a view. I am especially fond of Waterford, because of the good times I have had there. I was put off at first by the morbid look of the city. Admittedly there was something charmingly Continental about the way the narrow buildings leaned against each other along the quay, but the grayness, especially on a wet day, was forbidding. So it is with many an Irish town: the first impression can be depressing, but it fades quickly when the richness of the interior life is discovered. I think of Waterford now in terms of warmhearted friends, the lively amateur theater, the ballet dance of the glass blowers, the liberal spirit at the Quaker school, the song contests in the pubs, the barber who told me that he plays the drums several nights a week in a hotel quartet "not for the money but for the enjoyment of it," and the Tourist Board official who took me up to the golf course above the river and steered me through a garbage dump in order to show off the full panoramic beauty of the old port.

Despite the attractions, the intimate quality, of Ireland's provincial cities, they are often hard put to hold on to the more ambitious of their younger people. For many restive youths, the excitements are too few and the opportunities too limited. They go to Dublin—which may only be a steppingstone to London— where they find themselves competing for rented rooms with the more numerous country Irish. The latter are known to the "Dublin jackeens" (the established city dwellers) as "culchies" (uncouth peasants) who crowd into rented rooms and go to work in the shops and the offices and the car assembly plants. They delight in having money in their pockets for the first time and in being freed of the rural restraints of parents, priests and neighbors, but they are often homesick and seized by the anonymity of it all.

"In Dublin you have conviviality, but no friendship," wrote Brendan Behan. "And Dublin will give you loneliness, too—but no solitude." In Edna O'Brien's *The Lonely Girl* (which was

made into the film *Girl with Green Eyes*) the country-girl heroine
and her friend Baba hire a taxi to get a drunken boy friend
home: "We had no idea where he lived. It's funny that we
should have known him for a year but did not know where he
lived. Dublin is like that. We knew his local pub but not his
house."

The young men and women fresh off the farms are part of a
rapidly growing "bedsitter civilization" in Dublin. They kick
over fewer traces than those who go on to England, but they
become more questioning about simple religious or moral teachings, and they take their cues about behavior from others of
their age who have learned the ropes of city life. Much of their
time away from work is spent in search of companionship, the
lads huddling in the pubs or hanging about the street corners,
the girls going around in twos or threes, staring in the shop
windows and wishing they knew some boys. There are more
females than males in Dublin; it is the other way around in the
rest of the country. Dreams of romance and faraway places are
spun in the cinemas of Dublin, which thrive as perhaps nowhere else in the Western world. There are usually long queues
outside them. It is the only city I know where a man who is
brazenly approached by a woman on the street will hear whispered into his ear not words of erotic invitation but the scalper's
chant "Want a seat? Adelphi? Metropole? Capitol?"

There is a kind of innocence too about the way Dublin (except
for its private parties) curls up and goes to sleep by midnight, a
time of night marked by the clatter of people racing for the last
buses home and the girls thumbing lifts. The sight of this is a
reminder of how safe a city Dublin is, compared to most of the
world's capitals. The amount of serious crime in Ireland is exceedingly small, with only an occasional murder and few other
assaults. Drunkenness seems to be the biggest headache, and
yet, for all the Irishman's reputation as a drinking man, the
drunks are less evident than they are in, for example, such cities
as Oslo and Helsinki.

Boy and girl meet eventually in the dance halls, snack bars and "singing pubs," or perhaps at the ballad sessions which have become a lively part of the Dublin scene. Those who marry will marry earlier than their country cousins. They will do so without the usual fuss about a dowry and often without the complications of moving in with parents. Housing is hard to come by in Dublin, even though a tremendous number of homes have been built since the end of the war, but if both husband and wife are working they may be able to scrape up the rent or the down payment for a small semi-detached house in one of the nondescript neighborhoods which have none of the attractions of Dublin's more famous and atmospheric parts. Such "New Dubliners" become increasingly divorced from the countryside and its customs. A city wife is more the equal of her husband than a country wife: he earns the money, she runs the household and controls the upbringing of the children. Parental authority diminishes and the children go off on their own much sooner. There are many children. According to one sociologist, married Dublin Catholics probably have the highest urban fertility rate in the Western world. Thus Dublin just grows and grows, making ever more obsolete de Valera's words in 1938: "Let us resolve never to become a cosmopolitan people."

Dublin (or "Dark Pool") became the country's principal town more than a thousand years ago when the Vikings turned the little settlement into a naval base. By the early eighteenth century it had only sixty thousand people, less than a tenth of today's Greater Dublin population. Then it moved into its golden age, the Georgian period, when it prospered as the second city of the British Empire. While the Catholic Irish hovered dimly and humbly in the background like tattered stagehands, Continental nobility flocked to the salons of Dublin's aristocrats. The theaters rivaled those of London, and Handel himself conducted the world premiere of *Messiah* in the old Musick Hall on Fishamble Street. Red-brick Georgian town houses, gracefully crisp in design but adorned with fanlights and wrought-iron balconies, rose up about the residential squares and the handsome avenues on both sides of the River Liffey. A Wide Streets Commission saw to it that the nobility of the buildings was enhanced by space, sky and vistas that reached to the mountains.

The city acquired an elegance, "a splendor built on squalor," which continues to this day and gives the first-time visitor to the heart of Dublin the pleasurable sensation of stepping into another century. The old Parliament building (now the Bank of Ireland), the Four Courts, the great Custom House, Leinster House, many of the buildings of Trinity College, even the sprawling Guinness Brewery, all sprang up, phoenixlike, in an outburst of creative energy. Phoenix Park, in fact, was created then as one of the world's largest public pleasuregrounds. Its 1,752 acres, which could easily consume London's Hyde Park or New York's Central Park, give Dubliners a great slice of countryside (and a zoo, a racecourse and much else) close to the center of town.

After the Act of Union of 1800 destroyed its importance as a capital, Dublin increasingly became an Irish Catholic city. By the turn of the century it was known as one of the most slum-ridden cities in Europe. Thousands of families were jammed as thick as cockroaches into the ornate, high-ceilinged rooms of Georgian houses abandoned by the upper classes. Sean O'Casey in The Plough and the Stars spoke of the "vaults that are hidin' th' dead, instead of homes that are sheltherin' th' livin'." The city's death rate was double that of London. People were sleeping six to a bed in Mountjoy Square, and one newspaper compared Dublin's slum conditions to Dante's Inferno.

There are still some appalling tenements, and people still sigh about "dear, dirty Dublin." It is a mark of the shabbiness of much of the city that the makers of the movie The Spy Who Came In from the Cold filmed it as East Berlin. Slums are now exceptional, however, and in general the city has a look of middle-class respectability. It is growing outward instead of upward. There are endless rows of prosaic private homes instead of the apartment blocks and high-rise developments familiar elsewhere in Europe. Metropolitan Dublin is expected to have a million inhabitants within the next twenty years.

It is a frightening prospect, for Dublin is one of those cities— like Amsterdam, Kyoto, San Francisco—which have such singular personalities that an excess of expansion and "improvement" could squeeze the life out of them. The principle might be: more is less. The more that Dublin is taken over by lounge bars, parking lots, shopping centers, bowling alleys, industrial estates, baby skyscrapers and sleek hotels, the less there is of its special aura of raffish eccentricity. It is a pleasure to read a Thomas Kinsella poem describing Dublin as "the umpteenth city of confusion," but painful to see in a financial magazine the opinion that so much of Ireland's business is now concentrated in Dublin that it is "becoming more and more a city upon the periphery of the English Midlands."

What is most distressing to anyone who has fallen in love with the city is the way that the best of it is being whittled away day by day by natural forces, commercial greed or just plain indifference. A recently published book of sketches by Flora H. Mitchell of the most important and intriguing buildings and byways of the city bears the revealing title *Vanishing Dublin*. Many of the sketches are of fine old structures which have been torn down within only the last few years. Admittedly, a number of the handsomest Georgian houses are almost beyond saving because of poor construction in the first place and more than a century of neglect. But even the sturdier buildings are in danger so long as there are officials who would fill in the Grand Canal and clear away architectural treasures just to provide more parking space. One problem, as the Irish architect Niall Montgomery told me, is that "a lot of Irish people still do not feel that it is really their city." Dublin's grandeur is entirely the work of the old Anglo-Irish Ascendancy, not of

Irish Catholics. One important national figure who helped set fire to the Custom House as a revolutionary youth admits today that he still has the inclination to do it again.

It is, incidentally, one of the particular rewards of Dublin to come upon delightful elderly men who were very much a part of Ireland's struggle for independence. It is like being in New York, Boston or Philadelphia in the early 1800s and meeting old rebels who had been engaged in the American Revolution. But then history lurks around every corner in Dublin, for the city is a medley of centuries: a faint memory of the Vikings here, a touch of the medieval Irish there, evidence of the Georgians and the Victorians almost everywhere else, and the modern Irish making their mark with heroic statues, glassy buildings and one-way streets. Despite the constant demolition I have mentioned, history dies hard in Dublin. Look closely at the street postal boxes. Once painted red but now a bright green, they still reveal the crown of the British monarch. Within the gates of Dublin Castle, which used to be the seat of English power in Ireland, the Chapel Royal is now the Church of the Most Holy Trinity, but the thronelike red-plush seats for royalty remain. The priest who gave me a guided tour said in awe, "Just imagine, last Sunday there were two good holy nuns sitting there." Not far from the Castle is the ornate Olympia Theatre, a perfect relic of the gaslight age, and the Brazen Head Inn, more than three hundred years old and still going strong. Facing the Liffey is O'Meara's Irish House, a century-old pub, apparently designed by a superpatriot. There are round towers rising up from the roof and the exterior decorations depict such scenes as Grattan addressing the Irish Parliament for the last time and "Erin Weeping on a Stringless Harp."

Dublin is obviously a splendid city for casual strolling, though not always for casual dress. I recall setting off on a long walk one warm Sunday morning in July wearing slacks, a short-sleeved shirt and sunglasses. I was soon embarrassed to find that I was the only person on the streets so informally attired. Everyone else was in his or her Sunday best: the men in dark going-to-Mass suits and the women looking most refined in their carefully ironed dresses, veiled hats and white gloves. In a neighborhood not far from the Guinness works I came upon a shepherd with a stick and a dog hurrying a flock of sheep down an avenue. As I puzzled over this touch of the countryside in the middle of the capital city I found myself walking down Long Lane, a charming narrow street lined with neat little cottages which could as well have made up a village in the most bucolic backwater of Ireland. Other "working-class" areas I passed through were less appealing, but I could understand what Basil Clancy of *Hibernia* meant when he said, "This is one of the best cities in the world for a youngster to grow up in." And I could see why Edna O'Brien had said that Dublin is still the most congenial city to be poor in. Many of the children around the old tenements or the dreary new housing projects looked like Dickensian urchins, grimy as could be, but their faces were radiant and they raced about like terriers.

On such wanderings I have delighted in the signs. "The Sick and Indigent Roomkeepers' Society." "The Invalid Requisite and Baby Carriage Company." The pretentious "Turf Accountant" over innumerable betting shops. "Nelson's Pillar" still announced as a stop by the bus company a year and a half after Nelson came crashing down. The shop windows are fascinating, too. I have seen recordings of Pope Paul VI's visit to New York in 1965 gathering dust next to made-in-China "Lucky Shamrocks" cigarette lighters.

One day I chanced upon the house where Oscar Wilde once lived (next door to the Our Lady of Lourdes Girls' Club) and that inspired me to walk over to Eccles Street for a look at No. 7, where Leopold and Molly Bloom of *Ulysses* resided, according to James Joyce. I was sorry to find it demolished, with nothing left but a board fence. That night friends took me to Bailey's pub. There, mounted on a wall like an enormous Irish ikon, was the door from No. 7. I shouldn't have been surprised. Dublin, praise be, is still very greatly Joyce's city, still alive with the kind of characters he described as "the most hopeless, useless and inconsistent charlatans I have ever come across in the island or the Continent." But it is also true that the most flamboyant characters are vanishing, just as the Victorian pubs with their cut-glass mirrors and glassy-eyed patrons are dying off one by one. Dudley Walsh, a distinguished solicitor, said glumly that "the real Dublin is disappearing. You hardly hear the old accent any more. We're being taken over by people from County Mayo." Dubliners still talk, of course, as only Dubliners can talk, about everything under the sun, but without the old-time bitterness and vehemence. As Ireland mellows and the flaming past recedes, the Dubliner's list of pet hates becomes ever shorter.

Sentimentalists may regret the diminishing role of the traditional Dublin pub, but it should be recognized that it has often served as a kind of ordinary man's oasis in a desert of despair, a place where he could escape from the grim realities of life by drinking up the household money. Today's Dubliner still likes his pint at the end of the working day, but he can also be seen navigating through the rush-hour traffic in order to get home in time to take the wife and children out for a drive on a balmy summer's evening.

The most welcome change in Dublin is that Dubliners now have the means and the leisure time to enjoy the fullness of their city. It is a superbly sited metropolis, "wandering between hill and sea," which has just about everything a city should have, and all within arm's length. There are mountains, beaches and golf courses within half an hour's drive from the city center. There are botanical gardens, two universities, race tracks, sporting fields, excellent theaters and restaurants, cathedrals, museums, libraries, elegant shops and much more. Some things are in short supply, like the first-class concert hall which has been talked about for years and some good swimming pools, but Dublin is altogether a thoroughbred of a city. Dominic Behan, Brendan's talented younger brother, once suggested an answer to the Irish custom official's question, "Anything to declare?" It should be, "I declare to God, what could I bring you that you haven't already got?"

Chapter 3

NATIONAL CHARACTER

*People keep telling us that life is earnest, life is real,
but we're not so sure we want to be earnest and real.*

—IRISH PROFESSOR

*We're pragmatic. We say to the English and Americans,
"All right, if you're fools enough to believe all this nonsense about us, go to it."*

—SIOBHAN McKENNA

Ireland is said to be a place where the inevitable never happens
but the unexpected often does. The Irish, by and large, are
fatalists; they are not surprised when things go wrong. Things
went wrong for seven hundred years, but the Irish survived.
They have a capacity for endurance. They can always fall back
on their wit and their words. Dr. Conor Cruise O'Brien has
observed that "words are the weapons of the disarmed."

Camouflage

The Irishman is a chameleon, an expert at camouflage, who
changes the color of his personality according to his mood or
the surrounding conditions. He is fluid, elusive, evasive, eager
to please yet ever ready to take offense. In an Oriental way he
will not disagree with you too directly or reveal his full feelings.

You will learn about them later from third persons. Someone has said that an Irishman will never say anything about you to your face that he wouldn't rather say behind your back. Mara Farrell, a magazine columnist, wrote recently, "We are a nation of twisters—we shy away from speaking the truth." A century ago, Anthony Trollope found the Irish people "to be good-humoured, clever—and the working classes much more intelligent than those of England . . . But they are perverse, irrational, and but little bound by the love of truth."

Like all thumbnail sketches of national psychology and behavior, such characterizations—and no doubt all that follows in this chapter—are unfair, inexact and incomplete. They are perhaps unnecessary too, for the Irish without the help of critics have managed to make themselves one of the best-liked of all the peoples in the world. They are not always taken as seriously as they would like, but I have met few people who do not find them delightful and stimulating companions. They have a style —call it charm, blarney, the gift of the gab or whatever—which endears and endures. "I have always been proud of being Irish," wrote Ted Bonner, a journalist, after a trip abroad, "but to travel a lot is to be, in addition, *grateful* for being Irish. In almost any country it is an instant passport."

It is impossible, however, to speak of the Irish, past or present, without mentioning the peculiarities of their personality. There is something which I can only describe as the Irishness of the Irish, a way of behaving, a way of looking at life, which springs from many origins and influences. It is customary to speak of the Irish as Celts, especially when one sees them as so many fanciful and devil-may-care rascals, but they are actually a mixture of races, as a glance at Irish history makes clear. The Norsemen and the Normans, among others, drove deeply into the Irish bloodstream and contributed character as well as physical traits. Moreover, the Irish for centuries were suffused with religion and abused by their overlords. There were times in their history when their Irishness was all they had left. It was their whistle in the dark, their built-in survival kit. They became expert at passive resistance. They would slip and slide like blobs of quicksilver under a thumb. It is what makes the Irish so unsettling to the foreigner with an orderly mind; they seem so mentally untidy. As Disraeli said, "The Irish are an imaginative race, and it is said that imagination is too often accompanied by somewhat irregular logic."

I recall reading about the Irishman who told a stranger, "Of course I don't believe in fairies, even if they do exist." And I think of the hall porter in a Dublin hotel to whom I complained that my television set was not working. I was, after all, paying for the thing; would he see about having it fixed? "We can't do anything about it, you know," he said, most cheerfully. "There are thirty other rooms with broken televisions in them."

Let it be noted that I did not press the issue. I might have got results eventually, but I would have been made uncomfortably aware that I was making a fool of myself. What man in his right mind, after all, goes to Dublin to look at a television set in a hotel room? (Never mind why the hotel management thought it sensible to install TV in the first place.) A common Irish response to all manner of complaints is, "Ah, what does it matter, after all? Have another drink." An American business-man in London just back from a working trip to Dublin told me, "You know, the Irish really *are* full of blarney. The people I saw hadn't the slightest intention of doing what they said they would do—though they gave me a good time while they were saying it. Oh, of course, they'll do *something*. It will all work out in the end. They kept asking me why I was taking everything so seriously."

He put his finger on something very Irish: It will all work out in the end. The catlike Irish somehow always manage to land on their feet. They improvise. They cope. They thrive on adversity. I sometimes suspect that the Irish are secret anarchists, and that only the stern discipline of their Church keeps them on the rails.

In 1966, at the very height of the tourist season, the nation was hit by a three-month bank strike which would have brought the economy of any other Western country to a standstill. The Irish took it in their stride. With millions of pounds locked away in vaults, the circulating bank notes had to do double and triple duty and were soon reduced to confetti. Even though no one could cash them, checks were written and accepted, and when the checkbooks ran out people made their own. They wrote out their own money or IOUs on backs of envelopes and any scrap of paper. A barter system began to appear: so many eggs or fish for a bottle of whiskey. One could almost feel the disappointment when the strike ended, especially on the part of those people in debt (at least half the nation, I suppose) who had been given a ready-made excuse for not paying up.

The mental untidiness of the Irish, as already mentioned, is accompanied by a certain physical disorder. In contrast, say, to the Germans or the Swedes, the Irish are undisciplined in their civic deportment (though they are law-abiding about more significant matters). They are natural jaywalkers and litterbugs. They attach little importance to the harmony or style of their home furnishings and personal dress. The Irish are design blind anyway; the visual arts have little place in their lives. No one is perturbed about wearing a rumpled suit or a mackintosh which looks as stepped-on as a welcome mat. The usual status symbols count for little. Indeed, anyone too neatly groomed or too ostentatious in demonstrating that he can afford the best wines or the best Jaguar will soon be cut down to size by the stiletto tongues of the Irish. Sociability and conversational agility win higher marks than position or possessions. Ulick O'Connor, a versatile Irish writer, told me, "We have an aristocracy of personality. There a kind of classlessness in Irish society because we are interested in a man's mind and personality instead of his title or income. A commoner will be more readily accepted than a prince if he is a more interesting person."

It is indicative of both the democratic impulse of Ireland and its almost small-town intimacy that the President is widely referred to as "Dev" and that people speak knowingly of "Jack," "Charlie," "George" and the rest of the boys who happen to be the nation's foremost government ministers. De Valera is obliged to live in the President's Palace (once the Viceregal Lodge) in Phoenix Park, a residence much too grand for his taste, but most other politicians make a point of living modestly and proving that they are not putting on airs. The fact that expensive living by a politician would be immediately detected and much commented upon is one reason why there is little important corruption in Irish public life. (Nepotism is another story, but not a particularly shocking one.) The salaries of ministers are small —the Prime Minister makes only $7,920, plus $3,600 as a member of Parliament—and the public even begrudges them their official cars.

Ireland is so small a society that it is almost literally true that everyone of any consequence knows everyone else of consequence. Personal networks of friends and acquaintances are especially large, because many people work in several fields at once. Offhand, I know of a government official doubling as an opera singer, a hairdresser *cum* musician, a lawyer who is a poet, author and lecturer as well, and a journalist who runs an antique shop and serves as an anticensorship agitator. Ireland seems especially small because the Irish are such chronic gossips. No secret is kept, no reputation is safe. Appropriately, *The School for Scandal* was written by an Irishman about Irishmen. Herbert Moulton, an American writer much experienced in Ireland, once complained, "You can't get away with *anything* here!" To which he was told, "Ah, no, Dotey, there you're wrong. You can get away with anything, but everybody has to *know* you're getting away with it."

The intimacy of Dublin was most directly revealed to me when I told a personal story (about some lady tourists in Nepal) in the Pearl Bar one evening and then had it related back to me by entirely different people at two other places the next night. Lord Killanin, a large man in Irish business and cultural circles, told me, "Saying or doing anything in Ireland is like my jumping into that swimming pool—I could drown in my own waves."

The coziness of it all can be oppressive and protective at the same time. Many people are greatly inhibited by the fear of what the neighbors will say. Whatever they do out of the ordinary, they feel, will be found out and frowned upon. To cite an extreme case, I heard of a girl from one of the little islands off the Donegal coast who went to work in London and somehow allowed herself to be talked into making a brief appearance in a strip-tease film. As luck would have it, the movie was seen in a Soho cinema by two lads from the island who had also gone to England to work. When she next returned home she found backs turned against her. On the other hand, as Basil Clancy, editor of *Hibernia*, said, "Ireland is like the Dead Sea. You can't sink here." You might be able to become debauched in London, where presumably no one cares, but in Ireland there are always people looking after your welfare— like it or not.

To beatniks and Bohemians, Ireland is probably the squarest country in the world. To almost everyone else, however, it is a delicious country. There is a rhythm to the place which is almost Mediterranean. Everything seems so congenial and undemanding. There is a certain lackadaisicalness and disregard of time. (Or else a proper appreciation of time. Tell an Irishman that you haven't time to stop for a drink or a chat and he'll say, "You don't mean it! Sure, the man who made time made plenty of it.") People still see life as a dance instead of a race. The tendency is to look with suspicion upon any excessive expenditure of energy or too obvious display of ambition. National leaders, of course, go about urging the Irish to work harder and to pay attention to productivity. In the meantime, the Irish Tourist Board turns indolence to advantage. "Taking it easy is something of a national sport in Ireland," its advertisements boast. "You'll forgive inconveniences that would cause you to boil anywhere else."

The Irish climate, variously described as soporific or anesthetic, is often credited for the slothfulness which visitors keep finding in Ireland. My own feeling is that climate has little to do with it. The Irish have simply been conditioned to live from day to day, having little faith that today's exertions will be rewarded tomorrow. Their inclination is not to save or plan or otherwise show that they have confidence in the future. I have already remarked on this in suggesting that the Irish small farmer behaves almost as a transient on his own land. Even today, when Ireland at last seems to have a future, young people, like their elders, tend to bumble their way through life, largely because they are so poorly prepared for the business of modern living.

When I asked a foreign employer in Ireland how the Irish shape up as workers, he said, "Do you mean here or abroad? After all, the best people leave. They have to, because they are too frustrated if they stay. Those who do stay make it as pleasant as possible for themselves. Their whole idea is to make the job *easy*." The manager of a factory at Shannon told of how some workers, when the plant first opened, would just disappear for a number of days once they had enough money in their pockets, then return to the job after they had spent it all. But in time they became more reliable. Others have said that most young men and women come to a job without any skills whatsoever, but that once they are trained they become good and extremely loyal employees. "I am proud of my Irish workers," said a German executive at the Liebherr crane factory in Killarney. "I was preaching teamwork, always teamwork, but every Irishman is an individualist. It took some time, but now it is all right. Not perfect, but all right."

An Irish economics professor told me, "The three great failings of the Irish are: one, lack of application; two, lack of persistency; three, lack of thoroughness. We are feckless—there is no doubt about it. We need more of a challenge, more contact with other people so that we will be more aware of our failings and our backwardness."

Articulate Cannibals

As this last quotation will suggest, anyone seeking to sort out the nature of the Irish can at least go forward in the knowledge that nothing he can possibly say about them will be more cutting than what Irishmen have said and do say about themselves. As Samuel Johnson put it, "The Irish are a fair people; they never speak well of one another."

What the Irish seem to like least about themselves is their habit of belittling and backbiting. They have something in common with the Norwegians, who, according to Henrik Ibsen, "can only agree on one sole point: to drag down what is most lofty." Malice may be the premier Irish vice. The head of one of the big state industries said bluntly, "We are articulate cannibals." Almost every noted Irish author has written of the nation's talent for verbal sabotage. Shaw, for example: "A certain flippant, futile derision and belittlement seems to be peculiar to Dublin. . . . When I left Dublin I left (a few private friendships apart) no society that did not disgust me."

That was a long, long time ago, but only recently a publicist in Dublin told me, "We're a great people for disliking. There is a watchfulness about us. We're great ones for minding other people's business." And an editor said, "There is always somebody trying to stop someone else doing something in this country. We are a censorious, small-minded lot, quick to attribute base motives." An Irish social scientist gave me an example of the way "we don't trust ourselves." The teaching and practice of the social sciences were in bad shape in Ireland, he said, and the first step needed for improvement was the writing of a report outlining the deficiencies and making recommendations. He and his colleagues in a public-affairs institute were capable of producing the report, but they feared that it would be discounted if they wrote it. Their motives would be questioned, their qualifications derided, their recommendations ignored. So they called in a distinguished social scientist from Denmark to do the job. Because he was not an Irishman his conclusions were given serious attention.

The individual Irishman, of course, while having a poor opinion of everyone else, thinks very well of himself and does not take kindly to criticism. The Irishman's favorite motto is said to be, "Laugh at everything and everyone, but don't laugh at me." When a Dublin friend told me that each Irishman lives in a little world of his own I remembered Synge's description of an Aran Islander who "seems to have shut himself up in a world of individual conceits and theories."

This would appear to confirm what is so widely believed, that the Irishman is the supreme individualist—but is he? It seems to me just as true to say that he is a great conformist who is only too ready to accept authority and deride those who break with convention. Perhaps the balance is that within a rigid framework of conformity (for he is one of the most conservative of beings) the Irishman revels in his obstinacy. Like the Finns, another bedeviled and cheerfully fatalistic people who survived seven centuries of foreign domination, the Irish are disputatious and seldom capable of working cooperatively. The real wonder of Father McDyer's cooperatives in Glencolumbkille is that they exist at all. I asked a parish priest in Kerry about the chances of the local farmers getting together for their mutual benefit. "Not these bloody fellows," he said. "The first sunny day and they'll be fighting with each other to see who gets to use the tractor first."

Of all peoples it is the Russians who come most to mind

he centuries slumber in the remote areas of western Ireland. An old oman in a traditional black shawl trudges an empty, winding road.

All photographs by Brian Seed

In Donegal a widow knits while one of her four sons, briefly home from England, thatches the cottage roof.

A young shepherd follows his flock through the Sheeffry Hills of County Mayo. The solitude deepens with each passing year as the Irish abandon the countryside for the cities.

In Dublin the rooftops bristle with television aerials raised high to receive programs from Britain and Northern Ireland.

Traffic is heavy throughout the day on O'Connell Street.

The familiar pursuits and pleasures of the Irish resist the pressures of change. Gathering fuel for the family fire, children load a donkey cart with chunks of turf.

Two countrymen with glasses of stout talk in the doorway of an unassuming pub.

The ancient Gaelic game of hurling is played fast and rough in Dublin's Croke Park.

At the Abbey Tavern in Howth a ballad group sings of the days of famine and revolt.

Pupils in the small, old-fashioned schoolhouses as well as those in modern schools spend a major portion of their time learning Irish, the national language rarely spoken today by the mass of Irishmen.

Education is still greatly in the hands of the Catholic Church whose most controversial figure in Ireland is The Most Rev. Dr. John Charles McQuaid, Archbishop of Dublin.

The new generation of Irish priests, some of whom are shown during an ordination ceremony at Maynooth Seminary, are more questioning than their elders and more concerned with social justice.

The classic Irish wake has all but disappeared but a funeral is still an important community event.

(*Opposite*) Politics at the grass roots is the art of Oliver J. Flanagan, a Member of Parliament.

Three national leaders: Prime Minister Jack Lynch (*above*), President Eamon de Valera (*right*), and former Premier Sean Lemass (*below*), the architect of Irish prosperity.

Industrial expansion since the late 1950s has slowed Irish emigration and provided in foreign-owned factories thousands of new jobs for girls as well as men.

The computer plant *(below)* is part of a cluster of industries built next to Shannon Airport in the Irish west.

The head of Shannon's development, Brendan O'Regan, is one of a new breed of enterprising managers.

Another is Anthony J. O'Reilly, Managing Director of the state-owned Irish Sugar Company, whose office overlooks Georgian Dublin.

Irish culture, still dominated by writers, actors and talkers, is experiencing a belated breakthrough in the visual arts. Edward Delaney, seen here with his statue of Theobold Wolfe Tone, is outstanding among the young sculptors, painters and designers.

At Trinity College, a striking new library by English architects symbolizes the growth of higher education in the Irish Republic.

The Union Jack flying before the Belfast City Hall symbolizes the unflagging loyalties of Northern Ireland.

Former Prime Minister Terence M. O'Neill *(above)* lured foreign-owned companies to bolster an economy which had become dependent on shipbuilding *(above right)* and other traditional industries.

Although more prosperous than the Republic, Ulster retains the flavor of its Victorian pubs and the fervor of its Protestant and pro-British convictions.

(*Right*) Belfast urchins make scrap bonfires on the eve of Orangeman's Day.

After the annual parade, sash-wearing men of the Orange Order relax in the fields outside the capital.

when I contemplate the Irish. Considering that the Soviet Union
has more than three hundred times the land area and eighty
times the population, it may seem farfetched, but I have seen
the unkempt villages in many parts of Russia and experienced
the emotional force of Russian hospitality and the vagaries of
the Russian nature. To understand the Irish countryside one
can hardly do better than to read Chekhov's short stories on
rural life in old Russia. From out of a national past of hardship
and oppression the Russians have emerged as ambivalent personalities, capable of the most contradictory displays of emotion.
"I am thus and not thus," wrote Yevgeny Yevtushenko. "I am
industrious and lazy, determined and shiftless. I am . . . shy and
impudent, wicked and good; in me is a mixture of everything
from the west to the east, from enthusiasm to envy . . ." Wright
Miller, in *Russians as People*, said: "The average Russian can
be plunged for long periods into moods of either pessimism or
optimism, either apathy or concentrated effort, and under the
stimulus of persons around him he can also change his moods
rapidly and show that they are changed, yet he cannot be
called volatile or superficial. The root self-confidence and the
security in his community are always underneath."

So it is with the Irish, who are still—like the Russians—a
rural people. There is always ambivalence. The man I see in
one situation as a quiet, pious, good Catholic reveals himself
at another time to be a Rabelaisian character at heart. What the
"typical" Irishman seems most constantly to be is someone who
manages, one way or another, to get through the manifold
difficulties of life in Ireland. James Plunkett put it most candidly
in three lines in his short story "The Trusting and the Maimed":
"Life was a succession of small deceits and subterfuges, snatched
pleasures and social inconveniences. There was only one com-
mandment which demanded absolute regard, the eleventh com-
mandment—don't be caught. The rest could be discreetly
tampered with."

Stage Irishmen

What should be obvious by now is that Irish appearances deceive. It is true what they say about the Irish, but only sometimes. The "real" Irishman is least of all like the classic singing, dancing, fighting, drinking, lazy, loquacious rogue of stage, screen and the joke books. The stage Irishman was most graphically depicted in Bernard Shaw's *John Bull's Other Island* in the person of Tim Haffigan. When the gullible Englishman, Tom Broadbent, tells his Irish partner, Larry Doyle, that Tim behaved "just like an Irishman," Doyle all but explodes:

> Like an Irishman!! Is it possible that you don't know that all this top-o'-the-morning and broth-of-a-boy and more-power-to-your-elbow business is as peculiar to England as the Albert Hall concerts of Irish music are? No Irishman ever talks like that in Ireland, or ever did, or ever will. But when a thoroughly worthless Irishman comes to England, and finds the whole place full of romantic duffers like you, who will let him loaf and drink and sponge and brag as long as he flatters your sense of moral superiority by playing the fool and degrading himself and his country, he soon learns the antics that take you in. He picks them up at the theatre or the music hall.

Just how sensitive the Irish still are about stage Irishmen was revealed in a speech by then Prime Minister Sean Lemass several years ago when he attacked those "Irish journalists, playwrights and novelists who seem to think that the surest way to extract any royalties from British publishers is to depict the Irish not as they really are but as the British public have been led to imagine them. These people do not seem to understand that they are helping to sustain an anti-Irish propaganda which was originally devised during periods of cold war against Irish independence and to justify measures which were taken to prevent its attainment."

The trouble is that every time I am solemnly told in Ireland that the stage Irishman does not exist I meet one the next day. There may not be a brogue (which is something I have heard only in New York), but the general behavior—the torrent of words, the jokes, the songs, the devil-may-care jauntiness and the great fondness for alcohol—is enough to confirm every stereotype. I remember, for example, meeting a man named Paddy in Galway. He was every inch a figure of Irish fun. He was flush-faced, round-bellied, dressed like a walking slum (as someone once said of Brendan Behan) and full of that "crazy loveableness" which a Danish writer discovered in the Irish. As might be expected, Paddy's mind was a bottomless pit of amusing stories, which he told one after another, interrupting himself only to make sardonic observations about the deplorable state of affairs in Ireland. He said that the fish caught in the waters near Galway are sent by train to the market in Dublin, where they are purchased by wholesalers to be sent back by train to the fish shops in Galway. "B-b-by the t-t-time you b-b-b-buy them here," he said, "the f-f-fish are a l-l-little tired. But that's w-w-what is known as m-m-m-modern economics in Ireland." He had, as you see, a fearful stutter. Nothing daunted, however, he stuttered on for hours as we went about what passes for night life in Galway. At the end of it all he said jovially, "That w-w-was w-w-wonderful. There's n-n-nothing I like b-b-better than t-t-t-talking!"

On another evening I left the Abbey Theatre after attending an O'Casey play and heard two ladies speaking about the earthy Irish characters they had just seen on the stage. "Thank goodness," said one, "we don't have people like that around any more." Yet only ten minutes later I was seated in a disreputable old pub near the Moore Street market, drinking in the sight of carousing market women, a dancing midget, a muscular man in a pin-stripe suit singing "Danny Boy," and a skinny man with a bowler cocked on his head pounding an ancient piano.

I should mention, too, the time in the Shelbourne Hotel bar when a friend whispered in my ear, just before introducing me to one of the most famous of Irish writers, "Go easy, now. If you provoke him he's likely to drive a fork into your hand."

Characters all, but once their existence is admitted it is necessary to say that they are the exception to the rule. The representative Irishman has more in common with "Paddy Solemn," as the late humorist Myles na Gopaleen identified his serious, straitlaced countrymen. Popular beliefs to the contrary, the everyday Irishman is neither a romantic nor a sentimentalist but a stubborn realist who can be surprisingly reserved, subdued and even silent.

Sean O'Casey wrote:

> We Irish, when we think, and we often do this, are just as serious and sober as the Englishman; but we never hesitate to give a serious thought the benefit and halo of a laugh. That is why we are so often thought to be irresponsible whereas, in point of fact, we are critical realists, while Englishmen often mistake sentimental mutterings for everlasting truths.

I remember watching the Easter Rising anniversary parade in Dublin and being puzzled by the absence of cheering, weeping or any strong signs of emotion. I asked a nearby priest about it. "Oh, no," he said, "we are not so demonstrative as you might think. We are a quiet people." It might be noted that the Irish are not much of a kissing people either. Even when parents and children or husbands and wives are reunited after long absences there is embarrassment about too much display of feeling. As for sex (which I examine in Chapter 6), it seems in Ireland to be more of a function than a passion—a case of procreation without recreation.

No one who has ever been to a sporting event in Ireland, however, would dream of suggesting that the Irish are an unemotional people with no desire for bodily contact. When Croke Park in Dublin is bursting with ninety thousand people screaming for their favorites at the All-Ireland hurling or football finals, it is easy to believe that it is sport above all else which absorbs the passions of the Irish. And absorbs their physical energies as well, for there are hundreds of thousands of Irishmen who are regularly active in sports as well as devoted followers of teams and of racing animals. Sport is so closely woven into the national fabric that it is impossible to imagine the Irish as a people existing apart from horse jumping, horse racing, greyhound racing, hunting, fishing, hurling, football, rugby, soccer, golf, bowling, sailing and all the other activities which dominate conversations, fill up the newspapers and make gambling the great national industry.

Sport manages to override political boundaries, as the All-Irish teams of Republicans and Ulstermen demonstrate, but it also provokes some patriotic excesses. The Gaelic Athletic Association is a worthy and powerful Ireland-wide organization founded more than eighty years ago to save the traditional Irish sports from losing out to English games, but its reputation is clouded by the famous, or infamous, "G.A.A. ban." The ban forbids members of the more than three thousand clubs in Ireland to play "foreign games" (more recently described as "excluded games"), or to attend such contaminating contests, or even to go to a dance in their support, under threat of automatic expulsion. The "foreign games"—cricket, hockey, rugby and soccer—have a huge following in Ireland, but, understandably, it is the swift and rough games of Gaelic football and hurling which pull hardest on the Irishman's emotions. Hurling, which may be as many as four thousand years old, looks to me like organized mayhem. Two teams of fifteen men each, all of them wielding the curved "hurley" (a cross between a hockey stick and a baseball bat), race at top speed up and down the field after the hard, fist-sized ball in a spectacular display of stamina, dexterity and physical courage.

The self-confidence of such athletes is refreshing to see after witnessing the gawkiness and uncertainty of young Irishmen in other settings, particularly when they are obliged to make contact with girls. One need only go to a dance hall anywhere in rural Ireland to see how shyly and awkwardly young people approach each other. The major problem is getting the boys to ask the girls to dance in the first place, and then when they are on the floor and in motion they seem to have nothing to say to each other. A dance scheduled to begin at nine o'clock may not actually warm up until near eleven even though the band has been playing for two hours and one side of the hall is lined with anxious girls trying to look nonchalant. The boys slowly drift in from the pubs and then huddle like rabbits around the entrance, as if to make sure they will be able to make a quick getaway. "These kids never speak to each other unless they go to a dance hall," a showband leader said. "We're needed; we're a necessary institution. But some places you can play your heart out and you still can't break the ice."

As for the Irishman's reputation as a natural stage performer, Jim Fitzgerald, a leading theatrical director in Dublin, disposed of that by saying, "We are a nation of actors—mostly bad." Gunnar Rugheimer, just before leaving Ireland after his years with Irish Television, spoke of the great fallacy that "native wit and charm" would be enough to make TV a success in Ireland: "What happens most of the time when you take an ordinary Irishman and put him in front of a camera is the same thing that happens in any country. He becomes embarrassed and clams up."

The Irishmen encountered by tourists are well prepared to be as instantly talkative and totally hospitable as the Irish are supposed to be. In less travel-worn parts the Irish are just as gracious once they make a stranger's acquaintance, but there is a greater shyness about them than might be imagined. I have sat for hours in some country pubs where the fragments of conversation only occasionally offset the grunts, mutterings, suckings of pipe stems and gulpings of stout. I have long since learned not to thrust myself upon the Irish in public places; it is better to let some time elapse so that a conversation can gently come alive. The Irish Tourist Board has even felt it advisable to suggest to travelers that they look upon the Irishman in his pub as a kind of "shy and independent, though reasonably friendly cat" who is likely to retreat in alarm—either literally or by hiding behind the façade of the professional Irishman—at the too sudden approach of a well-intentioned stranger. "Let the Irishman come to you, which he (like the cat) will do, drawn by a natural friendly curiosity, if you but offer him time and the appearance of an amiable indifference."

A conversation, once under way, can be delightful. The truest of the beliefs about the Irish is that they have a way with words. The melodious speech is attractive to begin with, and then the Irish select their words with loving care, first rolling them about in their mouths like children sucking caramels. A fair number of the better-educated Irishmen I know work hard at emulating the instant wit, or cleverly contrived wit, of such native masters as Oscar Wilde, Oliver St. John Gogarty, and J. P. Mahaffy, the great Trinity College classicist and author of *Art of Conversation*. Not long ago I dined with an Irish scholar who all but drowned me in a torrent of witticisms and the most sarcastic dissections of the most eminent Irishmen. I staggered away marveling at such a brilliant tour de force—and remembered nothing.

Even the most ordinary Irishmen seem to be able to recollect the most telling quotation for the occasion, or else they quite unconsciously bring forth the most illuminating phrase to say what they mean. I remember arriving at a tearoom on the Aran Islands after a stormy ride from the mainland. An Irish visitor to the islands, noting my bilious appearance, said, by way of greeting, "Passage perilous maketh the port pleasant." A little later a young lady with whom I was discussing Irish habits said, quite out of the blue, "The Irish are dangerous coughers in church, you know." Would any girl but an Irish girl have said "dangerous"?

Although much is made of Irish wit, I find myself thinking of the talk one hears in Ireland as a kind of balm. There is a polite, soothing effect to much of ordinary speech. Ask a hotel clerk to awaken you in the morning and he does not just say, "Yes, sir. Eight-thirty. Good night," but, more gently, "Yes sir. Eight-thirty it is. That will be quite all right. Sleep well, now." On one occasion in a Waterford restaurant I thanked the waitress for giving me the bill with my coffee, as I had requested, so that I could get to the theater on time. "Sure," she smiled, "the service may be terrible, but we're always quick about bringin' the bill." In contrast, Edward Hyams in the *New Statesman* tells of an Irish friend who discovered the disadvantages of trying to use the exquisitely good-mannered forms of common Irish speech when in America. In a New York restaurant he asked, "I wonder, now, could I have an ice cream?" The curt answer: "Why not?"

As one might expect, Ireland's choicer conversations take place in the public houses. "We drink to loosen our tongues," someone told me, thus reinforcing my notion that the Irishman is not at all the thundering extrovert he is thought to be. Once loosened, the tongues have a disconcerting habit of saying the most outlandish things. People talk with apparent knowingness about anything under the sun, whether it is the size of the Prime Minister's bank account or the state of affairs in Outer Mongolia. Ernest Hemingway once complained that the Irish knew too many things that they had not earned the right to know. Much of the talk about the world outside Ireland comes under the heading of engaging naïveté or oratorical bravado. Even about Irish subjects many people will not let their lack of information stand in the way of the most conclusively stated opinions.

The pubs are hard places to avoid, for there are fourteen thousand of them in all Ireland, or one for every 320 people, and your Irish friends just naturally steer you in that direction. The pub is a booby trap, however, for anyone trying to take a true measure of Irish life. The fact is that the majority of Irish adults hardly ever set foot in a pub. Even though women are now welcomed in the lounge bars and in a number of pubs to a degree which would have been unthinkable a generation ago, most Irish females simply do not drink in public and may never touch a drop in their lives. And among the men there are more total abstainers than heavy drinkers. There are nearly half a million persons, or one sixth of all men, women and children in the land, who have pledged not to drink alcoholic beverages. The Pioneers are by far the most numerous of the abstainers, and can be identified by their Sacred Heart badges. Most of those who do drink go at it moderately: a couple of glasses of creamy Guinness and that's it for the night. Even those who behave like drunks may well have consumed only a modest amount; either the Irish have a poor head for alcohol or else they enjoy playing the part of the jolly carouser—as if determined to live up to the conception of Irish as powerful drinkers.

The country does, of course, have a major social problem in its alcoholics. Thousands of families exist in abject distress because the father (and sometimes the mother as well) drinks away the greater part of the income. The nation as a whole, however, is well down in the international tables for alcoholic consumption. The Irish, per capita, drink less beer than the British, the Germans, the Australians and many other beer-drinking nations, and the intake of spirits is far below that of the Americans and most European nations. Still, changing living standards are having their influence. There has been an increased consumption of whiskey and wine (more people are serving drinks at home) and a gradual movement away from heavy black stout, which accounts for over three quarters of the beer sold, to lighter beers.

Life in a Rut

I will admit, as I write this, that it is painful to go against form and portray the Irishman as something other than a glorious drinker and an altogether devil of a fellow. Nonetheless, there are far more homes than pubs in Ireland, and it is in the homes that one must look for the Irishman as he is most of the time. Away from the conviviality of the pub he is revealed as someone who is extraordinarily ordinary. He leads a far simpler and certainly less cultured and sophisticated life than other Europeans.

The food the Irish eat is indicative. They exist on eggs, bacon, sausages, cabbage, potatoes and more potatoes, with few green vegetables and little fruit. There is little variety in the meat and fish, and far too much dependence on tea, bread and sweets. Irish housewives, generally speaking, are indifferent, unimaginative cooks. The Irish tourist authorities have found it necessary to set up special cooking courses for many of the farm wives who take in guests under the Farmhouse Holiday program— otherwise the tourists would be subjected to identical dismally prepared dishes for meal after meal. A social scientist, looking at family life at a low-income housing estate, wrote that even where there is plenty of money "some of the mothers just haven't the ability to cook a decent meal for the children. Many of them have no idea how to cook meat. Bread, butter, tea, buns, sometimes chips cooked either at home or bought in the cafés—this is the staple diet."

Because of their small incomes and large numbers of children (a *third* of the families at this housing estate had nine or more children), most married couples in Ireland dwell in a deep rut of routine and count themselves lucky if they can avoid the worst pitfalls of debt and are able to take some kind of holiday each year. Ireland strikes the outsider as a land of ease, but in my experience it is anything but easy for the average adult trying to make a go of life. In fact, the amount of pure, unadulterated despair is woefully large, as Irish psychiatrists are the first to say.

An *Irish Times* reporter, Mary Maher, in a series of articles on the cost of living in Dublin, described a representative Dubliner, a twenty-eight-year-old motor assembler named Sullivan, as having "the strained look of a man racing against time and circumstances." He told her, "I have a certain sense of frustration about everything. I see other people with all the things I wish we had, and I don't know how they do it. I'm continuously trying to see where I can get a few bob extra."

There are many Irish families, certainly, that lead full and enriching lives, and many people who are visibly happy. Even those without money enough for amusements or material comforts are rewarded by participating in the amateur dramatic clubs, debating societies, patriotic organizations and religious, sport and business groups which can be found all around the country. And yet, for all that, a sympathetic observer of the Irish can go away with the uncomfortable impression that far too many people live resignedly rather than happily. There is a grumpy malaise about their existence and they seem to lack imagination or vitality enough to do anything about it. Discontent is married to inertia.

I find this not so much in the old, who usually seem content enough, or in the young, who are becoming aware of their potential, but in those from early to late middle age. They might be described as the lost generation of Irishmen. They were too young to have shared in the excitement of the independence struggle and are too old to enjoy or understand the greater opportunities and liberality of the last few years in Ireland. They were the first Irishmen in seven centuries to grow up in a free state, but their personal freedom was greatly circumscribed.

Their society was economically backward, stiflingly nationalistic and intellectually arid. As late as 1963 I heard Ireland described as "a concentration camp of the mind"—which is no longer true. The kind of Irishman who came out of this restricting atmosphere, if he stayed in Ireland, was likely to be so docile and downhearted that it amounted to a crime against the human spirit. I have met such Irishmen much too often.

One October evening in Dublin I dropped into a chips-with-everything place on O'Connell Street for a cup of coffee. A morose fellow at the same table divined that I was an American and proceeded to give me a rather jumbled account of world affairs, including his conviction that the Chinese Communists were planning an invasion of Europe. I asked him what he did for a living, and some other questions, and he replied as follows:

"I'm a house painter. Did you know that Brendan Behan was a house painter, too? I knew him. I could tell you a lot of stories about him. [He proceeded to tell half a dozen.] I have six brothers and four sisters. One of the sisters became a nun in America. My dream is to go to America, but I'll never get there. A lot of us go to England, you know. We call it 'the promised land.' Have you heard about the Irishman who went to work in London? He wrote back to his friend Paddy that it was wonderful—you spend your time just picking money off the streets. So Paddy went straight over to England, and when he came out of the station in London there's a pound note on the street right in front of him. He picks it up and says to himself, 'Sure, every word he said about the place is true.' Then he throws the money away and says, 'There's no sense starting off my life in England by working on a Sunday.'

"I've thought myself about emigrating, but I can't make up my mind. I don't like working here. We do a lot of backbiting on the job. You're working with a couple of fellows, and as soon as they see someone they haven't a good word for him. They'll say, 'There's a loafer if ever there was one,' even if they hardly know him. And you meet a lot of people who haven't any heart. People don't have the feelings they used to. If some old person came into a place like this we used to give up our seat, but now we just tell them to eff off. I'm not terribly religious, of course. I go to Mass. But we shouldn't hurt each other.

"There's not much to do here. I go to the films and gamble a little. Sometimes I just drink. I think about going out with girls, but only when I see them. The feeling passes soon enough. You know: out of sight, out of mind.

"A friend of mine told me, 'Why should I get married? I'd just breed a few pups as bad as meself.' I feel that way myself. I was hurt bad about a girl. She was putting the pressure on me to get married, but I just couldn't feel up to it. I felt, like, there was too much I'd be missing. A little like stopping living. You know how it is with us: your ma might say, 'Sure, what do you want to be thinking of marrying for—there's plenty of time.' Or your mates on the job will laugh at you for stepping out with a girl. They'll make jokes about it. You know the story about the Irish bachelor and the spinster? They go out together for twenty years and finally she says, 'Paddy, isn't it about time we got married?' And he says, 'Ah, sure, that's a ridiculous idea. Who'd ever have us?'

"Anyway, I don't think so much of the girls these days. If you have a car or they hear the rattle in your pocket, then they'll go out with you. They don't care about your personality —what you're really like. I'm thirty-one. I suppose I'll get married sometime. What will happen will happen. If I can't get the right girl, I'll have to take second best.

"I left school at fourteen. The Christian Brothers were all right, but I sometimes think I could have a better education. I could have learned something instead of a dead language. That's all Irish is, no matter what they say about it. I sometimes think I could have been something else than a house painter. I'd like to be on the stage. I have dreams, you see, and there are parts of them which are like pieces out of the films, and because these are things happening to me in the dreams I feel there's a message in it for me, but I don't know what it is. Still, it doesn't matter. Be satisfied with what you have! Look at Frank Sinatra. He has it all, but I read in a magazine that he isn't happy. The thing is to be happy."

The New Breed

This familiar Irishman, the hapless, hopeless dreamer, by his very presence puts into sharp relief the new breed of Irishmen who are beginning to emerge on the Irish scene. The contrast and conflict between the two was made the subject of a play called *Breakdown* by Eugene McCabe. Two former schoolmates, now in their mid-thirties, meet after many years. Ned Holloway, a small-town chartered accountant, "a neat gray monkish man," has gone to seed. His wife explains his office routine: "The main knack is never to be there—and hire a little girl to explain why." He spends most of his time playing billiards: "chalking his cue for deadly dictums about what's wrong with the country." C. J. Shine, on the other hand, went from fame as an international rugby player to success as "a tailor-made executive in fifty-guinea suits" who owns both a Jaguar and a fancy Protestant wife. Shine, who has gotten into some financial trouble, needs Holloway to doctor his books for him, but his old school chum, delighting in the irony of the situation, makes Shine crawl first, and then refuses. At the end of it all, Shine roars:

I'll not be broken by a little smirking ex-priest fiddling and fixing loop-holes for every little counter hack from here to Ballyduff, till the big wheel comes rolling, then he jumps in the ditch, all hocus pious pocus, and believes nothing! That's the funny part of it. We're moving here, soon we'll be humming and I mean to hum with them and you'll be standing on the sideline with your blurry Gaelic buffs, your bile and the whole bloody cringing crowd of boozey Jeremiahs . . . remember that . . . *watch* and *remember*.

To which Holloway says contemptuously, "It's the new national anthem. I'll write it down."

The playwright is obviously not fond of either the old-style or the new-style Irishman, but the Ireland of the future will see more Shines and fewer Holloways. It will also be marked by some who manage to combine cool intelligence and high ambition with a concern for public service. One of the most encouraging signs in Ireland today is the surfacing of outstanding young managerial men who have somehow thrown off the dead weight of Irish fatalism. A good many may be found in the business world, but the new breed is most evident in politics and in the state enterprises. George Colley, for example, while more of an Irish-language enthusiast than most of his colleagues, is a bright and aggressive politician who did not become nationally known until a few years ago. He made his name as a progressive minister for education (before moving on to the commerce and industry department) and he became one of the three principal contenders to succeed Sean Lemass as premier. Significantly, he is particularly thought of by the average Irishman as the politician who had the guts to stand up to the Bishop of Galway when the Bishop abused him at a public meeting. Michael McInerney, a veteran political correspondent, has described Colley and the other relatively young men in the Irish government as a "completely new, untried generation of political leaders" who "seem utterly unlike their fathers in dress and behaviour. They seem to have all the élan of the modern business entrepreneur. Immaculately dressed and groomed, they look remote and prosperous in their Mercedes cars; their speeches are well-informed, showing knowledge of the most modern techniques in industry, commerce and services."

The most striking of the new breed is Anthony J. O'Reilly, whom Ulick O'Connor described to me as "the prototype of the first really free Irishmen." Tony O'Reilly is a handsome six-foot-four-inch former international rugby hero who has an

Australian wife and (at last count) six children, including triplets. Full of fire and self-confidence, sharp of tongue as well as mind, he went to a Jesuit school and trained as a solicitor before becoming an industrial consultant in England. At the age of twenty-five he was back in Ireland as the first general manager of the Irish Milk Board. In this vital job of marketing the nation's surplus dairy products he moved with uncommon energy and was courageous enough to ignore the old taboos by doing business with Communist countries. In 1966, at thirty, he succeeded a respected man of twice his years as managing director of the huge Irish Sugar Company, a state enterprise which has embarked on some expensive adventures in freeze-dried food processing and which has created a new company in partnership with Heinz.

In common with others of his breed, O'Reilly is unencumbered by the old baggage of unrealistic national dreams. He is an arch-pragmatist—proud to be an Irishman, but well aware that the nation cannot prosper in splendid isolation. He deplores all the "wasted" years when Ireland seemed to be in a stupor, and he is concerned about "the failure of communication in this talkative country"—the difficulty of creating a response to modern ideas. But for Pope John and Sean Lemass, he probably would not be working in Ireland at all. It says something for the improved state of the nation that the O'Reillys are finding it challenging to stay at home. "These are the people," said an executive at the Guinness plant, "who are beginning to make things hum in this country." It is a new kind of Irish music.

Chapter 4

THE NEW REALISTS

There are old men in Ireland who will still change colour and clench their fists when the name de Valera is mentioned.

—PATRICK O'DONOVAN

The ironic tragedy of Irish history since 1922 is that, although we freed ourselves from the British, we did not acquire for ourselves British freedom; and that whilst in the same period Britain shed her empire, became humanitarian, set up the welfare state and became socialistic, we have clung to the outworn and outdated conservative attitudes which the British held forty years ago.

—S. P. IRWIN

"When I went to Ireland," an English friend told me, "everyone said I should never discuss politics or religion with the Irish. But, dammit, that's all people talk about!"

The Irish have always talked politics. It is the great national pastime. They are going at it today as vigorously as ever, but a new dimension has been added. The orthodox conservatism which has so marked the Irish political scene is giving way to what can only be described as incipient liberalism. There is a most visible impatience with business-as-usual politics and a sometimes startling outspokenness about the demands for more progressive political action.

This was nowhere more graphically demonstrated than on a late-evening Irish Television program in the spring of 1967. A blunt-spoken priest, Father Fergal O'Connor, gave warm endorsement to ideological socialism and proceeded to lambaste Irish politics and politicians. He spoke scornfully of the Labour Party as an ineffectual capitalist-oriented organization. He said that Fine Gael, the main opposition party, was on the right track with its new "Just Society" policy—but what a pity that so many of its members did not believe in it. As for the ruling party, Fianna Fail, "they just make up their policy as they go along." Said Father O'Connor, "We are governed by a small clique supported by a bunch of yes men."

Someone in the audience said all this was "unadulterated nonsense," but many Irishmen would agree with the priest. The nation's latent radicalism is rising slowly to the surface. Paradoxically, the current years of relative prosperity are producing greater demands for change than were ever seen in the years of economic depression. As one commentator, Dr. Louis Smith, has put it, "The standard of living has never been so high in Ireland as it is now. Yet the people have rarely been so discontented."

The economic advance of the nation since 1958 has led the public to expect a fast rate of progress, and some politicians, in their search for votes, have promised more than any government can deliver. The Irish seek the same wages and social benefits as those of the British, who have far greater numbers and resources, and a long history in industry and commerce. Individual incomes in Ireland are little more than half those of the British and a third of the Americans'. The disproportionate number of children and elderly persons in Ireland, plus all the housewives and the handicapped and unemployed, puts a heavy burden on the third of the nation which earns the money. Wages are increasing, but prices are rising and taxes are severe; for some income groups taxes are higher than in Britain. The country does not have the financial resources to satisfy all the demands. It has been called "a capitalist country without capital."

Leftward Movement

Bread-and-butter and social-security issues are in the fore-front of political thinking now that "we have stopped playing the patriot game," to quote a young politician. One result is the cautious leftward shift by all three political parties. The Labour Party now calls itself "socialist," a word once avoided in a country which has equated socialism with Soviet-style Communism. The two others are starting to behave like the Social Democratic parties on the Continent. As mentioned earlier, all the parties are affected by the youth movement, which is putting into the commanding posts younger men who were born in the 1920s and 1930s, after the independence struggle. There is a slow phasing out of the "humbug about the Irish language, Christianity and partition," as Dr. Noel Browne has described it. He has charged: "The love of our language and the understandable resentment of our people against the border were deliberately used to help distract their attention from the clear failure of our leaders to solve the serious social and economic problems which we still have."

None of these developments, however, has so far altered the fact that Ireland is phenomenal in the democratic world for the constancy and conservatism of its political life. The three dominant parties in the Republic, when combined with the two principal parties in the North, give the island a total of five right-wing and middle-of-the-road parties which have only a few individual left-wing voices raised against them. The trade-union movement in both ends of Ireland has only marginal political influence.

In Ulster, the Unionists, representing the great majority of

Protestants, have headed the government for nearly half a century, since the first days of the province's separate existence. In the Republic, Fianna Fail ("Warriors of Destiny") has been in power almost continually since 1932. Its domination has been interrupted only twice, for a total of six years, by coalition governments. For thirty-five years it has held close to half of the seats in the Dail, always with a long lead over Fine Gael ("the Irish Tribes"). As the oldest party of them all, Labour has remained on the fringe of things: a cautious third force with little rural strength and a surprisingly lukewarm appeal to urban Irishmen.

Political life in Northern Ireland (but *not* in the Republic) is wholly distorted by religious controversy. As one bit of Ulster graffiti expressed it, "Take religion out of politics and what have you got? No politics!" In the south, according to Proinsias MacAonghusa, a prominent left-wing commentator, "the outstanding feature of Irish political life for many years has been the broad consensus about aims between all major or relatively major groups, in spite of continuous and sometimes fierce disagreements about methods and personalities." Irish officials drumming for foreign investment can and do boast that Ireland is as stable and unrevolutionary a society as a wary businessman could hope for on this earth.

The Irish voter, who is against-the-government almost as a reflex action, is nonetheless just about the most predictable political animal this side of the Communist world. Generally speaking, he votes the way he or his family has always voted, depending on the position taken during the civil war of forty-five years ago. Most industrial workers vote for one or the other of the two main parties instead of for Labour, despite the example of the Labour Party's success in Britain. Even the tens of thousands of farmers who have been protesting against government farm politics do not seem to be wavering appreciably in their traditional loyalties. Most of them still support Fianna Fail, whose leaders they are so busy abusing.

Like the Democratic and Republican parties in the U.S.A., Fianna Fail and Fine Gael are more ideologically divided within themselves than they are from each other. Even then, the arguments are not so much about fundamentals as they are about priorities. The older hands are more concerned with the familiar patriotic issues of language and partition than the younger men. The latter are more anxious to push economic expansion and social-educational reforms. As the *Irish Times* has said:

> The realisation that our enemy is as much within us as without is one of the tasks to be driven home by the younger men in politics today. They kick themselves for all the dozy, self-satisfied years; for all the things undone in education, in agriculture, and other spheres; for the terrible self-satisfaction which allowed emigration to go on and on; for the small-minded pettifogging politics in which we have indulged, most particularly since the second World War, when other countries, shattered by the war, have rebuilt themselves entirely.

The Politicians

As their record in the United States would seem to prove, the Irish make artful politicians, and public interest in politics is huge. The percentage of voters who turn out to cast their ballots in an election is one of the highest of all the democratic states. During election times the politicians go into whirlwind action and the country throbs with the excitement of it all. A news item from a town in Connemara stated: "In the days before the Presidential election, excavations were made for the pipe-laying of a water-supply from the reservoir along the back road. When the votes had been cast, all excavations were filled up again, and there has been no word about a water-supply since."

In such a society the contact between the voters and their parliamentary representatives is on a close and often first-name basis. Most of the members of the 144-man Dail Eireann, the

Irish House of Commons (there is also a sixty-man Senate with restricted powers), are within easy driving distance of their constituencies and they spend much of their time in them. Appropriately enough, the atmosphere at Leinster House, the handsome eighteenth-century seat of the Irish Parliament, is like that of an oversized city hall.

With notable exceptions, the standard of the politicians is not high. Pull and personality count more than experience and ideas— but then this is not something exclusive to Ireland. What is especially Irish is the way the sons, widows and relatives of old heroes are conspicuous by their presence. The average politician is skillful at pulling wires, attending funerals and knowing everyone's name, but he is apt to have a narrow and often obstructionist outlook on large national issues. Dr. David Thornley, a leading political scientist, describes the majority of Dail members as overworked and underpaid local grievance men who have little time left over to do a proper legislative job.

The quality of parliamentary debate is low even if there are some brilliant flashes of oratory. It is amusing, of course, to read about the member who wants to make sure that topless dresses will be banned if they reach Ireland, or about the slanging matches between the wittier politicians, or about the latest charges of political favoritism. (Responding to accusations, Education Minister Donogh O'Malley has said candidly, "I have no hesitation, all things being equal, in supporting those who support us.") But the time wasted on trivia often prevents adequate discussion of the big issues—for example, the momentous question of Ireland's hoped-for entry into the European Common Market.

I once spent an evening in the community hall of the little western town of Grange, north of Sligo, listening to a discussion by local citizens about government suggestions that they provide farmhouse and other accommodation for tourists. It began on a high plane, with priestly blessings and factual speeches about the benefits that tourism would bring to the region, but in due course the whole thing bogged down in a meaningless row about road signs. So it is with the Irish Parliament: it has its moments of grandeur, but it all too often becomes little more than a gilded version of a squabble in a pub. There is a shortage of original and constructive ideas. MacAonghusa, whose tempestuous radicalism cost him his post as the Labour Party's vice-chairman, has said that what is most lacking in Irish politics "is an atmosphere of intellectual inquiry and intelligent criticism. Irish traditions usually penalize the inquiring mind in all fields. One of the dirtiest words in Irish politics is 'intellectual.' Sadly, it must be recorded that Irish parties appear to regard anyone with ideas as either a harmless lunatic or a dangerous nuisance, while at the same time claiming that they welcome new ideas and have open minds. And the depressing thing about it all is that there is no reason to believe that any great changes will come about for a long, long time."

Ireland has all manner of democratic instruments and constitutional safeguards. It has a free press and the exposing weapon of the parliamentary question. It has some outstanding political scientists. And, as I have said, it has an attentive public. Yet it is striking how much authority is confined to the few men who constitute the power elite and how autocratically they wield it. The government ministers have such power and so little effective opposition that they tend to become arrogant, as in the instances when individual ministers have sought to suppress or alter the news reports of the national radio-TV service. The senior civil servants and the heads of the big semi-state industries, plus a few key bankers and industrialists, are the other major decision makers. In the background, of course, is the hierarchy of the Roman Catholic Church, which functions more as an inhibiting than as a dictating force. The Church does not run the country, contrary to some outside opinion. The clergy is even criticized for not speaking out more often, in the manner of the exceptional Father O'Connor, about the slowness of the authorities to correct social evils. The Church's relationship with the national government is touchy at best. (After all, it had condemned the Rising of 1916 and sided all too often with the British rulers.) But private expressions of displeasure by the archbishops and the bishops carry much weight, and on the local level the priest is still often the most important man around.

Irish political leaders reflect the paternalism of the Church. Theirs is a father-knows-best attitude to a public which they often seem to distrust. The public, for its part, counts for little between election days. There are few civic groups with real influence, local or national. Parents have little say in the running of the schools. Such vocational organizations as the National Farmers' Association and the Irish Congress of Trade Unions are becoming more effective, but to date they have served only to illustrate the marginal importance of pressure groups—at least those outside the Church—in Irish politics.

In most respects the Irish are as free as any people in the world, but they have yet to know the fullness of individual liberty. They have the freedom to put politicians in and out of office, and they are free to live and work where and how they please, but their range of choices is narrow. Similarly, the Irish have many "rights," but there are limitations on self-expression. Everyone is conscious of all the things one does not do or say in Ireland. A few years ago, in an *Irish Press* series, "The Young Idea," an Irish student in Paris, Mary Kenny, wrote: "In going to school in Paris I was obliged to learn the Rights of Man off by heart; in drinking coffee in cafés I heard waiters and workers and artisans talking about *la liberté*. The great revelation that comes over so many of our exiles hit me slowly but with force. I discovered the meaning of democracy, the meaning of individual rights, the meaning of criticism, the meaning of the civil state of man."

She added that Ireland has priceless riches to give to "a world dimmed by the ungodly," but "how can she give them when the world laughs at her, considers her a nursery, a glass-protected shelter, protected from the world's naughtiness and realism, and therefore naïve and unrealistic and unfit for the combat?"

This too is changing. Irish voters are becoming more aware of the world and less ready to submit meekly to authority. It already appears that the cult of personality which has been a feature of Irish politics is passing. The age of the great men may be over. When Jack Lynch became prime minister late in 1966 he was just one of several relatively young ministers who were in competition for the job, and he was soon being described as "the first among equals." It seemed a far cry from the strongman days of William T. Cosgrave, who nursed the young democracy through its anguished early years; Eamon de Valera, who gave the nation a new respectability in the world and carried it unscathed through World War II; and Sean Lemass, the creator of confidence, who thrust Ireland into modern times.

Cosgrave, whose son Liam is now the leader of the opposition, died in 1965 at the age of eighty-five, secure in Irish history as one of the founders of the modern state. He survived a death sentence for his role in the Easter Rising and went on to become the chairman of the Provincial Government in 1922, and then president of the Executive Council (a post comparable to today's premiership) of the Irish Free State from 1923 to 1932. He was the leader of the opposition until his retirement in 1944. He had a generosity of spirit which was unusual among those senior politicians who lived through the quarrel over the treaty and the bloodshed of the civil war.

While leading Ireland through a stormy period of internal disorder, Cosgrave put the country's new parliamentary institutions to work. He saw to it that the rule of law prevailed in a bitterly divided land which might well have become, at least for a while, a police state. He was not the only figure of importance during the new state's first decade, but he proved himself to be the biggest democrat of them all by overruling those in his own government who would have held on to power by force. When de Valera's Fianna Fail Party gained the upper hand in the 1932 elections, Cosgrave quietly stepped aside.

Eamon de Valera

De Valera was already a world figure when he came to power. Sixteen years earlier he had, like Cosgrave, played a front-line role in the Rising and had only barely escaped execution. His birthplace was New York City. The date: 1882, a year of renewed famine and of violence against the English landlords. One foreign journalist wrote that Ireland was "not only the most distressful country in Europe, but in the whole wide world." De Valera's father was a Spanish musician who died two years after his son's birth, and his mother an immigrant Irishwoman who sent her child to Ireland before his third birthday. He became a scholarship student, a mathematics teacher, a Gaelic Leaguer, and then one of the original members of the rebellious Irish Volunteers shortly before World War I.

An ascetic, thin-lipped, seldom-smiling man, de Valera was Ireland's unswerving idealist who had the bearing and the assurance (and the guile) of a statesman long before Ireland became a state. He was involved in all the major events of the war years when the Irish rebels made Britain's difficulty Ireland's opportunity. When he was released from his life sentence in an English prison a year after the Rising, he returned home to find himself a national hero. He was elected president of the Sinn Fein ("Ourselves Alone") movement, which sought an independent all-Ireland republic, and of the Irish Volunteers, the military arm of the freedom movement. Soon Irish children were singing a new ballad:

> Up de Valera! he's the champion of the right,
> We'll follow him to battle 'neath the Orange, Green
>   and White,

And when next we challenge England we'll beat her in
   the fight,
And we'll crown de Valera king of Ireland!

Though still in his thirties, de Valera was the most influential
Irishman of his day. He was not able, however, to head off the
Treaty of 1921, which his closest colleagues signed in London
while he remained in Dublin. The treaty not only partitioned
Ireland, but obliged members of the Irish Parliament to pledge
their allegiance to the British Crown. As de Valera fought in
the political arena to prevent the treaty from coming into force,
republican extremists began an armed struggle which de Valera
later commanded, and which he finally brought to an end in
1923 when the Free State forces proved invincible. The orgy
of murders, executions and senseless destruction of property
poisoned Irish political life for decades to come. Many thousands
of Irishmen today, in an oversimplification of history, still
consider de Valera to be "the man who started the civil war."
I have been in pubs and restaurants when flush-faced men
stood up and reviled their President in the strongest possible
language.

Nonetheless, de Valera has always had a multitude of passionate supporters behind him. Within a decade after the civil war
he was leading the government and setting off on a campaign
to assert Ireland's sovereignty and self-sufficiency. (It was not
until 1948, however, that a sudden decision by John A. Costello's
coalition government proclaimed the Republic of Ireland and
withdrew it from the Commonwealth.) De Valera won world
acclaim for several speeches of high idealism at the League of
Nations, and his whole appearance and manner succeeded in
conveying an image of a proud and self-reliant nation. Even those
who thought him second-rate as a thinker had to admit that he
looked first-rate. One critic has said that it was "a case of a
Rolls-Royce chassis and a Ford engine." Another has spoken

of de Valera's "righteous self-belief." Senator Owen Sheehy Skeffington, however, is generous enough to say that "of Mr. de Valera it can truly be said that if he is vain, he has a lot to be vain about."

He was prime minister for more than two decades, moving up to the presidency in 1959. For some thirty-five years he has been the nation's foremost father figure, a role he has felt eminently well qualified to play: "Whenever I wanted to know what the Irish people wanted, I had only to examine my own heart, and it told me straight off . . ." He has idealized the way of life of his childhood: "Sometimes I think it would be a fine thing for us in this country if we could shut ourselves off from the rest of the world and get back to the simple life I knew as a boy in Bruree."

Such a viewpoint, touching as it is, meant that de Valera in his later years of power held back the nation from its natural progress; the Irish marked time instead of finding ways to move along with the social and economic developments of the age. For all his devotion to the Irish people, he was no crusader for the improvement of their standard of life. One commentator has said that de Valera "may well go down in history as the genius who took the socialism out of Irish Republicanism." Much was done during his years as prime minister, especially in housing, but much was not done. He did not carry out "the radical changes" necessary to provide for "the fundamental needs of our citizens," as he had promised in an unusual speech in 1932. As Senator Skeffington pointed out several years ago, de Valera was interested in education but "his interest has been mainly in the higher reaches. He has shown enlightened generosity to the universities, and has treated Trinity College with consistent fairness; he has helped to found most praiseworthy institutes of higher learning; but our primary school system has been allowed to remain—apart from the teaching of Irish—pretty well what it was when Pearse so vigorously condemned it as a 'murder machine.'"

As prime minister, de Valera was in a class by himself: an Olympian, righteous figure who became ever more remote from the realities of Irish life. He was not a man to be argued with; he had a habit of having things his way. He was the national schoolmaster, and the Parliament building was his lecture hall. General de Gaulle might well have learned his style from de Valera. Today, as President of Ireland, de Valera is a man to be admired. He is the nation's foremost historical monument and the world's most senior statesman. He is a living legend who received his first lessons in the ways of politics and revolution in the days of Queen Victoria.

Now in his mid-eighties, de Valera is still a courtly, active man who carries out a taxing schedule of ceremonial duties. He is at his best when he stands ramrod-straight and eagle-profiled in the cold wind and rain at the unveiling of a martyr's plaque or at yet another funeral of a younger colleague of the hard years. So close to blindness that he can see but little of the vast official residence he occupies or its beautifully manicured gardens, he usually has a military aide at his side who gently guides him about the physical obstacles of the world. In his office, however, where the bookshelves are heavy with the weight of the classics and the *Catholic Encyclopaedia*, he sits alone with callers, who are not always aware that the President can scarcely see them. At the end of each talk, he rises from his desk and leads his visitor across the room to the door, sending him off with a strong handshake. De Valera impresses his guests by remembering the names of people he met long years ago and recalling the details of events which have long since passed into the history books.

Although he is well aware of the changes under way in Ireland today, his exposition of the kind of country that ought to be is like a cry from the past. When I heard his views I recalled a comment by an editor in Cork that "for years, de Valera has responded to every problem by talking about the importance of the Irish language." He has said that restoration of Irish, "the sister language of Latin and Greek," is more important than independence itself. He holds to his dream of an Irish-speaking and God-fearing Ireland which would show the materialistic world how to live the simple Christian life. He will almost apologize for the expensive furnishings in his office; a crude desk and chair would do just as well. He speaks of the days when he was quite content with a thin mattress on the floor and a book to read in his small jail cell. The strength of his feelings on such matters makes it all the more intriguing that the man who was one of his closest deputies for over a third of a century, who was his choice as his successor to the premiership, should have been the great pragmatist who pulled the nation out of its dreamy past and hurled it into an ever more materialistic future.

Sean Lemass

As "the quiet man" and "the manager of Ireland," Sean Lemass never aroused anything like the passions which swirled about de Valera, or about such long-dead patriots as James Connolly and Michael Collins, and yet Lemass influenced and altered Ireland more decisively in this century than any man save de Valera. When he stepped down from the premiership in 1966, there were numerous tributes to his work but little real appreciation of what he had done, in his unflamboyant, business-like way, for the country. In the *Irish Times*, however, Michael McInerney wrote:

> Mr. Lemass changed Ireland radically in his seven years as Taoiseach [prime minister] and his 50 years of political life. It is to be remembered that he had a longer ministerial record than any Taoiseach, even including Mr. de Valera; for he was a minister for nearly 30 years, seven years longer than Dev. He will be remembered forever as the man who industrialized Ireland, who ended the longest cold war in history [the Republic versus Ulster], who took over from the magic

of a de Valera to the practical tasks. He consolidated national independence by consolidating economic growth. He joined an Economic United Kingdom without sacrificing sovereignty. Ireland owes him a lot.

Lemass was only fourteen when he joined the revolutionary underground. He was just sixteen, the youngest rebel of them all, when he spent four days with a rifle on the roof of Dublin's central post office during the Easter Rising. After the fighting he was imprisoned for several weeks and then, as the story goes, "the cops gave him a kick in the arse and told him to go home to his ma." As he grew into manhood, Lemass, whose brother Noel was slain in the Dublin hills, fought as an I.R.A. guerrilla. He went to jail four different times and became an officer on de Valera's staff during the civil war. He was captured by the pro-treaty forces and imprisoned once again for a year. "That boy is always on the run," said the father of the pretty girl he married in 1924. "He'll never make a home for you."

One of the founders of the Fianna Fail Party, Lemass became the youngest member of de Valera's cabinet when Fianna Fail came to power in 1932. He was de Valera's minister for industry and commerce during the long era of protectionism and isolationism, but as prime minister after 1959 he took the opposite course of expansive, outward-looking economic policies which admitted Ireland's need of foreign capital.

In his early years under de Valera, the young Lemass earned the affectionate Biblical nickname Benjamin (after Jacob's youngest son), but he escaped the fate of Anthony Eden, who never quite emerged from Churchill's long shadow, by proving himself to be a more imaginative and open-minded leader than the old warrior. As prime minister, Lemass was so different an Irish politician that it almost seemed as if the nation had been taken over by a glutton-for-work businessman who was a secret Social Democrat. He was not much of a social mixer. He was unexciting as a speaker, impatient with slackers, zealous about efficiency, and more excited by an increase in exports than by oratory about holy Ireland's destiny. While de Valera had the air of a lay archbishop, Lemass had the flair, and appearance, of a riverboat gambler.

When I first met him in 1963 he looked ten years younger than his age. His graying mustache, silver-streaked black hair and somewhat wolflike countenance provided a picture of a Continental Irishman. Indeed, Mrs. Lemass told me that her husband "must have some French ancestors. He looks sort of French." But his father was a Dublin hatter and the family had lived in Ireland for generations. Lemass was born in Dublin in 1899, and he learned his four R's (reading, 'riting, 'rithmetic and revolution) under the Christian Brothers. He never acquired any real fluency in the Irish language, but then neither did most of the politicians who supported the language restoration movement.

When I suggested to some of Lemass's friends that he was not exactly the typical Irishman, they agreed that he was more industrious and single-minded than most, but in private he was a hearty companion who liked to relax with his cronies, play poker and go off fishing, and who fussed over his wife, his four children and his numerous grandchildren. On one occasion I arranged with Mrs. Lemass to have a photographer take a picture of the whole family for an American magazine. On the appointed day we found that we had to squeeze twenty-four persons into the photograph—and they apologized for those who hadn't been able to make it.

Although politics is his game, and one which he has played with unrivaled skill, Sean Lemass will probably appeal to historians as Ireland's great practical economist. I once asked him where he had acquired his knowledge of economics. Because his formal schooling has been interrupted by the revolution, he said, he had begun his economic studies while in prison. However, most of his knowledge, "such as it is," was picked up on the job when he served in the Irish governments.

The success of Ireland in the past decade prompted the question why more had not been done earlier to expand the economy and improve the social services. Of course, said Lemass, the nation's resources were terribly limited in the early decades, but there was also a lack of the special knowledge needed to pull up a nation by its bootstraps. "I only wish we knew then a lot of the things we know now." He expanded on this in a public speech: "We were the first of the small countries to achieve freedom in this century, and we undertook the tasks of self-government with little to draw on from the experience of others, and little understanding in any country of the problems which a newly independent nation had to face. The newly freed countries of today can, from the beginning, call on many international institutions to advise and assist them, and to provide capital funds for their development. In the early days of our state, there were no facilities of this kind, and, indeed, the necessity for systematic planning of national economic development had not then been accepted anywhere, even in Russia."

The Irish Free State in 1932 was a country which looked as if it had been bypassed altogether by the Industrial Revolution. Partition had torn away the shipyards, the engineering works and the linen factories of Northern Ireland. The only industries of any consequence in the new state were based on agriculture. These were brewing, distilling, bacon curing, butter making, biscuit manufacturing, and the weaving of woolens and worsteds. Two thirds of the population lived on the land. Exports, especially of live cattle, were almost wholly agricultural, and almost all of them went to Great Britain, as always.

It was a simple farm economy which made only sparing use of machinery and chemical fertilizers. The barter system still existed in some parts. In the more remote islands and coastal areas life was about as primitive as it could possibly be in the twentieth century. The Irish depended on the British for almost all their consumer goods, and London continued to dominate private banking and other business. The economic dependence on Britain was galling to de Valera. One of the first orders of business for the incoming government was to make Ireland as self-sufficient as possible. It was a formidable undertaking.

Some progress had been made by the Cosgrave government, but the handful of small factories could hardly be seen on the preponderantly rural landscape. Even the agricultural side of things was unpromising. Much of the country was waterlogged or mountainous, and a lot of the arable land was undeveloped. The surrounding seas were full of fish, but the Irish had never developed a proper fishing industry. There were not enough forests left to build a worthwhile timber industry. Wood had to be imported. There was plenty of turf (peat) for burning in fireplaces, but no oil or coal to speak of, and few minerals. The nation had few skilled workers or experienced managers, and there was little capital. The long years of revolution, civil war and economic dislocation had left the Irish public weary, divided and demoralized.

This was the background as Lemass, only thirty-three and new to his first job in government, produced a plan for industrial development. The government soon began using quotas, restrictions and tariffs as bricks to build a protective wall so that new Irish factories making Irish goods for the Irish could survive. Many plants were founded within a few years' time, and they were able to supply much of the country's requirements. They were often low-grade goods, but they did the job. Irish economists I have consulted agree that it was necessary and wise to provide a shelter for native industry at that point in history. "The trouble is," said one, "that protection went on too long. We have had the devil's own time getting these companies into competitive shape to face up to free trade."

Protectionism was most intense in Ireland during the nearly five years of the "Economic War" with Britain in the 1930s. The conflict stemmed from the government's decision to withhold the payment of Land Annuities to the British. It is a complicated story, but the upshot was Britain's imposition of prohibitive tariffs on Irish imports. The Irish, in turn, placed stiffer tariffs on British imports. It meant hard times for the Irish, but there were at least two rewarding side effects. Austerity having suddenly become patriotic, the Irish learned to do without many of the British goods they were so fond of; "Be Irish, Buy Irish," was the new idea, even if the local products were often inferior. Secondly, many Irish farmers who could not sell their cattle to Britain began to switch over to tillage, thus helping the government's effort to achieve self-sufficiency in grain. Ireland was thereby in better shape to fend for itself during World War II.

Although the Irish government unquestionably favored free enterprise, it was faced with the fact that private firms did not have the capital or the ability to take on the big power, transport and industrial jobs which needed doing. Taking care not to make it seem like socialism in action, Lemass, under de Valera, created the variety of state-supported enterprises in sugar, shipping, aviation and much else which today loom so large in the Irish economy. Ireland had already nationalized its electricity—one of the first countries to do so. A small power plant was taken over and made the nucleus of a network which covers most of the nation.

Many other measures were taken—by the two coalition governments as well as Fianna Fail—to expand and protect the Irish economy during the depression years of the 1930s and through the war and the early postwar years. Ireland changed painfully slowly, however, and it was still far from being industrialized. In 1952, two decades after Lemass had set to work on the economy, live cattle and food and drink accounted for eighty per cent of exports. The industrial sector was still small. Farmers made up half the work force. Ireland was still an old-fashioned country, the land of the donkey cart and the potato patch.

The great limp forward drove up the emigration figures and produced the widespread conviction that Irish problems were beyond solution. As the population dwindled inexorably, the economic-growth rate slowed to a crawl, and then went backward. In 1957 the Irish voters decided that the coalition government was hopeless and brought Fianna Fail back to power with its greatest majority ever.

Once again, and still under de Valera, Sean Lemass was in charge of the economy. Another veteran minister, Dr. James Ryan, was given the responsibility for the nation's finances. Both men were anxious to accelerate the economy, but they lacked a master plan. Fortunately, the previous government just the year before had promoted an outstanding civil servant, Dr. Kenneth Whitaker, an Ulsterman from County Down, from the ranks of the Finance Department to the secretaryship. Whitaker and a few of his associates began to quietly work on a comprehensive program for economic development. One day in December 1957 he mentioned his ideas to Dr. Ryan. The enthusiastic Finance Minister took the Whitaker plan in its rough outline before the Cabinet, which, after much discussion, instructed Whitaker to go ahead with the preparation of what was to become the First Programme for Economic Expansion. It was launched late in 1958. Seven months afterward Sean Lemass succeeded de Valera as prime minister and was able at last to make modernization of the economy Ireland's first order of business.

Expansive Economy

As a recent government document has explained, the primary aim of the five-year plan was psychological: to "accelerate progress by strengthening public confidence, indicating the opportunities for development, and encouraging a progressive, expansionist outlook." Fearing the mood of despondency which might result from failure, the planners set an annual growth-rate target of a modest two per cent. It turned out to be over four per cent. At the same time, yearly emigration dropped amazingly from close to sixty thousand to twelve thousand in 1962–63. This, however, was due more to the economic slump in Britain than to better times in Ireland. Emigration has since fluctuated between fifteen and twenty-five thousand.

Even though the country's Second Programme (1964–70) has run into trouble and has disillusioned the economically unsophisticated who assumed that a high growth rate was now automatic, the boost to national morale by the upsurge after 1958 was colossal. Ireland was like a self-pitying plain woman who discovers that she has sex appeal after all. To foreign industrialists, the country's appeal lay in its labor surplus, political stability, literate citizenry, mild climate, reasonably well-developed power and transportation facilities, and handy geographical location between Western Europe and North America. Even so, a number of special inducements have been necessary to lure international manufacturers to Ireland. In particular, there are liberal grants to pay for factories, equipment and training. Extra cash is offered for setting up shop in the more depressed parts of the country. There is a ten-year holiday on export profits, with an additional five-year "tapering-off" period.

There are now more than 250 new international companies, but most are fairly small operations which seldom employ more than a few hundred people. In one recent year, thirty-five factories were opened for the manufacture of everything from socks, underwear and mink furs to garden tools, business machines and pharmaceutical products. Their parent companies are mainly British, but there are American, German, French, Austrian, Finnish and Italian owners as well. In the early years of the industrial drive there were widespread complaints that the government was "turning over Ireland to foreigners." In fact, it was not so much the foreign entrepreneurs who were causing concern as the wealthy Germans who came to the country, though never in great numbers, to buy up choice pieces of inexpensive Irish property as safe retreats in the nuclear age.

Particularly irritating was the way such foreigners would

block the pathways to beaches which had formerly been open to anyone, and put up "No Trespassing" signs to ward off Irishmen who were used to walking where they wished. People began scrawling "Irish Land for the Irish!" on walls, and a priest in Cork city asked, "Has the day really come when an Irishman can't go for a swim in his own sea?" A Bantry Bay fisherman grumbled, "We spent half our lives getting the British out. Now we're spending the other half coaxing the Germans in!" There was a great outcry when a German company erected a stolid modern hotel and a row of bungalows along the shore of a lake in Killarney, the country's most celebrated beauty area.

More recently the complaints have been about the French aircraft factory which never got around to making airplanes, and the other failures, but the country's general experience with the new industries has been good. The most eloquent part of the story is at Shannon, where the combination of the famous international airport, a new industrial estate and a new town has grafted a totally contemporary community onto an area which was generations behind the times.

"I saw the green hills of Ireland and I knew I had hit Europe on the nose," said Charles Lindbergh in 1927. Eight years earlier, Alcock and Brown, the first men to fly an airplane nonstop across the Atlantic, had landed in a Connemara bog. The west coast of Ireland, where the Atlantic cables first came ashore in Europe, was the natural place for ocean-spanning planes to set down. Shannon Airport was founded in the flying-boat days of the 1930s. It became the busiest refueling stop on the European side of the Atlantic after World War II when transatlantic air traffic began to soar. For a dozen years nearly half the passengers flying the North Atlantic were routed through Shannon. The Irish made it a customs-free airport in 1947, and travelers were delighted to find the world's greatest bargains among the cameras and whiskey bottles in the Shannon shop. It was the forerunner of the duty-free shops which can be found at international airports around the world.

Then, in the late 1950s, the big airlines began to introduce their new jets: great aircraft which did not need to refuel at the edge of Ireland before going on to New York, London or Paris. Shannon suddenly looked like a colossal white elephant, doomed to become yet another ruin on the Irish landscape. The coming of the jets, however, coincided almost exactly with the country's fresh determination to solve its economic woes. Instead of becoming one more reason for national despair, Shannon turned out to be the most visible example of awakening Ireland. Today, after having dropped by twenty-five per cent, passenger traffic at the airport is as high as it was in Shannon's best years. Employment has tripled in a decade. Some six thousand people now work at both the airport and the new industrial estate which adjoins it.

The air traffic has been saved largely because the government decided—against some compelling arguments—to preserve Shannon as Ireland's principal transatlantic airport. Non-Irish transatlantic carriers must land at Shannon instead of Dublin (they protest heatedly about it), and even Irish airliners must make a stop at Shannon on their Dublin–North America flights. But beyond this vital factor, the state-supported but independently managed Shannon Free Airport Development Company has done wonders by creating a large and thriving industrial estate and by enticing tens of thousands of tourists each year to the Shannon area. Credit goes first of all to Brendan O'Regan, the most Irish-looking Irishman I know. The son of a local hotelier and the originator of Shannon's duty-free shop, he is the head of Shannon development as well as a powerful figure in Irish tourism. His enthusiasm and free flow of ideas put him in the front rank of Ireland's new enterprisers.

By 1967 the industrial estate could boast thirty-six companies of many nationalities, making everything from textiles to industrial diamonds. General Electric of the U.S.A. is the major firm, employing a third of the estate's work force of 3,500 in the manufacture of components and complete radios. The companies were drawn to "the first air-age freeport" because of its peculiar advantages as a place for duty-free manufacturing and air-freighting. (And because of such inducements as building grants and freedom from taxes on exports, at least until 1983.) A British computer firm, for example, receives shipments of payroll punch cards flown across the Atlantic by American firms, processes them, and flies them back across the ocean, all in a matter of hours. An ambitious new warehousing program enables companies to store spare parts or extra stock cheaply at Shannon for rapid air delivery to overseas customers.

The air freight business has yet to live up to expectations, and there are many question marks about the whole Shannon conception, but there is no doubting the physical and psychological impact of its activities and example on the formerly depressed western area. Shannon Town itself is a wholly new community, complete with modern shopping center, which now has over eighteen hundred residents. Most of the Shannon workers, however, come from Limerick, a half-hour drive away. During the morning and evening rush hours the Limerick–Shannon highway is one of the busiest on the island, offering an almost frightening preview of a wholly industrialized Ireland, if it ever comes to that. Ennis, another nearby small city, has undergone something of a renaissance because of new industry and the tourists pouring in from Shannon Airport.

The Shannon complex would be nothing but wind and weeds, and dozens of industries elsewhere in the country would not exist at all, if it were not for Ireland's veiled socialism. The state companies account for a third of all manufacturing and employ a third of all industrial workers. The nation's largest single employer is Cora Iompair Eireann (C.I.E.), the rail, road, canal and sea transport corporation, which operates a chain of hotels for good measure. The best-known and one of the most successful of the national companies is Aer Lingus, or Irish International Airlines, which began humbly in 1936 with a single five-seater aircraft and now flies over a million passengers a year. Thanks in part to the "patriotic" sentiments of Irish-Americans as well as the traveling Irish, it has been outstanding among the transatlantic carriers for its consistently high passenger load.

The state is literally involved in everything from soup to nuts, from toffee to mattresses. There are some fifty state-sponsored boards and companies in production, communications, marketing, research, finance, promotion and development—and in such diverse activities as horse and greyhound racing and the financing of ships and films. The Irish National Stud is one of the more famous state organizations, but an enterprise like Bord na Mona, the Irish Peat Development Board, is far larger. It has turned the ancient Irish activity of turf cutting for home fuel into a vast, mechanized operation which employs six thousand persons and uses monster machines to produce nearly four million tons of turf each year from the country's largest bogs. Two thirds of the production is fed into electrical power stations, some of which are erected at the very edge of the bogs. Most of the rest goes into fireplaces.

Although Irish state enterprise is more sweeping than anything seen in Britain, Scandinavia or elsewhere in Western Europe, the "feel" of Ireland is still that of a society dedicated to free-enterprise capitalism. The greatest of the private concerns, Arthur Guinness Son and Company, still controlled by the Anglo-Irish Guinness family, has been a notably public-spirited organization which has operated as a little welfare state of its own. "This place is more secure than the civil service," one Guinness employee told me. It has always set the pace for the business community in wages and social benefits. It has never had a strike in its more than two hundred years of production. Guinness's innumerable benefactions have profoundly enhanced the social and cultural life of the Irish.

I first toured the sprawling St. James Gate Brewery in Dublin in 1948, when I was a wandering college student, low on funds and glad to receive a free glass of stout after peering at the gigantic vats of the biggest brewery in Europe. Guinness is Ireland's largest private employer, largest private taxpayer (one quarter of all excise revenue), largest industrial exporter and largest private customer for the Irish farmer's grain. Guinness stout accounts for three quarters of all the beer consumed by the Irish, and the company's Harp brand leads in sales of lager. Five million pints of the dark stout are consumed every day in Ireland and in some 120 other countries, but nowhere more enthusiastically than in Africa, where the slogan is "Guinness is Power." Many Africans believe it to be a splendid aphrodisiac.

While Guinness is still Ireland's colossus (though it is actually a modest-sized firm by the standards of larger nations), other private companies are coming alive after years of dusty lethargy, and a number of aggressive young businessmen are making their fortunes with new enterprises. Hugh McLaughlin, for example, has climbed from poverty in Donegal to wealth and influence as the major magazine publisher in Ireland. John Hinde, a photographer turned businessman, has built up a rapidly growing business color-printing millions of postcards and calendars for customers as farflung as Ethiopia and Miami Beach. The P. J. Carroll tobacco firm in recent years has begun to take the lion's share of the tobacco business in Ireland from its British competitors. It now occupies one of the capital's more glamorous new office buildings. The young company chief, Donal Carroll, is also governor of the powerful Bank of Ireland. In Waterford, the old cut-glass business, which had died out altogether, has been revived with startling results. The world demand for Waterford glass is so great that the company is unable to expand fast enough to keep up with the orders.

And at Tynagh, near Galway, an Irish emigrant named Patrick Hughes, who made himself a millionaire in Canadian mining after leaving Ireland in 1949, when he was twenty-five, has started a lead and zinc mining operation which has already proved to be one of the major industrial enterprises in Ireland. More than that, the discovery of a rich deposit of minerals in poorly endowed land gives one more boost to Irish morale.

Jack Lynch

When I called on the new Prime Minister, Jack Lynch, to talk about such changes in Ireland, I was struck by the contrast in personality between himself and Sean Lemass. The recently retired Premier (who remains in Parliament, but has become a director of a variety of private firms) would speak in the staccato style of a man in a hurry, as if he had to keep running at top speed to make sure that the country did not lose its hard-won momentum. Jack Lynch was more relaxed, as if to say that the nation was safely on the move, and that it was just a matter of intelligent administration to insure steady progress. He spoke at length about "the recent overoptimism" and "our state of euphoria" about the economic advances which made the slump in 1965–66 so upsetting. Now things were in hand again, he said, and all would be well.

Lynch is a tall, blue-eyed man with thinning sandy hair and the physical grace and self-assurance of a retired star athlete. He had been a hurling hero in his native Cork, where he was born just a year after the Rising of 1916. He was taught by the Christian Brothers and worked as a barrister before going into full-time politics. He rose swiftly to the upper reaches of government. When he emerged as the victor in the party skirmish for the premiership, the political commentators and pub pundits were hard pressed to think of anything to say against him, except that he was perhaps too decent, honest, considerate, modest and sincere to be an effective leader in the rough-and-tumble world of Irish politics. But then one observer noticed a remarkable thing: all three parties "are led by amiable, non-aggressive men who have established a unique consensus of political behaviour: they will not themselves knowingly wound an opponent or make extreme partisan declarations."

It is, in short, the end of an era. Lynch has said himself that he is the first prime minister of the post–civil-war generation:

"I am not affected by any past bitternesses. I see this as a period more of economic politics than of 'political' politics, if you know what I mean." What it means is realism in place of emotionalism, and the cool appraisals of technocrats instead of the impassioned arguments of patriots. "I guess we're growing up at last," said a Dublin friend, "but I'm not sure I like it. I hope we don't become too bloody reasonable."

Chapter 5

CHURCH AND STATE

Our faith is not superficial, but goes down to our roots, to our grass roots, and pervades every aspect of family and social life.

—The Bishop of Galway

The nuns teach you that "God is love," and if you don't learn it they rap you on the knuckles.

—A Dubliner

Religion matters in Ireland more than in any other country in the English-speaking world. It is even said that an Irish atheist is one who wishes to God he could believe in God. The island itself, of course, is divided on religious grounds. Northern Ireland, although one-third Roman Catholic, is the most passionately Protestant society I have ever encountered, and its anti-Catholics are wonders to behold. The Irish Republic, on the other hand, is pleasantly free of the nastier varieties of religious bigotry, largely because the Catholics are too numerous to feel insecure. The Protestants, who numbered 420,000 in the twenty-six counties a century ago, are down to about 130,000 in a nation of 2,750,000 Catholics. (There are over three thousand Jews.) In the pre-ecumenical days Catholic children used to chant:

> Proddy, Proddy on the wall,
> Half a loaf'd feed ya all!

In five years of living in London I have only once been asked my religion, if any, and that was by an Irish priest who came to lunch one day. In Ireland, people seldom put the question directly, out of sheer politeness, but it is easy to sense their desire to know just where one stands in the denominational spectrum. Because Catholics and Protestants alike are so conscious of their religious identity and attend church so faithfully, they are put off by anyone who claims to be a Christian yet has no affiliation, unless it be to something as vague as humanity. Atheists and agnostics are lumped together as people beyond the pale. In any event, Irish Catholics tend to refer to those outside the faith as "non-Catholic," to which some sensitive souls retort by describing the country as ninety-five per cent non-Protestant.

Catholicism

A visitor to Ireland soon understands why it is that the Irish are sometimes described as being more Catholic than the Pope. The impression of total Catholicism can begin on the flight to Dublin, for if it is an Irish Airlines plane it will be named after a saint. There may be several priests or nuns among the passengers, and then in the capital there are more to be seen on the streets, and in the shops and restaurants. There appear to be churches at every turn, but this may be only because the Irish churches (Catholic churches, at any rate) are busy places, with people moving in and out at all hours, weekdays and Sundays. It is quite a contrast to England, where most people rarely go to church and the cathedrals are primarily tourist attractions. In Dublin, ironically enough, the two cathedrals—Christ Church and St. Patrick's, where Jonathan Swift was dean in the early 1700s—are still in the hands of the Protestants. Since they were once Catholic, before the Reformation, it has often been proposed that the Protestants in their dwindling numbers be gracious enough to turn one of them over to the Catholics, who have no proper cathedral of their own.

In rural Ireland the oldest and often the most attractive churches are Protestant while the newer, plainer and sometimes startlingly modern structures are Roman Catholic. Three quarters of the Protestants are members of the Church of Ireland, a self-governing branch of the Anglican communion. For centuries it has been the stronghold of the Anglo-Irish. After the Act of Union in 1800 there was a single "United Church of England and Ireland" which, in Ireland, was primarily supported by tithes on Roman Catholic tenant farmers. Incessant Catholic agitation and census figures which revealed that less than a fifth of the Irish population belonged to the established church paved the way for the passage of Gladstone's Act of Disestablishment in 1869.

A visitor to Ireland today notices that the bookshops are full of religious works and that Catholic publications are thick on the newsstands. In the pubs, except when they are closed for the afternoon "holy hour," the "curates" (publicans) serve Parish Priests (glasses of black Guinness with a clerical collar of creamy foam). Volunteers of the St. Vincent de Paul Society and other Catholic charities collect contributions on the streets. The newspapers tell of the thousands of pilgrims who have climbed Croagh Patrick or of the hundreds flying off to Lourdes and other holy places on special pilgrimage flights. The comings and goings and pronouncements of bishops and priests are well reported. The newspaper headlines suggest the variety of religious activities and concerns. For example, "PSYCHOLOGY TESTS URGED FOR PRIESTS," "CARDINAL SPEAKS ON VALUE OF TEMPERANCE," "AFTERMATH OF COUNCIL TROUBLES THE POPE," "OPINION IN FAVOUR OF THE PILL IS STRONG," "SCRIPT WRITER REPLIES TO BISHOP'S CRITICISM."

Lionel Fleming, an Irish journalist and broadcaster returning home after a distinguished career abroad, wrote:

> Back here, I am struck by the preoccupation with clerical things; well remembered, yet half forgotten. It is natural for

the hairdresser to make conversation by talking of the late proceedings of the Vatican Council, though if any hairdresser did so in London I would have thought him round the bend. Hats off on the top of the bus as it passes a Catholic church. Fish on Friday. The collecting-box for the Missions in the local shop. Grottoes along the country road.

The Irish talk about religion incessantly, but as professional gossips and critics rather than as amateur theologians. They take the fundamentals of their faith for granted; what concern them are the personalities and everyday practices of the Church. The great questions about God and man are seldom heard amid the hubbub about this conservative bishop's latest outburst about immoral goings-on or that liberal bishop's call for a complete rethinking of education policies. The names of the Pope, of Jesus, Mary and the saints, and of God Himself, spring readily to the lips of Irishmen—though often in vain. As Oliver St. John Gogarty said:

> The plainer Dubliners amaze us
> By their so frequent use of "Jaysus!"
> Which makes me entertain the notion
> It is not always from devotion.

There are representatives of the Church at nearly all public functions, and the parish priests seem to be everywhere at once. The head of the Arts Council is a priest. The most prominent cooperative leader is a priest. Many of the most effective television performers are priests. The public schools are run by priests—and a smaller number of parsons and rabbis. The hospitals and other social institutions are so dependent on clerics and nuns that they would collapse without them. The statistics on the Church's forces are impressive: 6,000 priests, 13,000 nuns and 2,000 Christian Brothers in both parts of the island, plus 6,500 missionaries in seventy countries and 4,400 priests ordained for service in English-speaking countries.

The listings in the Irish telephone directory indicate just how wide a net the Church casts over the society. Just to take a portion of them:

Catholic Boy Scouts of Ireland
Catholic Commercial Club
Catholic Digest
Catholic Girl Guides (Dublin Diocese)
Catholic Girls' Hostel
Catholic Herald Ltd.
Catholic Protection & Rescue Society of Ireland
Catholic Scout Hall
Catholic Seafarers' Club
Catholic Social Service Conference
Catholic Social Welfare Bureau
Catholic Stage Guild
Catholic Travel Service
Catholic Truth Society of Ireland
Catholic University School
Catholic Women's Federation Ltd.
Catholic Young Men's Society
Catholic Young Men's Sports Club
Catholic Youth Council Football League

At every hand there is evidence of a society wholly embraced by a powerful and autocratic religious institution. Although the Constitution separates Church and state and guarantees freedom of worship, it singles out the Catholic Church in Article 44: "The State recognizes the special position of the Holy Catholic Apostolic and Roman Church as the guardian of the Faith professed by the great majority of the citizens." The Constitution elsewhere proscribes the introduction of legislation permitting divorce. The hierarchy of the Church—four archbishops and twenty-four bishops—presides over the Catholic faithful throughout the whole of Ireland, north and south. In fact, His Eminence, William Cardinal Conway, Primate of All Ireland, resides in Ulster, where he is the Archbishop of Armagh (one of the island's four ecclesiastical provinces which takes in all of Northern Ireland and a bit of the Republic as well). The hierarchy, needless to say, is the strongest pressure group in the country, and the everyday influence of the clergy is so great that it is easy to appreciate why the Irish have so often been described as priest-ridden. There is a character in Irish fiction who tells a rebellious friend, "There's no earthly use your beefing about religion. The stamp of the Church is on you. 'Tis on all of us. 'Tis on you since the day you were born and sooner or later they'll get you and you may as well give in and be done with it."

The Priests

Just as the image of a submissive, Church-controlled society comes into focus, however, the counterevidence begins to appear. You notice that much of the famous piety of the Irish Catholics is often a matter of lip service by people going through the motions; that churchgoing is little more than a social ritual for many people (a Sunday-morning obligation before the pleasures of the pub); and that subservience goes only so far. A government official said, "The influence of the priests in Ireland is greatly exaggerated. People look to them for guidance on moral or religious matters, but when they intervene in economics or politics they are usually ignored or laughed at. Look at Bishop Lucey in Cork. Of course he's a great man but he's been ranting for years about dirty books and the politicians in Dublin, and people just say, 'It's that bloody Lucey again!' "

Anticlericalism is rife in Ireland, but it has no element of anti-Christianity. Rather, it is faultfinding on a grand scale by Catholics frustrated by the conservatism of the Church or resentful of the high-handedness of individual priests and of their own sheeplike status. They say that the day is past when the priest was the only well-informed man in the parish. The laity, now better informed than at any other time in Irish history, has been allowed little say in the decision-making processes of the Church. (The whole question of lay participation, how-

ever, is being explored, and it is certain that changes will be
made.) Two of the most prominent young Irish leaders told me
that they would have given up their religion altogether if it had
not been for Pope John and the reforms he inspired.

Most of the famous Irish writers in this century have taken
the bishops and the priests to task for stifling individual freedom, for being obsessively preoccupied by sin and evil, or for
having a far too joyless approach to life altogether. What is new
is the increasing readiness of other people to speak out against
the clerical attitudes they dislike. (And a readiness to just go
ahead and break some of the rules, particularly in the matter
of birth control.) It is no longer unusual to read, for example,
that a speaker at a public meeting in Dublin denounced the
"prejudices, neuroses and legalistic posturing of an insular and
reactionary hierarchy, who seem to equate judicious progress
with heresy."

The average man's feelings about the clergy are likely to slip
out in casual conversation. One day in Kerry I asked a farmer
how to get to the parish priest's house. "It's just up the road a
few miles," he said. "You can't miss it, because it's not like any
farmer's house you'll ever see." He was only one of many who
suggested that the clergy live luxuriously, but I have seldom
found it so. In the poorer parts of the country the priest certainly has a higher standard of living than his small-farmer
neighbors, but it is not all that grand. Elsewhere the priests who
"do too well for themselves" are greatly outnumbered by those
who are just scraping by. The typical priest outside the teaching
orders receives no salary. He must depend on offerings, fees and
gifts, and in these days of rising living costs they hardly meet
his expenses, which include everything from the wage of his
housekeeper to the upkeep of his house and car. I came upon
one priest who was trying to find the money for wallpaper so
that he could receive visitors in his living room without being
ashamed.

It is still true that many Irish mothers are anxious to have at least one of their sons enter the priesthood, and are pleased if a daughter wishes to become a nun, but such vocations no longer have their old appeal. The Church is simply not getting its accustomed volume of recruits, and the dropout rate at the seminaries is high. Father Simon O'Beirne of Cork has spoken of the "significant decrease in the overall number of religious vocations at all levels—diocesan, regular clergy, brothers and sisters."

The priesthood offers security, but that seems to be less important in these more prosperous days. It offers immense opportunities for service, but at great cost to personal freedom in an age of growing individual expression. A priest cannot marry or have a romantic attachment. He is wholly under the command of his superiors; there is little he can say or do without their approval. Until recently priests could not go to the theater. The attendance of priests at horse races, where they used to be much in evidence, is forbidden. Their behavior is carefully scrutinized by a public which relishes a scandal involving a clergyman. In fairness, I should say that I have found a nice tolerance among a number of ordinary Irish people. One housewife who told of a priest who had been caught in a love affair said that most of her neighbors would place the blame on the woman for tempting the priest. "Sure," she said, "he's only a man, after all."

A columnist who said that "criticizing the clergy is as much an Irish national pastime nowadays as golf or courting" proposed the formation of an Irish Society for the Prevention of Mental Cruelty to the Clergy, because the rank and file of them are "the most exploited and misrepresented body of men in Europe." There is something to this. Although Irish society as a whole is still full of Church-inspired restraints and inhibitions which have been thrown off by other Western nations, it becomes increasingly difficult to believe that the individuals one meets are exploited or held down by their priests. My impression is that it is the priests who are people-ridden these days rather than the other way around.

There are instances, of course, of priests making life miserable for people because of their supposedly sinful behavior, and in a few northern places the barbaric custom of collecting money next to the coffin at funerals is still practiced. (In this "auctioning of the dead," the friends of the deceased shuffle by a table to hand their offerings to the priest. The names of the contributors and the amounts given are called out and the grand total is announced, after counting, to the waiting throng in the church. A person who had been held in high esteem by his neighbors will prove to be "a good class of corpse" and one which attracts large contributions.)

More familiar are the complaints about "the way the clergy have their hands in everything." An Australian resident of a western town said that he had been urged by the local priest to take the initiative in a vital community project. The priest felt he shouldn't take the lead himself, "because there had been so much resentment lately about the clergy 'interfering' in public affairs." What usually happens, however, is that the people in a parish quite happily divest themselves of their communal responsibilities by piling up everything on the shoulders of the priest. Several parish priests said that they would happily give up most of their many offices and welfare duties, including management of the local schools, "but if we don't do these things, no one else will."

On the national political scene, as mentioned in the previous chapter, the Church has a behind-the-scenes influence, but it can easily be exaggerated. If the great majority of ministers and legislators behave on the whole as the archbishops and the bishops wish them to behave, it is only because they are all Irish Catholics together. The Church, for example, is not the censor of books and films, but then it has no need to be. The laymen on the censorship boards have their own strong feelings about protecting their fellow citizens from "immoral works."

It is worth noting that de Valera, Lemass and the other leaders of Fianna Fail were excommunicated by the Church for their anti-treaty struggle in the 1920s. This proved to have awkward results after the party came to power a decade later and assumed an almost permanent command of Irish affairs. Ministerial relationships with the hierarchy have been cool, if not cold, rather than warm and intimate. The Prime Minister and two other ministers of the present government quite cheerfully related to me stories of occasions when they had, in effect, told individual bishops to mind their own business.

Significantly, the most frequently cited case of ecclesiastic interference happened as long ago as 1950–51, when a coalition government ruled the country. The formidable combination of the hierarchy and individual doctors of the Irish Medical Association managed to shoot down the Mother and Child Scheme which had been made possible by the de Valera government's Health Act of 1947 and which was now being implemented by Dr. Noel Browne, the crusading Minister for Health. The plan for free maternity care and free child welfare to age sixteen hardly seems revolutionary today, but it looked to the physicians like dangerous socialism and to the heads of the Church like a threat to their influence over Irish family life. The hierarchy expressed its objections most emphatically in confidential letters to Prime Minister John Costello, who decided to drop the idea. The public learned how strenuously the Church had fought the plan when Dr. Browne resigned from the government and made the correspondence public. The mother-and-child care sought by Dr. Browne was put into practice only a few years later by Fianna Fail when it returned to power.

Reactionaries and Radicals

Even though the hierarchy has since become more tolerant of social legislation, it is still widely accepted that the Church in Ireland is one of the most reactionary in the Catholic world. Of course, it has moved with the times. Mass is being said in the vernacular instead of in Latin. Mixed marriages (Catholic-Protestant) have become easier. Friendly relations with Protestants are being encouraged. But the Church leaders have been slow to respond to the challenges offered by the renovation movement of the Catholic Church. Desmond Fisher, formerly the editor of the *Catholic Herald*, has described the "whole Irish attitude at the Council" as "cautious, concerned about disturbing the 'simple faithful' and reluctant to change the existing disciplines too hastily."

Early in 1965, an Irish magazine, complaining about the hierarchy's lack of enthusiasm about the revitalization of the Church, said that "the Irish laity have still to be awakened to this exciting aspect of their lives, this Christian mission." When the Archbishop of Dublin returned from Rome later that year after the final Vatican Council session, he told his flock, "You may have been worried by much talk of changes to come. Allow me to reassure you. No change will worry the tranquillity of your Christian lives."

There was nothing reassuring about this, however, to those who felt that the leaders of the Church in Ireland were seriously out of step with the yearnings of the public for a more generous and openhearted Catholicism, and for the kind of Christian action which raises the quality of life in the community. There has been a special desire to improve relationships between Catholics and Protestants—to close the gap between them. Mrs. Janet Ryan, a Protestant married to a Catholic, wrote in the Catholic monthly *The Furrow* that one of the greatest difficulties of a mixed marriage is "the fact that Protestant and Catholics in Ireland have such different ways of life which extend beyond religion and include education from primary school to university, friends, social life—maybe even jobs."

One critic of the hierarchy, Gerald V. Breen, has said that the Catholic Church in Ireland "continues to be obsessed with doctrine and theology, about which we are all convinced, and neglects the urgent task of giving a lead in the translation of the Christian ethic into practical living." Despite the emphasis on doctrine and theology, it has been left to other nations to produce the great theologians. Ireland has in Maynooth College one of the most celebrated centers of higher ecclesiastical learning, but it has been a sterile institution for many years—or so it appears to Catholic thinkers in other lands who feel that the Irish have cut themselves off from the progressive movement of the Church in Western Europe and America.

The more dynamic and modern-minded priests at Maynooth, in the parishes, and at every level of the Church structure are frustrated by the elderly men, often well past the normal retirement age, who occupy most of the commanding positions and who are overcautious and suspicious of new ideas. In the normal course a priest does not get a parish of his own until he is well along in years, by which time his spirit has flagged and his energies have diminished. He may expect nothing more from his parishioners than "reflex-action Catholicism."

To many Irishmen, the Most Reverend John Charles McQuaid, Archbishop of Dublin and Primate of Ireland, is the foremost symbol of the Irish Church's behind-the-times character. The *Irish Times* in 1966 went so far as to say that "to those outside his flock he represents the very incarnation of all that it was believed Pope John with his loving heart was trying to rid his Church of—obscurantism, self-righteousness, arrogance and spiritual apartheid."

Dr. McQuaid was born in 1895, and he has been the Catholic Archbishop of Dublin (there is a Church of Ireland Archbishop as well) since 1940. His years as the most powerful religious figure in the most important Irish diocese have been distinguished by a large increase in the number of parishes, to meet the challenge of the city's growth, and by vigorous building programs which have added dozens of new churches and schools to the capital. He has had a great interest in sociology and social welfare. He founded, for example, the Catholic Social Service Conference, the Catholic Social Welfare Bureau and the Dublin

Institute of Catholic Sociology. He is the originator of a network of Church institutions to cope with the manifold social problems of a modern city. Even so, Dr. McQuaid is widely spoken of as the single greatest obstacle to the modernization of the Irish Church.

His role in the squashing of the Mother and Child Scheme is remembered only too well, and he is identified more than any other Church leader with the "Trinity ban," which prohibits, "under pain of mortal sin," Catholic youth attending Trinity College without special permission. While the ruling against Catholics atending non-Catholic schools is the work of the hierarchy as a whole and confirmed by the Holy See, it is Dr. McQuaid who seems particularly adamant about keeping Catholics out of Trinity. Although the college has a Protestant history, it is not a sectarian institution, and its student body includes about one thousand Catholics, most of whom are in open defiance of the ban. There are also some ninety Catholic members of the staff. Trinity has repeatedly invited Dr. McQuaid to appoint a chaplain to attend to the spiritual needs of the Catholic students.

The situation is full of absurdities, as one newspaper reader noted when he wrote: "Is Trinity College considered a greater menace to Irish faith and morals than employment in ungodly England or service in the British armed forces? As neither of the latter are renowned for piety or saintly living, why have they not been condemned bell, book and candle?" The University College of Dublin, which has the Church's blessing, is no more a Catholic university (although attended almost entirely by Catholics) than Trinity is Protestant. Catholics are not forbidden to attend Queen's University in Belfast, which has mostly Protestant students. When the Irish government early in 1967 made the momentous announcement that Trinity and the University College of Dublin would be merged, the ban looked more nonsensical than ever. It became just a matter of time before it would be lifted.

The Irish Church presents such a picture of rocklike permanency that it is hard to believe it is being shaken to its foundations by the blasts of change from the Vatican and the restiveness of its own maturing worshipers. The Irish radicals may complain about the slowness of it all, but drastic developments are under way. A decade from now the Church may have cast off its old-fashioned image altogether. It is already showing signs of becoming an innovating instead of a deterring force in Irish life. Cardinal Conway has said: "The directives of the Council are being steadily and methodically implemented in Ireland; every meeting of the bishops is predominantly concerned with this great task. . . . The *aggiornamento* is a much deeper thing than putting the Mass into the vernacular or the re-designing of churches. It involves above all a deep spiritual renewal, a re-adjustment of attitudes, a developed capacity to relate the unchanging Gospel to the circumstances of the modern world."

The ecumenical spirit is catching on quickly, among Protestants as well as Catholics, and Dr. McQuaid himself is often in the news as he meets Protestant leaders or entertains, for example, the Archbishop of Canterbury. After a meeting of the hierarchy in 1966, Catholics were told that mixed marriages may now take place before the high altar instead of at the side of a church; that Catholics may serve as the best man and as bridesmaids at the weddings of Protestant friends; and that they may attend Protestant funerals and baptisms.

Social Justice

There have been other developments as well, but perhaps none more significant than the increasing concern about the social wrongs in Ireland and the eagerness to create a truly just and compassionate society. It is almost as if the Irish have suddenly become aware that there is more to Christianity than regular Mass attendance and going to confession. Those who worry about the materialism which they say is sweeping the country sometimes ask, "Will the Irish remain Christian?" John Horgan, the theological correspondent of the *Irish Times*, looking at "the evidence of the society we have created since 1916 all around us—the way we treat our old people, our sick, the way we educate our children," said that "another question rears its head, and it is this: 'Will the Irish become Christian?'"

Until a few years ago there was an astonishing complacency about the fact that Ireland was decades behind other Western European nations in its health and welfare services. There was not only a meek acceptance of poverty and suffering but a strange lack of awareness by political and religious leaders of just how primitively the nation was caring for the sick, the handi-capped, the mentally ill, the delinquent young, the orphaned, the widowed, the itinerant families, and all the others who lived desperately in what de Valera chose to describe as "the foremost Christian nation in the world today." It was only after a suc-cession of factual and penetrating articles in the *Irish Times* by Michael Viney, a wise and concerned young English journalist (now an Irish citizen), that the extent of the neglect in a number of social areas became apparent.

James Connolly, Patrick Pearse and other champions of the independence movement had called for a social revolution to accompany the winning of political freedom, but the trauma of partition was so great that social issues were neglected. Political leaders concentrated on the border issue and the language movement. But, as a letter published in the Dublin *Evening Herald* said, "Language and borders do not matter to the unemployed, the hungry or the forgotten old people, many of whom die of genteel starvation." As a practical matter, of course, partition gravely upset the natural order of things on the island. Instead of being a unified nation with two large religious groups and a substantial working-class population, the Irish Free State became an overwhelmingly Catholic and rural society of small-property owners. It lacked humanitarian zeal or that "savage indignation" about the condition of man which tore at the heart of Jonathan Swift two centuries earlier.

The meeting of the first Dail in 1919, even before independence was secured, had produced some social sparks. The delegates were determined to abolish the "odious, degrading and foreign Poor Law system" which produced the notorious workhouses of the Famine era, and they were bent on improving on the dispensaries which provided elementary medical assistance to the very poor under humiliating conditions. Such enthusiasm was short-lived and was swept away in the political storms of the time. The country's hesitant social advance in the half century since then can be seen in the existence today of a number of the old workhouses as grim and soulless institutions for the old and the mentally ill, and in the continuation of the dispensaries as part of the national medical system. Until the postwar period the Irish governments were well pleased to leave the greater part of the nation's health and welfare work in the hands of the religious and charitable organizations. This not only seemed best for a strongly Catholic nation which emphasized almsgiving and family responsibilities, but it relieved the politicians of the burden of finding the massive funds to support social institutions. The involvement of public bodies in social action was strictly limited and was conducted largely on the local level.

Needless to say, those who could afford it received the best available medical care and social security while the poor and the unprotected had to depend on charity. The country was in a poor economic position and was little influenced by the social-justice movements under way on the Continent or even in Britain. The Irish clung to Victorian concepts of social care and took the attitude that "the poor are always with us"— a point of view which persists today. Even so, demands for better services grew and the religious orders which operated so many of the facilities found themselves hard pressed.

When a number of voluntary hospitals in the 1920s ran into

serious financial problems they raised money by operating sweepstakes and lotteries. A group of businessmen persuaded them to join in a single national lottery which would sell tickets on a massive scale and offer huge prizes. Thus was born the famous Irish Sweepstakes which has provided nearly $200 million to Irish hospitals and various medical needs since the early 1930s. The state has confined itself to the distribution of these funds. The three annual sweepstakes, each with a top prize of $140,000, are operated by a private, profit-making firm, the Hospitals' Trust (1940) Ltd., which has the appearance of being a charitable organization. It has grossed well over a billion dollars since it was extended special privileges—in particular, the right to sell Sweepstakes tickets abroad—by an Act of Parliament in 1933. The fact that more than four fifths of the total receipts are paid out in prizes, expenses and profits has earned the Sweepstakes some criticism. In November 1966 *Fortune* magazine noted that the fraction which goes to the hospitals is "probably less than the company would have had to pay in normal corporate taxes, were it not given official exemption."

After World War II the state assumed more responsibilities for Irish health conditions—taking over from local governments and moving into fields dominated by the Church—when it became apparent that some problems could be effectively handled only on a national scale. Tuberculosis, for example, was killing nearly 4,000 persons each year. Tens of thousands were afflicted with TB, but treatment was expensive and facilities were so short that many sufferers had to wait a year before obtaining a hospital bed. The illness was considered such a shameful "weakness" that victims would often not seek treatment until it was too late. Many were simply hidden away in their homes, out of sight of the neighbors. A mass radiography program was introduced, and when a coalition government came to power in 1948 a mighty assault on tuberculosis was launched by Dr. Noel Browne, the new Minister for Health.

Dr. Browne was a darkly handsome young man, still in his early thirties, who had made a name for himself as an impassioned advocate of an all-out attack on tuberculosis. Both his parents and other members of his family had died of the disease, and he had been a victim himself. As health minister he launched an expensive crash program to provide thousands of beds for TB patients in converted buildings and newly built sanatoria. He found the money by boldly spending the Health Department's capital of some £20 million, which had been raised over the years by the Hospitals' Sweepstakes, and by obtaining a £10-million mortgage on future Sweepstakes earnings. The drive was wondrously successful (thanks partly to the introduction of anti-TB drugs). Deaths from tuberculosis are now down to a few hundred a year and many of the sanatoria have been converted into mental homes or turned to other uses.

Dr. Browne's effort to do something equally dramatic about Ireland's shocking infant mortality rate produced the battle over the Mother and Child Scheme already mentioned. Ever since his resignation as health minister he has been one of the most vocal—and lonely—progressive voices in Ireland. He has lately served as the prickly conscience of the Labour Party (he became its vice-chairman in 1967), while in his professional life he has moved on to psychiatry, a natural field for a man who sees the Irish as a "frightened people" and Ireland as a "terribly unhealthy society."

At the time of the great health-plan controversy, the hierarchy's attitude was expressed by the bishop who declared, "The right to provide for health of children belongs to parents, not to the state. The state has the right to intervene only in a subsidiary capacity . . ." This was conventional Church wisdom, but, as has happened in all other Western countries, the state's role has become less and less subsidiary. The Irish bishops have gradually come to accept the greater involvement of the public authorities in welfare matters. The liberal Bishop of Ossory,

Dr. Peter Birch, has even said, "We ought to be both grateful and proud that modern improvements in social thinking have reduced the private demands on our pockets."

Ireland is now halfway to becoming a full-blown welfare state, and its record in some areas is one to be proud of. Infant mortality has been greatly lessened. The Irish are living to ripe old ages and benefiting from what Dr. Browne described as "a first-rate hospital system." He said, "We have some of the finest hospitals in the world." Treatment of infectious diseases is free. While Ireland does not have anything quite like Britain's comprehensive National Health Service, it does provide free service for the poor (the "lower-income group," about thirty per cent of the population) and a mixture of free and fee treatment for those in the middle-income group (fifty-five per cent). Higher-income families have to pay most of their medical costs.

The typical Irishman pays premiums in a government health-insurance plan and contributes to a social-security system which will give him about half of his wages when he retires. Monthly child allowances are given to all families with children, whatever their means. Public spending on health and welfare is huge today in comparison to just a decade ago, and there is every sign that the Irish governments will put ever greater emphasis on social as well as educational improvements. The political parties, in fact, are in stiff competition to prove that each is more socially aware than the others. Fine Gael, for example, the most conservative of the parties, is moving to the left under the banner of the "Just Society." Still wary of appearing to be too socialistic, the politicians like to say that their thoughts have been "informed and molded by the social doctrines contained in the papal encyclicals."

The converts to social action will have plenty to keep them busy for a long time. For all the progress that has been made, Ireland still lags well behind the rest of Europe in both its social thinking and the extent and quality of its social services. As a proportion of gross national product, Ireland's social spending is one of the very lowest in Europe. It is not one of the richer countries, but neither is Italy, which is well ahead of Ireland in the proportion of its social spending. While the welfare assistance I have described looks good on paper, it falls far short of the actual requirements of most of the so-called beneficiaries. Pensions are not payable until the age of seventy, and many pensioners must struggle to survive on less than eight dollars a week. Persons who qualify for free medical assistance tell appalling stories of the difficulties and indignities of getting it. The very people who seem to be most in need of tender care and loving kindness are often treated coldly and indifferently, if they receive help at all. Dr. Paul McQuaid, director of the Child Guidance Clinic at Mater Hospital in Dublin, has stated that Ireland's children's institutions have for too long been places of punishment, and he has urged a radical new approach to child care. One priest with a special concern for the elderly, Father Thomas J. Scully, has said, "never has our society been so efficient and affluent, yet never so impersonal and heartless."

The percentage of persons over sixty-five in Ireland is one of the highest in the world. More than half of the elderly are single or widowed, and many live in conditions of shattering loneliness. In an excellent series on the problems of growing old in Ireland, Michael Viney wrote: "The old are often left alone to cope with problems of poverty and poor housing, ill-health and loneliness. Some ten thousand are destined for the county homes and about half of these are sick. Almost a fifth of admissions in mental hospitals are of people aged sixty-five or more and nobody disputes that many of them would more properly be cared for elsewhere."

Having always heard of Irish family solidarity, I asked one eminent Irishman about the treatment of the elderly. "It's an old Irish custom," he said, "to throw our old people into institutions." Such a statement may be unfair, for the elderly have an honored place in many Irish homes, but it is true enough that there is a widespread callousness and lack of sympathy about the old and the deprived. The common attitude about the itinerants, the twelve hundred tinker families, is one of vast indifference. The fact that many itinerant children receive almost no education, and that their death rate is twice that of the national average, has not inspired heartfelt or imaginative efforts to improve their existence.

One popular argument against the welfare state in Ireland is that it will eliminate individual responsibility and neighborliness, yet a great many people do nothing more than make contributions to religious charities. There is far less individual involvement in social care than one would imagine. The Irish are inclined to push social problems under the rug, just as so many of the helpless are pushed into institutions and forgotten. Statements appear in the newspapers every so often that "today we are the best-fed people in the world with the best houses in Europe," ignoring the thousands living on little more than bread and tea, and forgetting the serious housing shortage and the great number of substandard dwellings. There is a refusal to face the facts. It is often claimed, for example, that Ireland has the lowest suicide rate in the world, thus demonstrating Irish contentment, but the nation's statistics on the subject, which count about seventy suicides a year, are highly suspect. Because of the shame of it all in Ireland, some medical men will go out of their way to call a suicide something else. A study of Dublin suicides published in Britain suggests that the true figure is at least two times greater than the official number.

There is a general insensitivity about the mentally ill and a reliance on old-fashioned treatment which emphasizes confinement in institutions instead of human contact. The stigma attached to mental troubles is perplexing in a country which, to put it crudely, is one of the maddest in the world. When Dean Jonathan Swift founded St. Patrick's Hospital in Dublin in 1725 as the first "lunatic asylum" in Ireland, he wrote:

He gave the little wealth he had
To build a house for fools and mad,
And showed by one satiric touch,
No nation wanted it so much.

Nearly half the hospital beds in Ireland are occupied by mental patients. In 1967 a government commission reported that "mental illness may be more prevalent in Ireland than in other countries" and said that the rate of hospital beds provided for the mentally ill "appears to be the highest in the world." (The figure of 7.3 psychiatric beds per 1,000 of the population compares with 4.5 in Northern Ireland, 4.6 in England and Wales, 4.3 in the United States, and 2.1 in France.) "At any given time, about one in every seventy of our people above the age of twenty-four years is in a mental hospital. When it is remembered that every mentally ill person brings stress into the lives of people around him, it will be clear that in Ireland mental illness poses a health problem of the first magnitude."

Apart from the large proportion of elderly persons in the population, the prevalence of mental disorders is blamed on the high emigration rate, the low marriage rate, problems of unemployment, the isolation of many people in a largely rural society, and a certain amount of inbreeding in more remote communities. Emigration, of course, is a kind of selection process which removes many of the young and vigorous from the society but not the old and the mentally disturbed.

There are estimated to be as many as 24,000 mentally handicapped (as against mentally ill) persons in the Republic, a high figure for a small country, and only a fraction of them are receiving specialized care. Almost all of the institutions dealing with the mentally handicapped are in the hands of religious orders which admit they are incapable of keeping up with the demand. Good and notable work is undoubtedly being done by private organizations in all social fields, but it is hard not to feel that the whole of Ireland's social services are severely handicapped by the heavy reliance on what is called the "charity approach" to welfare. At least, to hear the professionals tell it, there is a staggering amount of amateurism, duplication, inefficiency and general unpleasantness when so many religious orders are busy "taking care of their own." There is a whiff of the Victorian age every time a rheumatic old lady in a Dublin slum murmurs, "God bless them" when she is given ten shillings and a Christmas bag of coal by the good people of the Society of St. Vincent de Paul. One social worker spoke of "the outdated soup-kitchen and Christmas-handout approach to social problems." A Dublin friend explained, "The idea, you see, is that the poor exist in order to make the benevolent feel virtuous."

Dr. Ivor Browne, the forceful chief psychiatrist of the Dublin Health Authority and one of the most accomplished of the country's new breed of leaders, spoke of the wasteful fragmentation of the social services and said, "You can't excuse inefficiency just because it's charity." The efforts by such professionals as Browne merely to use state machinery to coordinate the religious welfare institutions are attacked as being communistic. The opposition to change is formidable, as is the resistance to modern ideas of social treatment. (Headline in Irish newspaper: PRIEST IS 'BEST PSYCHIATRIST IN WORLD,' SAYS JUDGE NEYLON.") One journalist, speaking about the silent struggle between the young social-action radicals and the elderly conservatives in the Dublin clergy, told of the time he was telephoned by a priest who wished to meet him at a secluded place. "He came in with his coat collar up like an I.R.A. man and whispered that he wanted me to look into the conditions at a certain juvenile home."

Whatever the confusion of the moment, the trend is toward a greater degree of social action by both Church and state which strikes at the fundamentals instead of just dispensing palliatives. A sorting-out process is already under way to see what can best be done by public authorities and what can be left to private agencies. Dr. Peter Birch, the Bishop of Ossory and one of the most impressive persons I met in Ireland, said that there should be no conflict between Church and state on social and educational matters in a country which is so heavily Roman Catholic. Catholic values would still apply, or at least they ought to, whether the work is in the hands of clerics or laymen. The great need, he said, is for cooperation in what is still a relatively poor country to make the best use of the existing resources.

Dr. Birch, who is a hero to the idealistic young priests coming out of the seminaries, is well known in Ireland as the great exception to the rule of the arch-conservative bishops and for having brought about a social resurgence in his diocese. The creation of a Social Service Centre in Kilkenny and the coordination of numerous volunteer bodies has had some superb results. Among other achievements is the exceptional amount of individual participation in welfare programs. "The old concept of charity as a handout," he said, "is giving way to a human presence."

Education

A decade ago a Dublin newspaper spoke of Irish education as "a stagnant pond." Today it looks more like an Atlantic storm. It is probably the most fervently discussed and debated of all subjects in Ireland. It dominates conversations in kitchens and sitting rooms all over the country. It has been constantly on the front pages during the past few years as a succession of studies have revealed just how antiquated and undemocratic the Irish educational system actually is, and as a succession of outstanding ministers for education have embarked on reforms.

Once again, it is a case of people who were benumbed or brainwashed into accepting things as they are, and fearing to criticize, suddenly finding their tongues and making it plain that they find the status quo intolerable. Irish parents are simply more aware than ever that their children are being badly educated, at least by the standards of advanced Western nations, and that educational opportunities are highly unequal. As one commentator has said, "Ireland's education is backward and based clearly and uncompromisingly on money and class. The child of the better-off parent will get the best education available, no matter how lacking in ability he may be; the working-class child, in most cases, will leave school at fourteen, no matter how talented he may be."

It did not surprise me to find that the Catholic Church controls the greater part of Irish education, but I have been astonished by the determination of the state, at least until the 1960s, to have as little to do with education as possible, and by the fact that the system has not changed in its essentials since the British days. If the colonial administrators were to return to Ireland today, they would be pleased to find that the Irish have carefully preserved their highly stratified educational structure, defects and all, and much of their philosophy of privilege. In education as in social welfare, the Irish carry on a number of British practices and viewpoints that the British themselves have long since discarded. While there are numerous reasons for this, including the innate conservatism of the Irish and the national propensity for the second-rate and for getting things on the cheap, it is the impact of religion which makes all the difference. As one leading educator, T. J. McElligott, has said, "State aid to Church schools was the only form of national education in England before 1870, and its continuation here is undoubtedly due to the strength of religious feeling in this country."

Separation is the operative word in Irish education. The state stands apart from the management of the schools. The primary- and secondary-school systems have almost nothing to do with each other. The many private secondary schools and the fewer number of state-run vocational schools go their separate ways. Catholics and Protestants are separated. Rich and poor are separated. Boys and girls are separated—and at the very time in their teens when they ought to be getting used to each other's company. The persons most directly involved with school-children seldom get together: there are few parent-teacher associations.

The denominational character of Irish education was made plain to me when I spent some days in a farmhouse about ten miles west of Sligo. When the girl in the family went off with her books each morning I assumed it was to the schoolhouse which was conveniently placed just a few minutes down the road. I discovered later that she stood waiting by the highway each morning and then went by bus into the city to attend a Roman Catholic school. The school within sight of the farm was for Protestants. There hardly seem to be enough Protestants in rural Ireland to warrant separate schools, but the Church of Ireland manages more than four hundred of them. Almost all are single-teacher schools. One teacher has said, "These schools are a disgrace. They exist for the prestige of the Church rather than for the education of the children."

The great majority of the primary schools are Catholic. They are deceptively called "national schools." The state lays down the ground rules and a uniform curriculum, and it pays teacher salaries and most of the cost of building and maintenance, but it is the parish priests who manage the schools under the command of their bishops. Irish parents pay tribute to the Church for having borne the burden of providing most of the education in Ireland over the centuries. They say that a unified primary-to-secondary nondenominational state school system would be out of character for Ireland, and they doubt that the country could afford it, anyway. (The Christian Brothers, for example, who teach in many of the secondary schools, do so at a fraction of the salaries that would have to be paid to regular teachers.) But the parents say, too, that the schools should be much better than they are. Although there are a good number of bright and modern buildings with excellent facilities, two thirds of the more than 4,800 primary schools for 490,000 pupils have only one or two teachers. Nearly half the buildings date back to the nineteenth century. Heating and sanitation are often bad, and the playground, if any, is frequently just a muddy field on the other side of the outhouse. Many schools have no means to stimulate interest in art or in subjects outside the limited and unimaginative curriculum. Civics has only recently been introduced. The Bishop of Ossory said that, "Our traditional education does not prepare us for book-loving or book-caring," and he spoke of the dearth of libraries: "Few of our young people are taught how to read and evaluate books in Irish schools."

Overcrowding in the schools is the worst physical problem. There is an average of thirty-four pupils per teacher, with some classes having fifty or more pupils, yet in some remote places a one-teacher schoolhouse may have only eight pupils. The trend now is toward large central schools, but it is slow going in the face of strong opposition. Several years ago the Bishop of Galway spoke of the Education Minister's plan to rationalize the one- and two-teacher schools as "a catastrophe, a major calamity for our Irish countryside." One impediment to improving conditions at the existing schools is the presence in many parishes of elderly, overworked or simply complacent priests who give only cursory attention to their school-management job. Several priests said flatly that it was high time to put Irish education in the hands of professionals.

Although one Catholic sociologist had said that "at the moment Irish society is characterized by a belief in education approaching a religious fervour," four out of every ten youngsters, or some seventeen thousand every year, receive no further education after compulsory attendance at the primary schools. Donogh O'Malley, the vigorous Minister for Education, called this "a dark stain on the national conscience." He said, "It means that some one-third of our people have been condemned —the great majority through no fault of their own—to be part-educated unskilled labour, always the weaker who go to the wall of unemployment or emigration."

In 1966, O'Malley created a sensation by announcing the

government's plan for "free post-primary education." It means that from now on the state will increase its grants to the secondary schools in order to cover the fees of the great majority of pupils. It will greatly accelerate the trend toward more education for more children. The school-leaving age is to be raised from fourteen to fifteen in 1970.

Until a few years ago the state assumed no responsibility for providing secondary education. Since 1924, however, it had supplied funds to the religious and other private schools to assist them with their costs and to pay most of the salaries of their teachers. The distance is wide between the fashionable schools with high fees, top teachers and snob appeal to the far larger number of schools run by priests and nuns where the fees are low and the quality of the education leaves much to be desired. (In all too many secondary-school classrooms, as in the primary schools, teachers are quick to use rulers, canes and other means of corporal punishment—not to mention some gross forms of humiliation—to maintain discipline.) A parallel vocational-school system provides a more technical education up to the age of sixteen in day and evening classes, but such schools do not enjoy the status of the others in the eyes of parents. The overwhelming emphasis in Irish education is on the arts subjects, with the result that the nation is failing to produce enough skilled young people for the technological age.

Although Ireland's Education Department used to think its only function was to pump money through the system, it has recently begun to take some initiative in providing education. Several secondary comprehensive schools have been started in needy parts of the country. The authorities, however, are quick to say that no one wants to turn the privately owned secondary schools into state institutions. Prime Minister Lynch describes the talk about this as "nonsensical" because "if Church and state could not work harmoniously together in Ireland, then they could not do so anywhere on earth."

It is in the realm of higher education that the more drastic changes are being made. The sixteen thousand university students in Ireland today will be doubled within the next decade. New universities will be created, and the present colleges in Dublin, Cork and Galway will have expanded roles to play. In the process, to quote Donogh O'Malley, "a most insidious form of partition on our own doorstep" will be eliminated: the division between "Protestant" Trinity College (Dublin University) and the "Roman Catholic" University College of Dublin (U.C.D.). In the greatest mixed marriage yet to be seen in Ireland, they will be combined to form a single, multidenominational University of Dublin.

Founded by Queen Elizabeth I in 1591, Trinity served for three and a half centuries as one of the bastions of the ruling Anglo-Irish. It has ranked just behind Oxford and Cambridge in social prestige in the British Isles. Its graduates include such notables as Jonathan Swift, William Congreve, Oliver Goldsmith, Edmund Burke, Theobald Wolfe Tone and Oscar Wilde. In modern times Trinity has sought to occupy a more natural and national position in independent Ireland, but, largely because of the Church's much-defied ban on attendance by Catholic students imposed in the 1930s, it has retained the atmosphere of the old Ascendancy days.

There are some 3,750 students at Trinity. Nearly half of them come from Britain and Northern Ireland, and over two-thirds are Protestants. The high proportion of students from outside the Republic has looked strange indeed as U.C.D. became achingly overcrowded and was in great need of Trinity's superior facilities for advanced scholarship. The government's announcement of the Trinity–U.C.D. merger would have unleashed a barrage of criticism a decade or so ago, but it was greeted in 1967 with warm and almost offhand approval as the right and inevitable thing to do in the ecumenical era. The Education Minister was eager to point out that he had not sought the approval of the hierarchy. The silence of the Catholic Archbishop of Dublin has been deafening.

The Language Struggle

Amid all the changes in Irish education, one stark fact remains: An extraordinary and destructive amount of time in the school life of every Irish youngster is spent in learning a language which is regularly spoken in Ireland and all the world by no more people than can fill a single football stadium. More than a third of the learning time in the primary schools is devoted to Irish, and it is a compulsory subject in the secondary and vocational schools. Pupils cannot receive their Primary, Intermediate or Leaving Certificates unless they pass examinations in Irish, no matter how brilliant their accomplishments in other subjects. In a number of schools, especially those in the fringe areas where Irish is still generally known, all subjects are taught in the old language.

The whole idea of the excessive emphasis on Irish is to produce successive waves of youth fluent in Irish so that one day it will truly be, as the Constitution says, the first language of the country. Gaelic revival has been the national policy since the earliest days of independence and the policy of the Irish patriots since the second half of the nineteenth century. Quite understandably, they saw this rich and ancient tongue—one of the very oldest of the European languages—as the shining badge of nationality. Once lost, it could never be recovered, and Ireland would no longer have a separate cultural identity. The British, as de Valera has said, would have won the final victory. Independence would be meaningless.

The trouble with the policy ("to restore the Irish language as a general medium of communication") is that it has not worked and it is not likely to. After decades of effort, at great cost, to force-feed Irish in the schools and encourage its use elsewhere in the land, less than twenty per cent of the Irish people have a fair knowledge of the language and only a fraction of them make any daily use of it. The movement has succeeded, of course, in saving Irish from disappearing altogether from everyday Irish life, but even in Kerry, West Cork and other Gaeltacht areas it is not exactly thriving. A commercial traveler in Cork said, "My work takes me into shops and offices all over southwest Ireland. When I started twenty-five years ago, I used to enjoy conversing in our native tongue with large numbers of people in all districts. Now, sad to relate, when I address young people in Irish, all I get in return is a blank stare and a snigger." When I asked a schoolboy in Cork whether he ever made use of Irish outside class, he said, "Only for a joke."

As many visitors have discovered, it is possible to travel for weeks all over Ireland and never hear a word of Irish spoken— not even if one drops into Parliament, where the language is only sporadically used, or attends one of those hysterical public debates about Irish, which must necessarily be conducted in English. Everyone *sees* the language constantly, however, because public signs are in Irish everywhere and often there is nothing but Irish. Visitors have been pleased with their recognition of such words as *aerphort* and *telefon*, but they are otherwise at a loss. One foreigner complained to the *Sunday Independent* about missing the bus to Wexford because the destination sign, under the new policy of the national transport company, was in the Irish equivalent, Loch Garman. The paper then conducted a little poll and found that only three out of ten persons questioned at the bus terminal had ever heard of Loch Garman.

Irish is not a simple language. It is so different from English and other European languages that it is Greek to a great many Irishmen, let alone the tourists. Take, for example, the following sentence from a report of a commission on language restoration: *"Tá treoir tugtha ag an Údarás Craolacháin do léiritheoirí nach ceart aon chaoi a ligean thart ina bhféadfaí an Ghaeilge a úsáid i gcláir, nuair is cuí sin."* In English, this means, "The Broadcasting Authority has instructed producers that no opportunity should be lost to use Irish in programs, where appropriate." When the classic Italian film *Bicycle Thief* was shown on Irish Television, with the dialogue in Italian and the subtitles in Irish, most of the population was left in the dark.

The language revival policy, though poorly thought out, was launched with great enthusiasm and high ambitions in the 1920s, but it soon began to flounder. Most of the outstanding language champions had been killed off, and the remaining political leaders were preoccupied with the civil war and more pressing matters. Governments claimed dedication to the cause, but no truly all-out effort was made to popularize Irish. It probably could not have been done without police-state methods; the impracticalities of supplanting English were enormous, and the people as a whole were disinterested, resented the imposition of Irish or simply could not see the point of it all. Neither the Church nor the business community did much to foster the language. Many politicians, including those who shouted loudest in English against English, did not really believe in the cause. There were powerful arguments that other nations —America, Canada, Australia—spoke English without losing their identity (but, of course, they are not little societies parked at the very edge of England). Even some of the most dedicated Irish-speakers doubted that restoration was possible. The revivalists pointed out that Hebrew has been largely restored in the new Jewish state in Palestine, but, as one authority said, "The Israelis need a common language. We do not. We already have one, the wrong one, according to some, but we cannot make the right one necessary now."

The viewpoint of the average Irishman was well expressed some years ago by Myles na Gopaleen:

> Let it be said first and foremost that I am in favour of the cultivation of the Irish language because it is ancient, beautiful and very interesting for being quite apart from all the tongues of Europe . . . but the modest proposal to revive

Irish as the common everyday language of the plain people of Ireland, I regard as arrant nonsense, the sort of thing that has never been done in the history of the world. And if it could be done . . . it would be highly undesirable: English is a world language and we are lucky to have it, particularly as we have embroidered it with the tweedy fol-de-lols and porter stains which are unmistakeably Irish and proud of it.

When the governments went halfheartedly about the business of revival it was left to the influential Gaelic League and other private organizations to promote the language cause with vigor. Their more passionate members often went to extremes in demanding the use of Irish at every turn and saying that the only true Irishmen were Irish-speakers. Cynicism has been one reaction. I have heard Irish described as "our great sacred cow" and "the chastity belt to keep the country pure." Indignation is another. Said a poet who was abused by revivalist hotheads during a poetry recital for reading a Patrick Pearse poem in English, "Imagine! You can't even read a poem in English that was written in English by the founder of the country without your patriotism being questioned."

While the more sober language enthusiasts undoubtedly have deep and admirable feelings about traditional Irish culture, it must be said that the great emotionalism about the language reveals the Irish inferiority complex. It is startling to hear Irishmen say that they will become nothing but second-rate Englishmen unless Irish prevails, when it is clear that the Irish have spoken English for centuries while remaining incorrigibly Irish. In fact, the Irish long ago proved that they could beat the British at their own game by using English with unrivaled talent. It is a sign of growing national maturity that the language issue is now being dealt with more realistically, or at least less hypocritically. The ambitions about Irish have been scaled down. Most politicians I have interviewed said that it would be nice if Irish could be widely spoken someday but English will always be the principal language—especially now that Ireland is drawing so close to Britain economically and dealing so much with other nations. Recent statements by major political parties more closely reflect the popular feeling that too high a priority has been given to Irish revival for too long. It has been the tail that has wagged the national dog, distracting attention from other problems and disfiguring the whole of Irish education.

The newly formed Language Freedom Movement, which has touched off a violent battle of words, expresses the widespread resentment of "compulsory Irish." It is being realized that the schoolchildren have been victimized by the language policy. Because Ireland has not made use of modern teaching techniques, they have been badly taught, very often by teachers who can barely speak the language themselves. (The ultimate is reached in the Latin classes in the all-Irish schools. This is described as teaching one dead language through another dead language.) The sad result is that many and perhaps most schoolchildren are essentially hostile to Irish, as are their parents. A woman in Dublin expressed a common view when she said, "I was forced to learn the language in school, but now I have a psychological block against it. I couldn't tell you a word."

Since the Irish dislike being forced to do anything, it has been proposed that the best way to get them to speak Irish is to ban the language. A more practical solution would be to teach Irish more imaginatively in the first place, and as an integral part of cultural studies within a drastically improved educational system. The usual question-and-answer parrot learning in Ireland, with its relentless cramming for examinations, does not open wide the minds of the young or inspire them with a zest for knowledge. Yet, paradoxically, Irishmen at all social levels have always had a tremendous respect for knowledge and intellectual attainments, a willingness to make conversational forays into any subject, a gift for abstract and imaginative thinking, and a love of learning for its own sake. Although Irish education is pleasantly old-fashioned in its attention to classical knowledge, it somehow manages to make the learning process a heartless conveyor belt clanking its way toward specific occupations. It is not the dearth of Irish-speakers but the cramping of native genius which is likely to keep Ireland from achieving its own kind of small-nation greatness.

Chapter 6

LOVE AND MARRIAGE

An Irishman is the only man in the world who will clamber over the bodies of a dozen naked women in order to get to a bottle of stout.

—DUBLIN JOURNALIST

We Irishwomen are almost collectors' pieces for sociologists. Irishmen are completely kinked in their attitude to women.

—MONICA McENROY

Ireland is a country where marriage has been defined as "permission to sin." It is a society which has long held the view "that God, in creating desire for woman in man, had been guilty of a lapse of taste." It is a man's country where men are the rulers and mothers enjoy power in a behind-the-scenes matriarchy. Well known for its late marriages and numerous bachelors and spinsters, it is perhaps the one place in the world where men most effectively manage to continue their bachelor pursuits (which have little to do with sex) after marriage. It has the greatest percentage of virgins, the fewest divorces (since divorce is forbidden) and the least-emancipated women in the English-speaking world.

Ireland has long believed itself to be a particularly moral society, an island of innocence in a dark sea of sexual abandon. The Irish have been the first to cast stones at the sinning Swedes, the swinging British and the promiscuous Americans. All countries but Ireland seemed to be wallowing in sensuality and unclean living. Only in Ireland, it was felt, were the innocent saved from dirty books, filthy films, Kinsey Reports, birth control and brassiere advertisements. Saved, too, from sex education, with the result that a modern Irish girl will turn to a magazine to ask, "Can French kissing lead to pregnancy? I am deeply involved with a boy who, I think, kisses this way. I am not easy in my mind."

By and large, Ireland is still a notably old-fashioned society in matters of love and marriage. At first exposure, it is a refreshing experience after regular contact with the sex-drenched world of America and Western Europe. As in the Soviet Union, where puritanism is even more officially endorsed, there is a startling dearth of erotic films, girlie magazines, titillating advertisements and seductively dressed young women. It appears to be, and in many respects it most definitely is, the most de-sexed nation on earth. Some years ago Edmund J. Murray, a Catholic scholar, wrote: "Ninety-five per cent of Ireland's eligible women would marry tomorrow were the eligible men of the nation to transfer their affections from horses and dogs and football matches and 'pubs' to the nobler activities of courtship and marriage." A while ago, during a stay at Glengarriff in southwest Ireland, I ran into a Dublin friend who said he had a pair of weddings to attend. His two male cousins had finally decided to marry. Each was over forty years of age. Thinking about their twenty or more years of bachelorhood and how they might have been gay dogs with the women, I asked, "Do you think there has been any romance in their lives?" My friend replied, "Oh, yes, there's been romance in their lives. They both love football."

And what if a maiden should encounter a man who is more interested in making love than watching football? The advice given by one Irish columnist was that she should whisper short prayers in his ear when he becomes overly amorous.

Sexual Inequality

It is no easy thing being an Irish female. She is dealt a double injustice. Marriage is harder come by and fraught with greater burdens than in most other Western countries, and yet there is little scope for a woman's talents outside marriage. In most cases it is either a state of third-class citizenship, a nunnery or the boat to England. To quote an exceptionally candid Dublin girl, "If God sent me a letter saying I would never get married I think I'd go out and make love with any man who asked me. There's no life for a woman here outside marriage. It's the be-all and end-all. This is a terrible country for a single woman, and especially in Dublin, where there are so many more women than men."

Except in the crucial matter of bringing up their children, and often controlling their lives well into adulthood, women take a back seat in Ireland. In the home they are subservient to their husbands. (One housewife, in a somewhat extreme case, said, "My husband wants a detailed account of every penny I spend, but I have no idea of what he spends on cigarettes, drink, horses, etc. If I seem to save anything, he cuts the house-keeping the following week by that amount. . . . I have to beg for the price of stockings and clothes for myself and the children.") Outside the home they are expected to know their place and do "women's work." There are no women in the Irish Cabinet and only four females among the 144 members of the Dail. (Women traditionally acquire a seat in Parliament as widows of popular M.P.s, not in their own right.) Although government departments are swarming with typists and other office girls, there are few women in important posts. In any event, state and semi-state employment contracts carry a clause which obliges a woman to give up her job if she marries.

Although Sybil Connolly is a success as a fashion designer, and Siobhan McKenna is notable as an actress, and other women have done well in the arts and professions, men are dominant almost everywhere. Using 1961 census figures, there were only 941 women listed as "administrative, executive and managerial workers" as against 12,439 men. Women dentists are outnumbered ten to one, and women physicians and surgeons five to one. In the legal professions there are seventeen men for every woman. Of 2,744 engineers, only one is a woman.

Ireland, of course, is not unusual in its conviction that a woman's place is in the home. Only a few countries, particularly in Scandinavia and the Communist world, have made substantial progress toward equal opportunities for women and full use of their talents—and they are only partway there. What is special in Ireland is the extent of male superiority and the unprotesting submission of the female to her inferior status. *Nova*, an English women's magazine, has said that the Irish woman "might be considered the last victim of slavery in Western Europe." While this exaggerates, and forgets Spain and Portugal, it is at least suggestive. Women are likely to be inferior so long as religion continues to be an overwhelming force in Irish life. The Roman Catholic Church, the greatest of the male strongholds, sets the pattern for the separation and the imbalance of power of the sexes. There are twice as many nuns as clergymen, but the hierarchy is all male and no one imagines that it could be otherwise. Even in Sweden the acceptance of women priests in the state Lutheran Church came only after a bitter and prolonged struggle.

Boys and girls are separated in Irish secondary schools, and twice as many males as females go on to higher education. In numerous farmhouses the wife does not sit down to eat until the men of the family have finished their meal. The typical husband never helps in the kitchen and assists with the children only when the mood strikes him. He has a separate social life with his male friends while his wife stays home. All this is slowly changing, of course; young couples in urban flats may carry on like their counterparts in Britain, though with the arrival of children and the dimming of the early glow of marital love the husband is likely to drift back into the company of his old pals.

It is now a fading memory in Ireland that there were some formidable women in public life in the early years of this century. Lady Gregory was a patron of the Irish literary revival and a founder of the Abbey Theatre. Countess Constance de Markievicz commanded an armed force in the Easter Rising and later became the most prominent of a number of distinguished women deputies in the earliest days of the Irish Dail. Today there are several important women's organizations, but they have little influence beyond the domestic world. Only an occasional voice is raised against the heavy discrimination that women encounter and the universal condition of unequal pay for equal work. Only infrequent cries are heard against the convention, taken for granted in a Catholic land, that a woman must labor on a marital treadmill and bear ever more children, however unwanted they are, however ill or exhausted she may be.

Monica McEnroy, a singularly courageous commentator on the battle of the sexes in Ireland, has insisted, "The women of Ireland, especially the young married women, *must stop being afraid*. We must stop being afraid of our husbands; afraid of our bishops; afraid of our doctors; afraid of everyone."

Norma Crosbie, the vivacious wife of a prominent Cork editor, is one of a number of educated women who are attempting to shake the female half of the nation out of its lethargy. "You promise in church to love, honor and obey," she exhorts her classes of young housewives, "but then you part when you come out of the church door, and your husband becomes just a boarder in your home. Now that he has found a housekeeper he is free to go out with the boys again. Don't let him!"

In a newspaper series on the life of the working girls in Dublin, Mary Maher wrote that "it is startling to meet them en masse, for they appear to be the most faceless, voiceless, resolutely purposeless people any society could produce. They offer no opinions; they enter no arguments; and it is difficult not to suspect that they know no facts." She told me with great disgust—for she is a young American journalist who has settled in Ireland—"They're so placid! They're vegetables! They're afraid to think anything in case they scare off some eligible man they might meet. Marriage is what they pray for, but a huge percentage of them will never marry. If you ask what they will do in that case they just look blank. They have no plans. They're just waiting. They only *exist*."

Many women are so grateful to have a husband at all that they put up with much in their married lives that women in other countries would consider intolerable. Dr. Ivor Browne, as head of the largest mental-hospital group in the country, described Irish housewives as "overwhelmed" by debts, children, neglectful husbands and the multiple difficulties of their lives. "You get the feeling that from the day they married they never get their heads above water, that things are just going from bad to worse."

Married life in Ireland is conceivably no worse than it is elsewhere in the world, but I am not persuaded that it is any better, as so many of the Irish fondly believe. When questioned, most women claim to be content and many say they are happy. They compare their lot to that of their neighbors, not to remote women in more prosperous or emancipated countries, and they are secure in their conventionality. The Irish tendency, in any event, is to idealize marriage. Even if one's husband is a trial, the children can be cared for with overflowing devotion.

Arranged marriages are now out of fashion (though matchmakers may still be found in rural Ireland), and most girls will insist on romance before marriage, but the glorification of the homemaker continues. When viewing the excessively high divorce rates in the United States and the ever-increasing popularity of divorce in Britain and on the Continent, the Irish are inclined to congratulate themselves on the permanency and stability of their marriages. They marry with the understanding that it is a lifetime proposition. The idea of marrying again is unthinkable. But, as already stated, divorce is forbidden in Ireland, and remarriage in Ireland by anyone divorced abroad is likely to be considered bigamous in Irish courts.

The great unknown is the number of Irish men and women who would end their marriages if they were permitted to. Probably very few at first, because of the stigma attached, but the number who would *want* to might be considerable. As matters stand, many couples live together in bitterness and many are separated. The poet L. A. G. Strong, who died a decade ago, wrote:

> Have I wife? Bedam I have!
>   But we was badly mated:
> I hit her a great clout one night,
>   And now we're separated.
>
> And mornin's, going to my work,
>   I meet her on the quay:
> "Good mornin' to ye, ma'am," says I;
>   "To hell with ye," says she.

Married Bachelors

Some years ago an American priest wrote that "without doubt, the strangest species of male on the face of the earth today is the Irish bachelor. He is the enigma and mystery of the world." Although a quarter of Irish men never marry at all (which is the one reason why as many as ten thousand Irish girls flee the country each year), the average young man expects to marry and feels that he ought to. But he does not get around to it until his thirtieth birthday. I have asked many Irishmen why this is so. A frequent answer is that while they wouldn't mind a nice warm wife sharing their bed they are fearful of the inevitable and unavoidable sequence of children and mounting debts. Before the Famine the Irish married early and had a soaring birth rate. Ever since the Famine the consciousness of the economic burdens of matrimony has been intense. And with it, as a natural accompaniment, has been a conception of marriage as a straitjacket.

"A young man in this country who is engaged to be married," writes Seamus Heaney, "is regarded with sympathetic puzzlement by his elder married friends. They convey to him a sense not so much of climax as finale. 'It's a blister you'll sit on for the rest of your days.' Images of strangulation and fettering recur—the knot, the noose, hitched, tied up—and euphemisms such as 'having the job done.' When he returns from the honeymoon, they admit him to their company with a new intimacy— he finds himself part of a secret order of broken spirits."

In rural Ireland the son who remains on the land after his brothers have gone off to the towns or overseas may be discouraged from seriously contemplating marriage until middle age, or else discouraged from marrying at all, because Mother cannot stand the thought of a rival female in the household with whom she must share her boy's affections. At the same time, those of his sisters who have not emigrated may have surrendered themselves to spinsterhood and a life of waiting on their parents, brother and whatever elderly relatives may be in the household.

An article in the *Journal of the Irish Medical Association* spoke of the "pathological constellation, not uncommon in Ireland, . . . where both parents are dead and gone, but several brothers and sisters are still clinging together ('keeping the family together') into middle-age. If one asks, why did you never marry, the response often is, 'Oh, I couldn't, I had to look after my brothers.' "

I have seen the elderly Irish mother described as just about "the most jealous and unreasoning female on the face of the earth." Harsh words, and yet by pampering and then clinging desperately to her dear boy she makes him a victim of her possessiveness and he turns out to be something less than a full man. While bachelors in other lands can hardly wait to have a flat of their own and a life of their own, he finds it easier just staying at home with Mother. If he does decide to marry he may unconsciously look for a mother substitute. Even then, he continues until his mother's death to turn to her frequently for advice and comfort.

Such an Irishman is best described as a married bachelor. According to one marriage counselor, his principal purpose is to make sure that marriage "is going to interfere as little as possible with his established routine. His wife is a king-size hot-water bottle who also cooks his food and pays his bills and produces his heirs. . . . In the intimate side of marriage he behaves as if he were slightly ashamed of having deserted his male friends and his bachelorhood. He takes what should be the happy, leisurely love-making of marriage like a silent connubial supper of cold rice pudding. A rapid sex routine is effected, as if his wife is some stray creature with whom he is sinning and hopes he may never see again."

Though many Irish wives are preconditioned to such behavior, having seen its like in their own fathers and uncles, they resent it deeply. But as they turn from their husbands to lavish their affection on their sons, and then, in later years, strive to "protect" the sons from scheming girls wishing to marry them, they carry on the vicious circle of maternal possessiveness and male selfishness.

All of this is familiar to anyone who knows the Irish scene, but it is difficult to say how "typical" such husbands and wives are. There is little hard sociological evidence on the subject, and the old social patterns in Ireland are breaking down, anyway. Young people are no longer tied so closely to home. They have greater personal freedom and they are already marrying earlier than their parents did. Girls now reaching maturity will not, after being exposed to television and women's magazines, so readily tolerate a bachelor husband.

Family Planning

I have emphasized the sorrier side of Irish marriages and no doubt have done an injustice to every blissfully married couple in the Republic. Most of the people I know well in Ireland do not fit the image I have drawn, but then these are among the better-educated and more emancipated of the Irish. I am seeking to reveal the conditions of the "ordinary" Irish Catholic husbands and wives. They live in a state of far greater tension than one would suppose from the sweet and serene atmosphere of the country. Apart from ever present economic worries, nothing puts such heavy strain on them as the mixture of normal sexual desire and the fear of an unwanted pregnancy.

Most Irish husbands and wives want children, and usually more children than other Europeans would wish. A flock of handsome children is a prideful thing in an Irish community. But a newborn child every year, for year after year, is another story, and usually a sad one. "Father," said one beleaguered mother to a priest-sociologist, "I've been married fifteen years and in that time I met with every misfortune, even twins."

Until lately there was a dumb acceptance of unwanted pregnancies as the Will of God, with nothing to be done about it except, as the celibate priests advised, for husbands and wives to sleep separately. Birth control was a taboo subject. People rarely spoke about family planning. The "rhythm method" sanctioned by the Church was tried, but, in the long run, found wanting. People knew about but seldom mentioned the tragedies of mothers no longer fit for childbearing who died giving birth, of family life destroyed because of the burden of too many children, of women driven to mental breakdowns by the multiple pressures of their lives. With rare and brave exceptions, the authorities were silent, the press mute.

What has happened in the last few years has been a dramatic breaking of the silence. Dr. A. P. Barry, for example, who is a consulting gynecologist and president of the Irish Medical Association, said that "a horrifying number of young married women are being treated by psychiatrists for nervous exhaustion and mental exhaustion following childbirth." The fact that eminent foreign Catholics had proposed reconsideration of the Church's stand on birth control, and that the Pope was thinking about it, seemed to open the door to discussion more widely than ever. At the same time, the birth-control "Pill" (any of a variety of ovulation-suppressing tablets) found its way to Ireland and came into rapid use under the guise of prescriptions for various ailments. "If I don't supply it to my patients," said a Catholic physician in a town near the Ulster border, "they'll go to some Protestant doctor on the other side and get it from him." Women who would never have dreamed of using a "mechanical device," as the usual contraceptives are known in the Republic, found it possible to justify their use of the Pill. And particularly after the newspapers and magazines, in a burst of enlightenment, began to speak frankly about family planning.

Monica McEnroy said in a *Woman's Way* series on contraception:

> Married woman in the Republic of Ireland, whatever their size of family, whatever their state of health, personal wishes or religious principles, are forced to accept total celibacy or chance the "safe period" as their only means of conception control.
>
> As a Roman Catholic hospital nurse, midwife and mother, I regard this as a national scandal. . . .
>
> What we all want to know is when the Irish clinics are going to start dealing with married women patients according to their medical requirements and let us make our own decisions on the matter of Church rules.

An eminent physician, contributing to a lively newspaper correspondence about overburdened mothers and unwanted children, said: "These tragedies are predictable and preventable.

Use of the safe period must be regarded as far too haphazard a method of prevention when the price in terms of health is so high."

Then, one night in October 1966, a new height in candor was reached when Irish Television presented a program entitled "Too Many Children?" Put on late in the evening, it was introduced by a young female announcer as "an adult subject, treated in an adult way, and we feel that it should be viewed only by an adult audience." It was a simply structured program, with Michael Viney playing tape-recorded interviews with "mothers of big families struggling to make ends meet" and asking for comments on their problems from a priest, a psychiatrist, a gynecologist and a social worker. I recorded the program in a Dublin hotel room and felt at times that I was witnessing a historic breakthrough in Irish life, for if *this* could be said on such a family medium as television, then anything could be said from now on in Ireland.

Viney began by mentioning the paradox of Ireland's great loss of population over the years while having a fertility rate more than twice that of England or America—"one of the highest in the civilized world." A fifth of all Irish mothers, he said, have seven or more children; some six thousand have twelve or more children. "And as a general rule the families with the least money tend to have the most children."

And then the voices of the women. Said one, "My mother had seventeen children. Every year she had 'em. I have five children now. If I knew I was going to have some more that way, by section birth, I'd dump myself in the river. I'd just like to know whether I was finished having children so I could settle down." And another, "I got married in November 1956. That will be ten years next November, and I'm expecting my tenth baby. The babies just come around every year. It happened that way. One year two babies came. I think this one will have to be the last, because I'm really not able to go on any longer."

Dr. Ivor Browne, the psychiatrist, commented that his patients had no confidence in the rhythm method of family planning which, according to the priest on the program, Father Enda McDonagh, a noted professor of moral theology, was "the only method which has been endorsed as in accordance with the divine laws of human dignity and human sexuality." Browne's opinion was that "it is just nonsense to talk about a safe period." The gynecologist, Dr. Declan Meagher, said the so-called safe period works only for a minority of women though it is the most common family-planning method used in the Irish Republic. "But it is supplemented in many cases," he added, "by the use of the withdrawal technique or coitus interruptus. This is a very prevalent practice."

Viney said, "Most psychologists would agree, I think, that coitus interruptus is emotionally unsatisfying for both husband and wife. Would you agree?" Dr. Meagher answered, "Yes, I would think it is not only emotionally unsatisfying but also physically unsatisfying and gives rise to frustration, and, I think, added to this, the moral guilt which follows leads to a considerable unhappiness in many marriages." He stated that a recent survey of Catholic gynecologists in Ireland revealed that twenty-five per cent of them prescribe the Pill directly as a contraceptive, "and those who didn't use the Pill as a contraceptive expressed the wish that they would like to if permitted by their conscience." (The number of Irish women actually using the Pill, however, is apparently still less than five per cent.)

Every so often, like a Greek chorus, the voices of the mothers came in:

We should have some way of putting a stop to having large families, because the children are suffering for it. I did discuss family planning with the priest once, and he turned around and said I was healthy enough, well enough and young enough to have them. He wouldn't give me absolution . . . I didn't go to confession for a while over that.

Well, I couldn't stop. I just kept on having them. And I think it's wrong. . . . Anyone in poor health should get a break in the family.

Family planning is a good thing. I mean, if I knew what I know now I wouldn't have as many children. I definitely wouldn't. I really think it's the best thing that ever came into this country is family planning and I think there should be more done about it. I really do.

Father McDonagh, himself a liberal-minded priest, was much on the defensive throughout the program. He said that "the difficulty facing the Roman Catholic Church is: do contraceptive means, admittedly more efficient, enhance our humanity or reduce it?" He said it was reasonable to think that having to watch the calendar or a temperature chart to see which nights are "safe" for intercourse is damaging to the spontaneity of love. Nonetheless, the rhythm method "at the moment" was the only one approved by the Church. In closing the program, Viney said that "any day now a pronouncement from the Pope may well take this whole issue a big step further."

It was a noteworthy television program, but the response to it was even more indicative of changing times in Ireland. Whereas a few years ago an avalanche of complaints about "indecency" might have fallen on the television studios, now there were only a few stray telephone calls to offset the letters of praise. Inevitably a rural mother of six wrote to say, "We were taught by our Christian doctrine that such things shouldn't be named amongst us," but more typical was the message which said, "All the priests in our area join me in this note of commendation."

The dilemma of Catholic clergymen in Ireland about the birth-control issue was made most plain to me when a middle-aged priest in a remote western parish acknowledged that he would personally like to recommend the Pill or some reliable contraceptive to the overstressed mothers of large and poor families. "But I can't," he said plaintively. "I can't say a thing until the Pope acts."

Other priests, of course, were far less liberal and obviously would find it painful to have to go along with any loosening of the Church's traditional attitude to birth control. They were already greatly disturbed by what they felt to be a crumbling of morality in Ireland, and acceptance of the Pill would only make it worse. All about them they could see signs of sinful thoughts and sinful behavior. People were talking publicly about sex as never before. They were behaving more immodestly and paying less attention to their bishops and priests.

I could see their point. When individual bishops denounced the mention of nighties on a television program or tried to forbid late-night dancing, they received little but hoots of laughter and sarcastic press comments for their trouble. When Irish authoress Edna O'Brien, whose sexually candid novels have been banned in Ireland, returns home from London she is greeted as a celebrity, pictured on the front pages, and asked to air her views on television before a panel of teen-agers.

Sex used to be something no decent person would mention— something that one should have as little to do with as possible. Sex was usually equated with sin, and morality was discussed more in relation to sex than anything else. Many a married couple would turn their religious pictures to the wall before making love. Boys were taught to believe that girls were "dangerous occasions of sin," and girls learned to deny their natural feelings. Edna O'Brien has said, "I don't think I have any pleasure in any part of my body, because my first and initial body thoughts were blackened by the fear of sin and therefore I think of my body as a vehicle for sin, a sort of tabernacle of sin." (This was several years ago. She tells me that she has since managed to move on beyond her fears.)

In its sex life, Ireland, seemingly so virtuous, has been a sick society. The gulf between what is preached and what is practiced is wide. The doctrine on relationships between male and female has been almost a denial of life itself, reaching extremes in those pious parishes of some years ago when the sexes would be separated in church and other public places. Young men and women would be reviled for "keeping company" or for showing any inclination toward romance. Recently a Jesuit priest, the Reverend Robert Nash, said in a sermon about "the false god of lust" that "an exaggerated fear of sex is almost as bad as an excessive love of it."

The Irish people have long indulged in self-deception. When James Joyce wrote about the sexual appetites of the Dubliners he knew, he was savagely attacked, as has been every Irish author to this day who writes honestly about such matters. Girls foolish enough to get pregnant have been thrown not only out of their homes but out of the country. A significant percentage of the mothers of illegitimate babies in London are girls who conceive in Ireland and deliver in Britain. It is an indictment of contemporary Ireland that the Greater London Council should find it necessary to maintain an office in Dublin in order to help such unwed mothers find a place for themselves and their babies at home.

The Guilt of Innocence

Given the strictures against sex in Ireland, it is a wonder that Irish girls get into trouble at all, but, as one woman has written, "daughters are getting out of hand everywhere." A young English businessman who spent several bachelor years in Dublin said that "with a little effort you could get an Irish girl to sleep with you, but she would say, 'Now, don't be using a contraceptive; I don't want to commit a sin.'"

What passes for innocence in Ireland is usually ignorance. The youth of Ireland have not only been given a warped view of sex but have been denied, by both their parents and society in general, the most rudimentary practical information. In today's world, when so many temptations are placed before the young, a nation can be guilty of innocence.

In his brilliant autobiography *Vive Moi!*, Sean O'Faolain has written of his own days of innocence:

> There is one thing I do blame, I must blame, because it caused me so much suffering as a boy— the delicate-mindedness, or overprotectiveness, or mealy-mouthedness, whichever it was, of the Irish Church, and the sentimentalised picture of life, especially in relation to sex, that it presented to us through its teaching orders and from the pulpit, except when some tough Redemptorist took over to give us a bit of straightforward, realistic hell. I think it chiefly was overprotectiveness; as if they believed that if nobody mentioned sex organs we would not notice that we had them. . . . A worse result of this niceness and genteelism of my clerical teachers was that, as boys, whatever we learned, mostly incorrect, about our bodies was learned in dark corners and huddles of shame, from brutal words and coarse jokes that associated all passion with filth. Whenever I think of the turbulence and agony of nubile youth, the terror of a boy at his first discovery of his manhood, of a young girl at her first experience of womanhood, I can only rage at our pious elders who so sweetly, so virtuously, so loftily and benevolently sent us naked to the wolf of life.

O'Faolain was twenty years old and midway through Cork University before he learned how childbirth worked. He had written a little poem with a line about "Mother Ireland's teeming navel." A medical-student friend, reading this, pointed out that "so far as his knowledge of the history of medicine went no mother had yet been known to eject a baby through her belly-button."

To judge by the letters sent to the advice columnists of Irish newspapers and magazines, an amazing amount of ignorance about sex lingers on. Angela Macnamara's *Woman's Way* column "Can You Help Me?" has printed such appeals as the following:

> How is it that some girls become pregnant before they are married? I have been told this is wrong.

> This is my first time having a boy-friend. Would courting make me pregnant? I have been in a convent for six years and don't know very much about dating boys.

> Is it only virgins who can wear white when getting married? If so, is it a sin for others to do so?

> Is it wrong to think about things to do with sex? I'm always thinking and imagining all sorts of things about it. I've only had a few dates and I behaved properly, so why do I have the sort of thoughts which are not proper at all? Should I confess them?

> I am nearly eighteen . . . I have been going out for a year with a very nice boy whom I love . . . Is it possible to have intercourse without being aware of it at the time?

> I am a bachelor of twenty-seven and find your page most helpful as I never received any sex education.

The fact that such letters are printed at all, and are answered with frankness, is a major departure from the traditional Irish conspiracy of silence about sex. But of course many adults are horrified. A "mother of ten," writing to Angela Macnamara about her advice column in the *Sunday Press*, fumed, "You are giving our young people rotten ideas to ponder over. I would love to see someone setting fire to you." Caroline Mitchell, an editor of *Woman's Way*, told me of a woman who came storming into her office to complain that her son was being corrupted by reading the "dirty letters" which the magazine prints. Asked how old the boy was, the mother said twenty-one.

"But surely he's old enough to know his own mind," said the editor. The irate mother exclaimed, "He has the mind of a fifteen-year-old, and God grant he stays that way!"

Although the new candor about sex is an advance, it remains within a rigid Catholic framework. Chastity is still paramount. There is no tolerance or thinly disguised approval at all of premarital relations, as there is in Britain and on much of the Continent. The advice-to-the-lovelorn columnists, who are themselves confessors of sorts, seldom give opinions which would offend a reasonably tolerant clergyman. One woman wrote, "I am getting married shortly. Is sex relationship permitted at all hours, or only for the purpose of procreation?" The feeble response was, "The answer to your problem will be given by your confessor." Another asked, "Can a woman become pregnant if she has sexual intercourse at any time of the month, or is it only when she has her periods?" She was given the badly needed facts of life, but the columnist felt it necessary to add, "Outside marriage it is unnecessary to know these details."

There is something ostrichlike about this view, for if anything is clear in modern Ireland it is the increase of premarital sexual activity, by which I mean the whole range of intimacies. In the country's more simple and sheltered days it probably was true that most young women—and men—had but little intimate experience before marriage. Dating was almost nonexistent, and adults were ever watchful. Today, the influence of outside ideas and the opportunities for sexual experience are greater than ever.

While parents, priests and school authorities convince themselves that old attitudes still suit changing conditions, and fail grievously to prepare the young for "the wolf of life," Irish boys and girls cope as best they can with the extraordinary temptations and pressures of modern times. Those who emigrate are so many innocents abroad—frail craft without moorings. Supposedly they have been provided with moral armor after hearing so much about the sin of sex, but in many cases the "morality" which keeps them "pure" is not a matter of conviction but a fear of losing reputation. Being caught is the greatest sin of all. Once out of Ireland, and away from the gaze of the home community, being judged "respectable" loses some of its importance in face of the desire to be popular.

Those young people who stay in Ireland but leave home to work in Dublin or the smaller cities are in a somewhat comparable situation, though the restraints are greater. Because most youngsters of fifteen or sixteen are already finished with school and going to work, they try to behave like grownups and overcome their appalling ignorance and immaturity. The girls are particularly susceptible to the dream-world cajoleries of films, advertisements, popular magazines and pop idols. Their heads have little inside them but thoughts of boys, dates, dances and the ways and means of achieving popularity. Their sole ambition in life is to "do a steady line" with a boy and marry as early as possible. With exceptions, of course, they see no other life for themselves, for they have been taught to seek no other.

The sexual pressure on the girls is considerable. Because so many eligible males seem afraid of them or are just not interested (and yet outright homosexuality in Ireland is either rare or well concealed), the girls are at a disadvantage at the hands of those who find them more interesting than their male companions. Such young men, who are inclined to see girls more as sex objects than as persons worth knowing for their own sake, have something of a buyer's choice. Many of the hundreds of dance halls all over the country operate almost like cattle fairs. One hotel manager said, "A dance here is like an auction. The boys come to look over the merchandise. The whole idea is to decide which girls will give out the most and then get them to go off with you after the dance, if you know what I mean." On the other hand, the girls at such dances complain about the difficulty of persuading a boy to take them home. There is, in any event, a frenzied character to the whole exercise, with the forbidden fruits of sex charging the atmosphere. The music is appropriately wild and deafening.

One of the most important social developments in Ireland in the past decade has been the boom in dancing in huge new ballrooms to the music of showbands. It is a far cry from the old-time crossroads dancing or the more sedate gatherings in parish halls. There are some six hundred showbands, so called because each has about eight instrumentalists, including one or two who sing also, and they put on something of a show as well as provide electronically powered dance music. Because the showbands altogether may draw more than half a million Irish youth a week (at seven to ten shillings a head) into the dance halls, it amounts to a fair-sized national industry. In some rural towns the ballroom, with space for two to three thousand people, is the biggest building and the biggest money-making enterprise in the area. The advertisements of the various ballrooms in the newspapers cover whole pages.

On dance nights the halls are ringed with cars, some of them purchased at great sacrifice by small-farm families in order to keep the boys from emigrating. I have met young people who go dancing three nights a week even though they have no money for anything else. They say they have nothing else to do and no other possibility of meeting the opposite sex. Their parents are often greatly disturbed by the whole thing, especially when they hear about the "close dancing" that goes on, but they feel they can no longer forbid their youngsters to go out with the crowd. "Times are changing," they say. Those adults who most vigorously denounce the dancing craze admit that they have done nothing about encouraging less "dangerous" means for young people to enjoy each other's company. Their instinct is still to separate the sexes.

The sexual attitudes of Irish youth today are more or less comparable to those in America or Britain a generation ago. The new permissiveness of Western society is only beginning to creep into Ireland. "I'm really quite liberal," said a girl in

Galway. "I've read *The Carpetbaggers!*" There is still a greater resistance to all-out experience than in most other countries, but it increasingly becomes a matter of technical virginity. "Because a boy and a girl agree that they shouldn't go all the way," said a pretty receptionist in Waterford, "she will let him take a great many liberties. It's a substitute for the real thing, I guess." It is widely felt that anything goes, so long as it stops just short of the finish line. Some, of course, go across the finish line. They take their chances in a game which can only be described as Irish roulette. The cost of loving is often high. "I didn't think once counted," said one pregnant girl.

Whether puritanical, promiscuous, or, as is usually the case, just confused, all the young men and women in Ireland are affected by the difficulty of enjoying an easy and natural relationship with each other. It is unusual, except in some university circles, for a boy and a girl simply to seek out each other's company for reasons of mind and personality—in short, to have no designs on each other beyond the pleasures of friendship and mutual interests. They have not been encouraged by society to regard persons of the opposite sex as individuals, and they themselves suffer from an insufficient awareness of their own individuality. They tend to huddle in the security of their own sex group, with the result that young men and women almost face each other as enemy forces. In the Irish battle of the sexes there are frantic skirmishes and long periods of delaying tactics. When marriage comes at last it has the look of a victory for one and a defeat for the other.

Like everything else in Ireland, of course, things work out and life goes on, but the element of joy in romance and marriage is too often missing. Only the luckier few know what it is to love merrily and live together tenderly.

Chapter 7

THE TROUBLED ARTS

For sheer philistinism it is hard to match Ireland among European nations. We are profoundly unappreciative of the arts and of civilized living.

—THE DUBLIN MAGAZINE

It takes both courage and patience to live in Ireland.

—SEAN O'CASEY

"Because we have the reputation of being priest-ridden and clerically dominated we are inclined to be sensitive about our Censorship of Publications code. I do not suffer from any such inferiority complex in relation to those matters." So said Senator John B. O'Quigley during a debate on a censorship revision bill in the Irish Parliament one June afternoon in 1967. "Let us not be the slightest bit put about by criticisms that have been made by ourselves of ourselves and of ourselves by other people because of our Censorship of Publications Acts and the manner in which they have been operated. If one looks at the film *Ulysses*—"

At which point Senator Garret FitzGerald interrupted to ask, "How?"

How indeed? Although *Ulysses* is a serious motion picture based on the work of the greatest Irish writer of the age, and although it is about Dubliners and was filmed in Ireland with Irish actors, it cannot be seen by Irish adults. They are protected from such disturbing influences by what has been, for nearly forty years, the most elaborate and zealously conducted censorship apparatus of any democratic nation in the world. It is a machine which has banned more than ten thousand books, including many of the major works of modern literature, and hundreds of films, including some of the finest productions of the most renowned international directors.

Censorship

While the salaried film censor looks at some three million feet of motion pictures each year to make sure that no "indecent, obscene or blasphemous" movie reaches the screen in Ireland, a five-man (unpaid) Censorship of Publications Board reads— or skims—some five hundred books and numerous periodicals which customs officials or members of the public have "recommended" to it as candidates for banishment. And in case any publisher or producer wishes to challenge a banning, there are appeal boards which will take another look at the offending work. The censors are hard-working individuals, predominantly men of late middle age, who take their policing duties seriously and do not consider themselves to be anti-intellectual. (Some years ago Arland Ussher gave, in *The Face and Mind of Ireland*, his conclusion that "censorship is maintained, primarily, for the purpose of baiting the intellectuals.") The censors are not necessarily humorless or sanctimonious persons. Judge J. C. Conroy, the white-haired chairman of the Censorship Board, is a hearty, likable man who says, "If anything, the Irish character is a bit bawdy, including my own. I'm no prude."

Judge Conroy and his associates, all of whom have full-time jobs apart from their censorship work, are on the lookout for books and magazines which "have no purpose but to corrupt." He recently told an interviewer, "If you open a book and the father rapes his daughter on the first page you don't have to read any further. If it's a paperback there's probably a picture of it on the cover, anyway. It's the hard-cover book, which could be a serious one, that gives you trouble. You can read a hundred pages and think there's nothing to it, and then on the next page you've got something really bad."

Given the stern history of Irish censorship, it was certain that the film *Ulysses* would be banned. It has been forbidden, after all, in a number of countries and otherwise denounced by moralists the world over for looking too frankly under the covers of Dublin life and for recording too faithfully the earthiness of Irish speech. ("The attitude of many is that Ireland is a country where foul language is unheard of," Dr. Owen Sheehy Skeffington told the Irish Senate, "but nobody walking through the streets of Dublin and listening to the prattle of infants can fail to collect a large number of four-letter words.") What cannot be said with certainty any more, however, is that this film or any other will remain banned in Ireland for long, or that in the future any particular film, book or magazine will be censored at all. Like so much else in Ireland, censorship is not what it used to be.

The machinery of censorship remains intact, but the age of lunacy—the blind, blundering and occasionally vicious crusade to protect the supposedly innocent Irish from the wickedness of the world—is over. In contrast to the hysterical days when an Irish writer had to worry about whether a single letter of the alphabet would incur the wrath of the censors (if he spoke of a woman's "breasts" instead of her "breast"), the control of literature and films is now being conducted with ever more sanity and common sense. The censors are no longer so heavy-handed. Whereas 600 to 700 books were banned each year a decade ago, there were 442 banned in 1963, 353 in 1964, 288 in 1965 and 158 in 1966. The Irish public as well as the censors has become so much more tolerant of mildly erotic material in the last few years that Ireland can no longer be described as the most prim and proper country on earth. Recently a travel writer felt called upon to advise prospective Irish visitors to the Soviet Union that among the things the tourist is not allowed to bring into Russia is "pornographic literature," and added, "Under this head would fall many paperback books on sale in Ireland."

In 1965 a thirty-year-old Catholic schoolteacher named John McGahern, who had won acclaim and awards for his sensitive first novel, *The Barracks*, was again in the news after the publication of his second book, *The Dark*. His moving and intimate account of adolescence in a bleak corner of the Irish west, of self-doubt, "self-abuse" and clerical celibacy, earned him high praise from British and Irish critics. The book was too strong for the censors, however, and it was banned. It was one of the most criticized instances of censorship in years, and then a major controversy developed when McGahern was informed by his school that his teaching contract would not be renewed. Not only had he written a "dirty" book, but he had married a Finnish girl in a registry office instead of in church. Many liberal Irishmen were dismayed when the author left Ireland to live abroad (he is now in London), for it seemed that nothing had changed. The exiled Irish writer has been an all too familiar figure. James Joyce, who himself had left Ireland as a youth, once spoke of his homeland as "the old sow that eats her farrow."

A year after McGahern's departure, however, a member of the Censorship of Publications Appeal Board with whom I sat down stressed that things were really improving after all. "We're concerned only with outright pornography now," he said. "You just have to look at the titles. The old Censorship Board had a devastating effect on Irish writers, but I feel today that no writer of worth will go unread or unsupported in Ireland—despite the McGahern case, and that was pure idiocy."

The more broad-minded attitude of the Irish was dramatically illustrated by the manner of the passage of the 1967 Censorship of Publications Bill by the two houses of the Irish Parliament. It called for a modification (though nothing too drastic) of the

Censorship Acts of 1929 and 1946. The aim of the young Minister for Justice, Brian Lenihan, under whose office the censors operate, was to reduce the ban on offending books from forever to something like twenty years. He also sought to make it possible to appeal against a banning at any time (but only once) and not, as the law required, within only the first twelve months of the restriction order. Although some warning cries were raised against creeping immorality, the debates in the Dail and the Senate were responsible and remarkably unemotional. The Irish public took it all most calmly, and the Church was silent. To the delight and surprise of Lenihan, the legislators were so agreeable about the whole business that he was able to reduce the banning period to twelve instead of twenty years. A Justice Department official told me later, "It was amazing how the bill passed so easily, with only an odd voice raised against it. Ten years ago a minister wouldn't have dared introduce a bill like this."

One immediate effect of the new act was to "unban" some five to six thousand books: those works which had been on the Irish blacklist for more than a dozen years. The stigma was withdrawn from many worthy volumes which deserved to be made freely available in Ireland, but the country was not flooded by a tidal wave of "dirty" books. The majority of the books which have been banned in Ireland are trash by any standard— *Hot Dames on Cold Slabs*, *The Flesh Merchants*, *Lust Money Stud*, *The Passion Attic*—and they are such fly-by-night works that they are not likely to reappear on the Irish scene.

The mellowing of Irish censorship has received little attention outside Ireland, largely because it has made so little impact inside Ireland. Apart from a handful of anticensorship writers, liberal thinkers and other persons derisively identified as "intellectuals," it is non-Irishmen instead of the natives who have been most agitated about censorship over the years. American author Paul Blanshard, for example, wrote in *The Irish and Catholic Power* (1953):

Like Spain's Inquisition under Torquemada the Irish Book Censorship is not so much famous as infamous. It is probably the best-known feature of the Irish clerical Republic. At one time or another the censorship has victimized almost every distinguished writer of fiction in the non-Irish world and it has brought under its blight Ireland's greatest poets, dramatists, and scholars.

To the ordinary Irishman such indignation by a foreigner is puzzling, not to say annoying, for he does not see what the fuss is all about. In no way does he feel affected by censorship. If he reads books at all (there are few good bookshops to be found outside the major cities), he thinks it is enough of a job just trying to keep up with all the wholesome, uncensored works. He sees nothing wrong about a Christian community using censorship as a means of social protection. "This is a moral country," a Dublin housewife told me, "and we want it to stay that way." The Catholic Archbishop of Dublin has rightly said, "Our good, ordinary people accept and want censorship because they accept the natural and Christian moral law."

As for the people who want to taste the forbidden fruit, they are able to do so—though sometimes with a little effort. No visit to Belfast or London is complete without bringing back a few banned books for yourself and friends. Novels like *The Dark* are well circulated after the censors make them notorious. "All the girls on our switchboard are reading *The Adventurers*," a Telefis Eireann announcer told me, "and that's about as raw a book as you can get." Not long ago at a crowded public meeting in Limerick, the Reverend Peter Connolly, a noted scholar-priest, spoke at length and with considerable enthusiasm about the work of Edna O'Brien, who was sitting next to him on the platform. She is currently Ireland's leader of the banned. Every one of the five novels she has written has been censored. (*The Country Girls*, a touching and often humorous account of growing up in rural Ireland, has been translated into Dutch for use in the schoolrooms of Holland.) When Father Connolly asked members of the audience whether they had read any of her books, a forest of hands went into the air.

"Bannable" books are often available in the shops for weeks before the censors get around to them. Now that the paperback revolution has reached Ireland, more and more books escape the notice of the self-appointed guardians of public morality. Or else the censors just don't care as much as they used to. In a leading Dublin bookshop the manager swept his hand over some neat piles of freshly minted books and said, "There are dozens of books here which we could never have sold ten years ago."

It should also be recorded that there is no censorship of the Irish theater. Official censorship, anyway. During this century there have been frequent rows about controversial dramas and a number of cases of plays suppressed because of unofficial pressure by the clergy or laymen. A production of Tennessee Williams' *Rose Tattoo* was closed by police action in 1957. The following year there was an uproar over the Dublin Theatre Festival's plans to stage a new Sean O'Casey play and *Bloomsday*, a dramatization of scenes from *Ulysses*. Behind-the-scenes pressure from the Church and direct objections by a trade-union organization led to the withdrawal of the plays. It is hard to imagine such incidents happening in Ireland today. *Rose Tattoo* and *Bloomsday*, in fact, were performed just a few years ago. Irish playwrights and producers now have such a degree of free expression that foreign visitors to the Abbey or the Gate Theatre (once described as "Sodom and Begorrah") are sometimes astonished at the rough language they hear. "It's all changing for the better," said Lord Killanin, the chairman of the Theatre Festival. "I don't think Dublin can be shocked any more. I think we've beat them."

Why, then, write at length about censorship at all?

Because it continues to be an extraordinary and deeply entrenched fact of Irish life. Because the national desire for censorship and the admitted need of it make a terrible indictment of the society, for it says that the Irish are too susceptible, too poorly educated and too emotionally immature to be able to cope with the world as it is. And because the arts in Ireland have been faltering for decades instead of flourishing, and it is hard not to suspect that censorship, or what is called "the climate of repression," has had something to do with it.

It must be said as well, in all honesty, that it is a subject any writer would find difficult to avoid if he is concerned at all about individual liberty. I have lived and worked in places where I was censored and spied upon, and where faceless officials decided which books and newspapers were safe for me and everyone else to read. I remember debating the meaning of freedom with Russian students in the very graveyard outside Moscow where Boris Pasternak lies buried. All of this may seem remote from conditions in Ireland. The mass of Irishmen are well satisfied with the freedoms they enjoy. Foreign visitors to this friendliest of nations are rarely troubled about the books they carry. And Irish censorship, in any event, is concerned about sex, not politics, and it does not even apply to anti-Catholic literature.

Nonetheless, it gives me a chill to read that copies of a new novel by a leading Irish author, Patrick Boyle, were seized by customs officials who considered it a likely candidate for banning. (As it turned out, the censors let it pass.) Or to be told by an Irish writer who lives near Ulster that he has the books he orders from London sent to a neighbor across the border to make sure the packages reach him unopened. Or to hear Professor James Dooge tell the story of the time a customs officer examining his suitcase at Dublin Airport came upon the book *When the Kissing Had to Stop*. This provocatively titled work by Constantine Fitzgibbon has as its main theme, as the professor says, "the danger of liberal thought, of liberalism, and how they can lead to a Communist takeover." The customs man "was so sure this book was banned that he went three times through the list of prohibited publications with increasing disappointment and I am sure he ended up with a firm conviction that our Censorship Board, for all their activity, were not really doing their job 100 per cent effectively."

I also find myself wondering about the superemphasis on sex as the only important moral issue, and about the readiness of otherwise self-assured people to have other people decide what is good for them to read. One evening in Davy Byrnes', sitting with a lady journalist from Sweden and an Irish married couple, I asked a bright young official of the Department of External Affairs what he thought about censorship. He said forthrightly that he was against it altogether, "except for pornography, of course." I asked what he meant by pornography. "Well," he replied, "it's obvious. *Playboy* magazine, for instance." I admitted that *Playboy* (banned in Ireland) had more than its share of attractive girls in an advanced state of undress, but said that it offered quite an assortment of intelligent articles as well, often by celebrated writers and public figures.

"Yes," he said, "but I wouldn't trust myself to read it."

"Why not?"

"Because I couldn't just look at the articles. I would have to look at the pictures too. That's where the editor is so clever: he forces you to look at the naked girls."

"Well, is that so terrible? Will it do you any harm?"

"Yes. It will appeal to my basest emotions."

Evil Literature

Ireland, of course, is not the only country which has raised barriers against words and pictures which might appeal to anyone's "basest emotions." The permissiveness now seen in America and Britain is of very recent origin after a long history of erratic control. The English are only now freeing their theater from the censoring hand of the Lord Chamberlain. France under General de Gaulle has become more, not less, censorial. Norway has been the scene of periodic anti-pornography drives in the last few years, and Finland has recently tried and convicted an author for blasphemy. Australia has a history of banning books with an almost Irish alacrity.

It is not that Irish censorship is unique; it is simply that it has been carried out at times "with a savagery that seemed pathological," as the late Irish author Francis McManus said. It is a manifestation of what the writer Mary Holland describes as "the dark side of Irish Catholicism, the darting, furtive guilt about sex which begins at our first convent kindergarten and maims too many of us for too many years afterwards." Although Church-inspired, it is a secular censorship system operated on a national scale with the approval of all political parties. It goes well beyond the relatively liberal controls of other democratic societies. It is imperiously conducted through an apparatus, described as "simple, silent and effective," which is outside the judicial system. The decisions of the censors are not open to court appeal. Even when a book goes before the Appeal Board it is an undefended prisoner.

Under British rule there was a degree of censorship through the old Obscene Publications Act, but the weighty restrictions on what the Irish can read were imposed by the Irish themselves. During the 1920s many of the most ardent advocates of censorship joined in a campaign called "the Angelic Warfare for Maintaining the National Virtue of our Country." In that feverish time W. B. Yeats was one of the few who took the calm view. He said, "I think you can leave the arts, superior or inferior, to the general conscience of mankind." A Committee of Inquiry into Evil Literature in 1926 led to the Censorship of Publications Act of 1929 and the first Censorship Board in 1930. The five censors, appointed by the Minister for Justice, were given the power to prohibit any book deemed to be "indecent or obscene" or which advocates "unnatural" birth control or the procurement of abortion. It was up to customs officers to seize banned books entering the country. Under a 1946 refinement they were given the additional authority to apprehend books which, in their inexpert opinion, *ought to be* banned. Significantly, the 1967 act makes no change in this procedure—humiliating as it has been for individual travelers to be told they are carrying salacious literature. (It is also noteworthy that the new twelve-year banning limit does not apply to birth-control books; they still get life sentences.)

"It is certainly right," said Sean Lemass recently, "that great writers who have survived the test of time should be read. Our first Censorship Board went a bit mad in this regard." The early censors banned not only obvious pornography but so many works of art—everything from *Point Counter Point* to *1984*—that the most prominent names on the blacklist amounted to a literary hall of fame. It was the individual books, not the authors, which were censored, but as the list grew ever longer it was difficult to think of a distinguished writer whose work was not represented.

Some of the authors, in no particular order: Tolstoy, Voltaire, Freud, Zola, Maupassant, Balzac, Mann, Proust, Sartre, Dreiser, Hemingway, Forester, Faulkner, Bromfield, O'Hara, Caldwell, Steinbeck, Sholokov, Fitzgerald, Saroyan, Salinger, Dos Passos, Koestler, Maugham, Moravia, Orwell, Colette, Pritchett, Gide, Gorki, Rolland, Durrell, Bellow, Capote, Mailer, Murdoch, Michener, Schulberg, Silone, Donleavy, Greene, Cary, Snow, Sinclair Lewis, Wyndham Lewis, Irwin Shaw, Aldous Huxley, Tennessee Williams, Dylan Thomas.

Almost every Irish writer whose work has won international acclaim in modern times has been on the blacklist. The names include Bernard Shaw, Sean O'Casey, James Joyce (for *Stephen Hero*, not *Ulysses*), Samuel Beckett, Oliver St. John Gogarty, George Moore, Frank O'Connor, Liam O'Flaherty, Sean O'Faolain, Austin Clarke, Brendan Behan, Kate O'Brien and Edna O'Brien.

The titles and authors are set down in the *Register of Prohibited Publications* and its supplementary lists. One reads this gargantuan work today with mounting disbelief, thinking it impossible that anyone should want to ban such books as *The Age of Reason*, *The African Queen* or *And Quiet Flows the Don*. Or that anyone would find great harm in the pages of *Tales of the South Pacific*, *The Catcher in the Rye*, *Zorba the Greek* or *Borstal Boy*. Dr. Kinsey's reports and many other scholarly studies of sexual behavior are mixed in with such titillating junk as *The Shameless Nude* and *The Grateful Mistress*. The banned periodicals are mainly magazines with a sexual emphasis. *Uncensored Confessions* was a predictable victim. It is an old story, of course, that such popular English Sunday papers as *News of the World* and *The People* have regularly removed their more fragrant sex and crime articles from the Irish editions, for fear of annoying the censors, replacing them with pious accounts of the Pope and pilgrimages.

It is hard to say what the effect of censorship has been on Irish authors. Some informants in Dublin point to the long list of writers who left Ireland because of what Edna O'Brien (who lives in London) calls "its totally stifling atmosphere." Yet, some might have left in any event for the experiences and challenges of larger and less provincial nations. It was Brendan Behan's opinion that "straightforward censorship is fairly harmless—no Irish writer is really injured by it. He is damaged by the indirect and unauthorized censorship which goes beyond the reasonable suppression of pornography."

Behan may have been referring to those librarians who outcensor the censors, the bishops who put their weight against this book or that play, or those priests and teachers who have persuaded Ireland's younger generation to look upon various writers as shameless sinners. "I grew up thinking of Frank O'Connor as a dirty old man," an Irish friend told me. "When I finally read his books I was mortified." When Sean O'Faolain's first volume of short stories was banned he felt "very much like a man suddenly plucked from the privacy of his study and shoved naked into the pillory to be pelted by his fellow citizens with rotten vegetables." It is one of the more heartening developments of the 1960s that the once-pilloried authors have begun to win public approval. Television has helped. After an appearance by Kate O'Brien, TV critic Ken Gray wrote:

> What I found most interesting was the thought that here— if we are to accept the evaluation of our Censorship Board— here, in this sincere, sensitive and intellectual woman, is a pornographer, a writer of "dirty" books. Could anything be more ridiculous? Her view of life, her approach to her work, as evidenced by her responses in this interview alone, showed her to be every bit as wicked and corrupt as a typical Mother Superior.

Irish film censorship has always received less attention and international notoriety than book censorship, even though it has been in existence longer and affects a far greater portion of the population. Ever since the 1920s no movie has been allowed exhibition in public without a certificate from the film censor. There is hardly a country in the world without a system for policing the cinema; Ireland's is just stricter than most.

The work is carried on quietly, with no announcements of bannings and cuts apart from an annual disclosure of statistics. Although some individual cases receive publicity, the public generally does not know what it is missing except when certain films at the most torrid moments become as choppy as the Irish Sea. A reviewer of *Suddenly Last Summer* wrote that the censor's cuts in the picture were so deep that the whole point of it was lost: "It took about forty years of film censorship here to decide that the Irish public could be trusted to know that there was such a thing as adultery, so maybe by the turn of the century they might also be let into the secret that homosexuality exists."

One man serves as film censor, a full-time job which a former occupant of the office described as being caught between the Devil and the Holy See. The present censor, Dr. Christopher

Macken, is a physician and ex-politician who sees one or two feature-length films and several shorts and trailers almost every working day. It hurts my eyes just to look at the figures: 1,016 films of varying lengths seen in 1966, of which 878 were passed without cuts, 89 were passed with cuts, and 49 were rejected. Members of the Appeal Board looked at 77 films and quite often overruled the censor.

One of Dublin's word coiners has said that the object of film censorship is to prevent the "Californication" of the country. If so, it isn't working. What is pathetic about the exercise is that the serious films which deal searchingly with real-life human experience are likely to be mutilated or forbidden, while Hollywood's production-line fantasy movies, all money and glamour and violence, fill the theaters. The Irish are allowed to see *Girl Happy*, *Bikini Beach*, *The Swingin' Set* and the James Bond films, but not such works as *The Silence* and *La Dolce Vita*. Even *Girl with Green Eyes*, a bittersweet slice of Irish life which was filmed in Dublin, was banned. *Of Human Bondage*, also filmed in Dublin and much concerned with the wages of sin, was at first rejected but eventually was allowed to be screened with cuts.

Although most of the motion pictures which circulate in Ireland are made for unsophisticated audiences, the people who take the cinema seriously have a better opportunity than ever to see films like *La Notte* and *Dear John*. Despite everything said so far, the film censor is becoming lenient and a sensible system of issuing general and limited certificates permits adult films to be seen by adult audiences; previously no one could see a movie which was ruled unsuitable for children. Distributors are raising their sights, and film societies are mushrooming. Once again, television's impact is important. It becomes ever more futile to protect people from the facts of life in books and films when they are exposed to them in their own living rooms on TV. British television in particular, with its frank documentaries and discussion programs as well as its life-in-the-raw dramas and off-color comedy shows, is changing the whole censorship equation in Ireland.

Improved standards of education are having their influence, too, according to Senator Donall O'Conallain. "Would it be unreasonable," he said to his colleagues in the Irish Senate, "or would it be discounting original sin too much, to hope that we would one day reach a point where censorship would no longer be necessary, where every Irishman would have attained that degree of sophistication and maturity that he would say, as the Roman writer Terence was able to say of himself two thousand years ago, 'I am a man and reckon nothing human alien to me'?"

Semi-Culture

As the Irish advance toward sophistication, what about the state of the arts in Ireland today? The condition of the theater? The caliber of the writers? The work of the poets, the playwrights and the painters? The fact that people outside Ireland ask such questions is revealing, and complimentary to the Irish, for their reputation as a creative and imaginative people lingers on despite what Irish critics themselves describe as "the paralysis of the arts."

It is a well-deserved reputation. If it is too fanciful to say that every Irishman is a poet at heart, then at least it is true that there are legions of Irishmen who are sure they could be distinguished men of letters if only they did not have to spend their days at the tiresome business of earning a living. As a matter of fact, I have encountered a startling number of people in Ireland who are scribbling away at something or other in their spare time, even if only a book review for an obscure periodical or a wickedly scathing letter to a newspaper. Ulick O'Connor, himself an attorney who has a successful second career as a poet, author and public speaker, tells in his biography of Oliver St. John Gogarty of the time in 1924 when the physician-poet returned home after some years in England: "As he got off the boat at the North Wall, a sailor approached him. 'Excuse me, Senator,' he said, 'there's a few stanzas in me pocket I'd like you to look over sometime.' He was back in Dublin."

Ireland's literary heritage is so deeply rooted that there are books with such titles as *1,000 Years of Irish Poetry* and *1,000 Years of Irish Prose.* The very name Abbey Theatre evokes visions of Great Moments in Irish Drama: the founding of the Irish Literary Theatre, *The Playboy of the Western World, Juno and the Paycock*, and Yeats thundering at a riotous audience, "You have disgraced yourselves again!" The roster of the Irish men of letters is unbelievably illustrious for a small nation. To speak of Congreve, Farquhar, Goldsmith, Sheridan, Swift, Synge, Shaw, Wilde, Yeats, Joyce, O'Casey, Colum, Clarke, Beckett, O'Connor, O'Flaherty and O'Faolain is only to begin the list of noted dramatists, authors and poets.

The Irish are well aware that their independent nation is very greatly the product of poets and dreamers: men like Patrick Pearse, Thomas MacDonagh and Joseph Plunkett, three of the martyrs of the 1916 Rising, who used words as weapons and swept a nation to its feet. AE (George Russell) called the poets "the gilding on the prow of the vessel"—which makes it all the more remarkable that the intellectual climate in Ireland should have turned so cold after freedom was won. "The birth of a terrible beauty," the Irish writer Benedict Kiely has said, "ended only in the establishment of a grocer's republic." Other commentators have spoken of Ireland as "a cultural desert" and "an intellectual slum."

Is Ireland today as bad as all that? No. In their distress Ireland's own critics are prone to exaggeration. But the condition of the Irish arts is not at all as good as it reasonably should be, and it falls far short of the enormous potential of the country. The day may come, and I believe it is now on its way, when there will be an outburst of cultural enthusiasm on the part of the Irish people. Parents will demand that the schools provide their children with something more than the bare minimum in art and music appreciation, orchestras will blossom in the cities, new libraries and theaters will be built, the average man will try his hand at painting or an instrument, critical standards will rise, and the artists and writers will become honored and popularly supported figures who need not go abroad to make their talent felt. A statement by Jim Fitzgerald, a leading theatrical director, about the Irish drama may be applicable to the arts in general: "We are in a stagnant phase now, but there is nowhere to go but up."

Wherever one looks there is evidence both of inertia and of fresh activity. The visual arts in particular have been in a sorry state. Despite the heritage of the Celtic and medieval artists, the Irish of modern times have contributed little that is truly outstanding to the world's fund of paintings, sculpture and architecture. (Jack Butler Yeats, brother of the poet, was Ireland's best-known artist until his death in 1957. Louis le Brocquy is the only painter today with a solid international reputation. Edward Delaney and Oisin Kelly are the most interesting sculptors. Michael Scott, whose work includes the new Abbey Theatre as well as Dublin's bus terminal and television center, has long been the foremost architect.) A team of Scandinavian experts who were invited to make an assessment of Irish design reported that one of the first things they noticed was "the manner in which today's Irish culture has developed a distinct leaning toward literature, theater, the spoken word and abstract thinking, rather than creation by hand or machine and the visual arts—the other side of human activity in civilization."

Irish schoolchildren are probably the most aesthetically deprived in all Europe. The schools do little to encourage the study of art. "Drawing" was dropped as an obligatory subject in the primary schools immediately after independence, almost as if it were something nastily English. The Irish Arts Council, which is financed by the state (£50,000 in 1967) and has a priest as its director, has sought to stimulate interest in the fine arts, but, as one of its reports states, this is no easy task "where there is little traditional conception of the place of art in life." (The Arts Council must struggle along on less than half the funds available to its counterpart in Ulster, and must do its work with a far smaller staff. Mervyn Wall, the novelist who is secretary of the Council, said frankly, "The government of Northern Ireland has shown itself to be more concerned about cultural development than the Republic. We are terribly satisfied with what is third-rate.") Painters and sculptors have an exceedingly hard time just surviving in Ireland. The ones I have met are inclined to vent their wrath on the Arts Council, sometimes quite unfairly, for being too conservative and tightfisted. One night in Bailey's pub a painter named Michael Caine said, "I went to them for some money, and they told me, 'We only give to groups.' 'Dammit,' I said, 'I'm a group! There's me, my wife and my two kids!' "

The brighter side of the story is that the artists, for all their difficulties, are more numerous and more productive today than they have been in decades, if not centuries. The creative spark seems to have leaped quite suddenly from Irish literature to the visual arts. Not only are the young painters, sculptors, engravers and designers producing imaginative work, but their chances of being exhibited these days are greater than ever. The art galleries of Dublin are becoming exciting places, and the National Gallery itself, under its energetic new director, James White, has undergone a wondrous rejuvenation.

One of the most significant and far-reaching developments is the founding, at a cost to the government of over £100,000, of the Kilkenny Design Workshop in the converted stables and grooms' quarters of Kilkenny Castle. Annual subsidies enable Irish and foreign designers to work together to improve the look of Irish manufactures. The dismal appearance of all too many Irish exports prompted the investment, but the results are likely to have a beneficial effect on the visual arts as well as commerce. Traditional Celtic designs are being used in jewelry, silverware and fabrics with impressive results.

The same mixture of inertia and activity can be found in Irish music. The composers and the professional musicians have a poor time of it, and efforts to raise the level of public taste are hamstrung by a dearth of funds (although half the Arts Council grants go to music) and a general indifference. Dublin's classical-music lovers still await the oft-promised Kennedy Memorial Hall, and so many other discouraging things have happened, including the loss of a quarter of the Radio Telefis Eireann Symphony Orchestra to the newly formed Ulster Orchestra, that one anguished critic said, "The lights of Irish music are being put out one by one." And yet as one moves about the country there seems to be something going on everywhere: concerts and string quartets in Dublin, operas in Kilrush and Castlebar, school orchestras playing away, amateur musical groups flourishing, and the sounds of music wafting out of pubs and restored castles.

A visitor's personal impression of the Irish arts obviously depends greatly on when he goes to Ireland, how much he moves about and how much he cares. On one journey of less than a month, devoted mainly to political and economic interviewing, I went to a performance of Bizet's *The Pearl Fishers* at the Waterford Light Opera Festival on the night of arrival. I then managed to work in the following during the succeeding days: Synge's *Riders to the Sea* at an amateur theater in Waterford, O'Casey's *The Plough and the Stars* at the Abbey, Beckett's *Endgame* in a tiny Trinity College theater, ten plays during the fortnight of the Dublin Theatre Festival, a visit to the Wexford Festival Opera, an afternoon at the Kilkenny Design Workshops, an evening at the International Film Theatre, and much time spent at poetry readings (a fine Dublin specialty) and art exhibitions.

This kind of travelogue of the arts hardly describes the day-to-day cultural life of the Irish, but it does suggest variety and vitality. The action is greatest in the realm of popular music, which in today's Ireland means much more than Sinatra, the Beatles or the native showband singers. "Rousing roof-ripping Irish ballad sessions," as the *Independent* has said, seem to be Ireland's answer to the night clubs and discotheques of London, Paris and Rome. A whole new and highly commercialized ballad world has sprung up in the pubs and taverns of Ireland within the past few years. Several groups like the Dubliners and the Clancy Brothers have become recording stars and have made foreign tours. One waspish friend said that "anyone who can carry a tune in this country becomes a ballad singer." It is intriguing to see young people who yawn at the talk of the patriotic past listening raptly to such ballads as "The Wife of the Bold Tenant Farmer," "The Heroes of Selton Hill," "Lament of the Evicted Irish Peasant" and "Ireland, I Wish You Were Free!"

What should be stressed is the fun of it all. An *Irish Times* columnist observed that "a kind of floating population of voices, guitars, tin whistles, spoons and banjos is now welcomed in pubs which a few years ago unceremoniously bounced anyone merry enough to lift an isolated voice in song." The merriest of all events is the all-Ireland Fleadh Cheoil, or Feast of Music, for the singers, dancers, fiddlers, pipers and other performers of traditional Irish music. It is held annually in a different town on the Whitsun weekend as the grand climax of a series of regional music carnivals. The round-the-clock music-making attracts some sixty thousand people, many of whom do little sleeping and a lot of drinking. Sometimes things get a little out of hand. "It's the biggest bash we've got on this benighted island," one university youth told me.

Troubled Theater

Cultural festivals are now as much a part of Ireland as horses and hurling. Although the Cork Film Festival is the most international gathering, with many nations represented, it is the Dublin Theatre Festival which comes closest to achieving the stature of the major Continental events. During the two weeks the dedicated playgoer can see a dozen dramas at a variety of theaters, attend earnest discussions about the state of the theater, and take part in the late-night social whirl. London and New York critics turn up, intellectuals rub shoulders with character actors, some people chase other people's wives, and a good time is had by all. Although most of the new Irish plays never get out of Ireland, worthy as they may be, there have been several successes during the Festival's first decade. Hugh Leonard's *Stephen D*, for example, was a London hit, and Brian Friel's *Philadelphia, Here I Come!* was a success on Broadway before appearing in the West End.

Since the Festival serves as a showcase for the latest work of Irish playwrights, it would seem to be a good thing for Irish drama, but it is often accused of contributing to the malaise of the theater. So much of what Ireland has to offer in the dramatic arts is concentrated now in the Festival fortnight that it is said to leave the other fifty weeks barren. The Festival has been described as "the lipstick on the corpse of the Irish theater." And this statement has appeared in *The Dublin Magazine*: "We pride ourselves on our appreciation of the drama, but despite this the Irish theatre lay down and died some years ago, and the Theatre Festival is no more than an annual exhibition of its dead body."

Such hyperbole ignores the fact that there are eight theaters regularly operating in Dublin, if one includes the Gas Company Theatre out in Dun Laoghaire, the experimental Lantern Theatre in a Merrion Square basement, and the tiny Peacock Theatre, which is an offshoot of the Abbey and specializes in Irish language plays. At the time of writing, three of the eight are offering the light musical revues which so delight Dubliners (e.g., *Gaels of Laughter* and *The Good Olde Days*), but the others are doing serious drama.

Critics are also inclined to overlook the amateur dramatic groups. There are more than eight hundred of them putting on plays in church halls and any spare auditorium in all parts of the land. Regional drama competitions lead up to an all-Ireland contest which is one of Ireland's most important cultural events. Even though a playwright gets a royalty of only £5 ($12) for each performance by an amateur group, the number of local drama societies anxious to do new Irish plays means that a popular playwright can earn a fair income within his own country even if he is seldom performed abroad. The most prolific and successful of the breed is John Keane, a Listowel publican who writes with wit and compassion of his fellow Kerrymen.

It is Brian Friel, an Ulster-born, Belfast-educated former schoolteacher and short-story writer who has attracted the most notice during the last few years. *Philadelphia, Here I Come!* achieved high praise in and out of Ireland for its controlled sentimentality and the clever use of two actors to play the private and public selves of the leading character. The drama crams into the last night of his leave-taking all the hopefulness and heartbreak of a young man who must tear himself away from his native village if he is ever to get on the jet to America, "a vast, restless place that doesn't give a curse about the past." The craftsmanship of such playwrights as Friel, Hugh Leonard and Eugene McCabe would seem to suggest that the Irish theater is not so badly off after all, but there is much that is wrong.

Not so many years ago, when Dubliners were much more of a theatergoing people, at least three permanent companies were operating at the same time. They provided year-round employment, even if at low pay, for actors, designers, stagehands and other employes. Economic pressures forced two of them to close, while the Abbey performers carried on under most unsatisfactory conditions. Talent left the country in droves, and the standards of acting fell dismayingly. Every big theater, including the Abbey, has been forced to worry excessively about whether a production is good box office, with the result that few unorthodox or experimental plays are attempted. Compared to a small nation like Finland, which has superlative theaters in every corner of the country, Ireland gives poor support to the drama. The subsidy of the Dublin Theatre Festival (£20,000) is, according to Eugene McCabe, "so small that it's farcical, but far from funny." He has given a playwright's view of the problem:

> When we talk of theatre—English, German, French, Swedish, Spanish—we imply a formidable heritage of dramatic writing, a dynamic policy or approach to it, vigorous critical standards, realistic subsidies, and, most vital of all, a discerning theatre-going public. If you have this you can have theatre on a high level all year round. In this sense we don't have theatre here at all. The dramatic writing we have got is remarkable in quality, but we don't have enough of it to form a backbone for solid indigenous theatre. There is the Abbey—a lovely new chassis, same old engine, backfiring now for over thirty years and in no danger whatsoever of exploding—and for the rest it is a scramble to survive.
>
> Can we have theatre? In time, perhaps, but the obstacles are considerable. All our best actors, directors, designers and writers go elsewhere until such time as pay, prestige and public are sufficient to attract them back. The Guthries, Cusacks Kennys, McGowrans, Becketts, O'Tooles and the dozens of other theatrical talents of all sorts and size would, I imagine, work willingly from time to time if we had a theatre which could give them work for development.

It is the Abbey Theatre which is the repository of almost all the hopes for Irish drama—and the setting of endless recrimination. As actor-writer Gabriel Fallon has said, "There was never a period in the Theatre's history when its plays and/or its players were not decried, when its value as a worthwhile theatrical institution was not seriously questioned, when its imminent death was not proclaimed with unconcealed satisfaction."

It is fashionable to say that the Abbey is not what is used to be. To which one retort is, "It never was!" But there were some great times during the early years. The Abbey as such was founded soon after the turn of the century, but the idea of it was announced in 1898 by William Butler Yeats, Lady Gregory and the dramatist Edward Martyn: "We propose to have performed certain Celtic and Irish plays which, whatever their degree of excellence, shall be written with a high ambition, and so build a Celtic and Irish school of dramatic literature." Yeats later spoke of the need to "make the theatre a place of intellectual excitement—a place where the mind goes to be liberated." The political and religious establishment was in no mood for such liberation, however, and the public, puritanical down to its toes, was easily shocked.

There were riots in 1899 when audiences cried, "Blasphemy!" at performances of Yeats's *The Countess Cathleen*. There was an uproar in 1907 when the word "shift," a woman's undergarment, was spoken in *The Playboy of the Western World*. A distraught Lady Gregory telegraphed Yeats in London, "Audience broke up in disorder at word 'shift.' What should I do?" Yeats replied, "Leave it on." There even were riots by Irish-Americans about the unflattering picture of rural Irishmen given in the same play, when the company toured America in 1911. The Abbey was at its most exciting in the early 1920s, when it produced Sean O'Casey's magnificent three, *Shadow of a Gunman*, *Juno and the Paycock* and *The Plough and the Stars*. Inevitably, given the conflicts and the hypersensitive nationalism of the time, the plays were boisterously denounced. The depiction of a whore in the third of the plays caused storms in the theater and stoning of the cast. One critic insisted that there were no prostitutes in Dublin, despite the city's red-light reputation and the omnipresent streetwalkers. O'Casey went off to London in disgust and then decided to stay away for good when the Abbey rejected his next work, *The Silver Tassie*.

His departure may have taken the life out of the Abbey. It slumped into a kind of Gaelic preciousness. From the mid-1930s until his resignation in 1966, the Abbey's managing director was

Ernest Blythe, an Ulster Presbyterian and former finance minister with a passion for the Irish language and no theatrical background. Under the daring and professional leadership of Hilton Edwards and Micheal MacLiammoir, it was the Gate Theatre instead of the Abbey which did the most exciting work after the 1920s. Some of their recruits went on to become stage and screen stars, including Orson Welles, James Mason and Geraldine Fitzgerald. The Abbey, of course, has produced such superb performers as Barry Fitzgerald, Sara Allgood, Cyril Cusack, Siobhan McKenna and May Craig, but it lost some notable acting and writing talent as well. Peter O'Toole applied for a job when he was nineteen, but he was told to go away and learn the Irish language.

When the old Abbey Theatre burned down in 1951, forcing the players into temporary quarters, there were high hopes that a new building would bring about a revitalization of the company. It took all of sixteen years, however, before the Abbey players were given a new home. It is a squarish blond-brick building, austere on the outside but handsomely appointed within. Naturally enough, the critics and theatergoers found much to complain about. With only 628 seats, it seemed too small for the country's national theater. The exterior design was likened to a mortuary or a lion's house at the zoo. The opening performance, a dramatic scrapbook of the Abbey's finest hours, was a disaster. Since then, however, there has been a succession of fine productions, and the new management, young and ambitious, is well on its way to recovering the Abbey's lost prestige.

The Writers

Two Irish university debating teams which met recently clashed over the question whether Ireland is "a writer's purgatory." Judging by the way some writers have been treated in the past, there is probably a good case for calling it a kind of hell. But the worst days are over and there is no reason, apart from his own yearnings and the problems of making money in a small market, for a writer to go into exile. It is probably as unfair to look for another Joyce in Ireland today as it is to seek a new Ibsen or Strindberg in Norway and Sweden, but it is worth noting that no one even comes close. Perhaps things have become too bland and comfortable. According to Marese Murphy, a Dublin journalist, "The dearth of major writers in this relatively free era suggests that repression of some kind—or at least conflict—is essential for creativity in the Irish artist."

It is almost a commentary on the situation that two of the more significant literary events at present are the new respectability of James Joyce in Ireland and the belated discovery by readers outside Ireland of the comic genius of the late Flann O'Brien.

Not only is *Ulysses* now out in the open after years as ar under-the-counter item in the bookshops, but the author himself is spoken of these days with more reverence than revulsion Furthermore, like Shakespeare in England and Hans Christiar Andersen in Denmark, he has become a national tourist attraction. Visitors are taken on "Joycean tours" of Dublin; the Martello Tower at Sandycove, where the fictional Stephan Dedalus and Buck Mulligan lived, has been turned into a museum; and Joyce addicts from the world over gather in Dublin on "Bloomsday" (June 16) each year to compare notes and attend lectures on such esoteric matters as Joyce's place in the world of cybernetics and "The Phallic Tree of *Finnegans Wake*." The film *Ulysses*, although banned, has inspired many an Irishman to read Joyce for the first time. Not everyone approves, of course. A popular point of view was expressed by a Dublin *Evening Press* reader named J. J. Murphy when he said in a letter to the editor: "I had not read much of Mr. Joyce, nor do I intend to. Mr. Joyce, in my mind, was a dirt bird, and I don't care how much of a 'Joyce revival' is brought about by the release of a pornographic motion picture. I still prefer to think for myself."

Flann O'Brien is—or has been until lately—a name known only to the more literate Irishmen and a small fraternity of foreigners who discovered years ago that he was the single Irish writer who came within striking distance of Joyce. Flann O'Brien is one of the two pseudonyms of Brian Nolan, a onetime civil servant and spectacularly gifted poetry-prose writer who was best known to the Irish public as Myles na Gopaleen, the satirical columnist of the *Irish Times*. In his newspaper pieces he mercilessly exposed the hypocrisies and pomposities of present-day Ireland, while in his novels he revealed a blazing talent for comic invention and scholarship of Joycean proportions. His "true comic spirit" was praised by Joyce himself when his first book, *At Swim-Two-Birds*, appeared in 1939, a year when the world had other things to think about than the cyclonic imaginings of an unknown twenty-seven-year-old Irishman. It became, in Benedict Kiely's words, "the secret treasure of a few." After the war the novel occasionally surfaced, to the ardent cheers of its champions—William Saroyan, Graham Greene and V. S. Pritchett among them. John Wain described it in 1962 as "a Gargantuan comic novel which makes a simultaneous exploration, on four or five levels, of Irish civilization," and later as "just about the only real masterpiece in English that is far too little read and discussed." The book did not begin to win a wide readership until 1966, when the author suddenly died at age fifty-four. Now his three other novels, *The Hard Life*, *The Dalkey Archive* and *The Third Policeman*, are all on view for the first time, and the Flann O'Brien cult is showing all the signs of becoming a movement.

Of the Irish novelists now at work, one of the most accomplished is Brian Moore, best known for *The Luck of Ginger Coffey* (which was made into a splendid film), but, as a Belfast man who has spent most of his writing life outside Ireland, he

cannot be claimed by the Republic. Apart from the still-surviv-
ing members of the older generation of writers and such exceptional short-story writers as Mary Lavin and James Plunkett, I
have most enjoyed reading John McGahern, John Broderick and
Edna O'Brien (not *all* of their books, however), probably because each has written so effectively of the spiritual poverty
and the furtive passions of rural Ireland. Although they and a
number of other writers have brought about something of a
revival of the Irish novel in the last half-dozen years, the novelists as a whole have been slow to come to grips with the new
forces which are wrenching the Irish out of their dozy habits.
The poets and the short-story writers seem to be more attentive
to the drama of change in Ireland. John Montague, for example,
who is one of the better younger-generation poets, has written
a short story, "A Change of Management," which has one character saying, resignedly, "I'm a bumbler, and the age of bumblers
is past." A new class of men is taking over: "Practical, hardheaded people," as one of them says in the story, "who are not
afraid to face the priests, the politicians, the whole vast bog of
the Irish middle-class, and woo something positive out of it."
To which an old-line Irishman groans, "They'll murder us with
activity!"

It is the poets, in fact, who are the most vital literary figures
these days—so much so that Ireland is in the midst of a poetic
renaissance. Patrick Kavanagh died in 1967 after a long and
tempestuous career, but such veterans as Padraic Colum (born
1881) and Austin Clarke (1896) are still going strong. So many
younger poets are at work that a new volume of Irish poetry appears almost every month. Thomas Kinsella, Brendan Kennelly,
Richard Murphy, Rivers Carew, Eavan Boland, Timothy Brown-
low and Richard Weber are only some of the more impressive
poets. The most important man in Irish poetry, however, is a publisher: Liam Miller, an ex-architect and man of manifold talents
whose Dolmen Press has been the discoverer and mainstay of a
host of outstanding poets. He is an almost Biblical-looking man

with a black Brillo beard, heavy-lidded eyes, drawn cheeks, and the weight of Irish culture heavy on his shoulders. Besides his publishing work he edits a poetry magazine, masterminds the Lantern Theatre, designs theatrical sets, writes articles and reviews, and conducts an informal literary salon. Until he started the Dolmen Press in his bedroom in 1951, Ireland had been deprived for thirty years of a publisher willing and able to gamble on imaginative writing.

Edward Delaney

It had been my intention to speak in detail of a single poet, or perhaps a novelist, by way of showing some of the problems and pleasures of being an artist in Ireland. Someone, ideally, who had decided to stay in the country despite the frustrations and the claustrophobic atmosphere so often mentioned. Someone successful, yet not numbed by success, who might have something to say about the state of the nation. Then an odd thing happened. The poets, the writers and the journalists I saw kept saying that I ought to "ring up Eddie—you know, Edward Delaney, the sculptor."

All I knew about Delaney was the fact that his large statue of Thomas Davis in the center of College Green in Dublin was the subject of a national controversy after its unveiling one day in 1966. The conservative Irish had been used to conventional and lifelike hero-on-horseback or orator-pointing-finger sculpture. This is what they expected in a statue honoring the Protestant poet-rebel of the ill-fated Young Ireland movement of the 1840s. Instead, Delaney's statue was bold, stark and modern, and it faced a strange cluster of spindly angels blowing water out of long horns. "It was like letting a nude woman loose in the streets," Delaney was to tell me, "or some new form of animal in the zoo. People didn't know what to make of it." I had also read a piece about Delaney by Proinsias MacAonghusa in a new magazine called *Scene*, a kind of Irish *Esquire*. It began:

Edward Delaney is Ireland's best-known sculptor. He is a young, tall, lean man with lengthy and unruly dark hair, who comes from Claremorris in Mayo and lives with his pretty wife and three young children in Dun Laoghaire. In a land not noted for its support of the visual arts, he has had a good deal of success in getting patronage from the State and its subsidiary bodies. The Irish taxpayer has not been ungenerous to him and he is very conscious of this. Unlike most people he appears to feel that he owes his country something, even when that country acts the philistine.

When I telephoned Delaney he apologized for living in the outskirts of Dublin instead of in the center of town. "If you want to get any work done," he said, "you can't live in Dublin. When I lived in the city there were always people dropping in unannounced and staying all night. You know what it's like: the I-missed-my-bus-going-home kind of thing. Out here, the people—the man on the street—they think I'm a scrap merchant. I do my own casting, and they see me buying off the tinkers and piling up scrap metal. In the pubs they know I back horses and follow football, and that's all we talk about."

Delaney and his family live in a cul-de-sac, in two small one-story houses knocked together to make a contiguous studio and living quarters, with his furnaces blazing away in the back yard. I could see that it was something of a problem living in the midst of enormous chunks of metal, enough finished pieces of sculpture to fill a small museum, and little bronze figures hanging from the clotheslines with the baby's diapers.

Delaney's nervous energy makes up for a dozen relaxed Irishmen. The words spill out at a machine-gun pace. He has a wild streak of humor and a sense of the ridiculous which was probably brought to a fine point during his beatnik days. "I was four or five years in Dublin and never did a thing. I couldn't get any support and I couldn't afford to work. I used to sit on the library steps with Brendan Behan, talking about how bad life was and all that." He finally won a scholarship in 1953 and went off to the Academy of Fine Arts in Munich. In the following years he received substantial assistance from Germany and Italy as well as Ireland, and he worked for a time as a craftsman with the American forces in Germany, but the pull of home was always strong.

"It's amazing to go out of Ireland for a while and when you come back you have to find out what has been going on almost as a day-to-day thing. I know every poet in Ireland, every musician, every fiddle player. It's a large family. It's not like getting into the vastness of a place like Rome, where you could have three or four artists living on one street and you don't know who they are and you're not interested in finding out. But here if a fellow turns out a bloody painting with two nude figures on it, Jaysus!—everyone is saying he's changed his style again. It's a very parochial thing."

When I saw Delaney he was completing work on a striking eleven-foot statue of Theobald Wolfe Tone which now stands in St. Stephen's Green. His reputation is such that he could stay permanently in Ireland and do very well for himself. "I've got it very good here," he admitted, "but I have this itchiness. I'm trying to get out of Ireland, but I can't because I've got all this work to do. I'd like to move out for two or three years and see the place from the outside again. I want to think. Ireland can be very, very nice if you're looking for peace to work, but after a time it can get so boring!" On the other hand, Delaney is not so sure he ought to leave. His criticisms of modern Ireland could fill a book and he is particularly incensed about the grudging support that official Ireland gives its artists. "If we're going to go on and do something better than what has been happening in the last fifty years," he said, "then I think people like myself have to stay at home."

Chapter 8

THE NEUROTIC NORTH

We are not an independent country—nor, indeed do we want to be. We remain British and proud of it. But within that overall British framework we have a wide measure of discretion to deal with our own difficulties as we think best.

—CAPTAIN TERENCE O'NEILL

The peculiar tragedy of Belfast lies not in the fact that its citizens hate each other, but that they do so in the name of Christ.

—DR. JAMES SCOTT

On a memorable day during World War II when Belfast was under German air attack, the fire companies of Dublin, despite the Free State's neutrality and the bitterness of partition, were ordered by Prime Minister de Valera to race up the coast to help save the capital of Northern Ireland.

Dublin is that close to Belfast—an easy morning's drive. Northern Ireland, otherwise known as Ulster, is as near to "southern" Ireland as flesh is to bone. For many Irish housewives living along the two-hundred-mile frontier it is an everyday matter to bicycle across the line for the cheaper groceries of the North. To the majority of people in the Irish Republic, however, Ulster is practically a foreign country. "Northern Ireland just doesn't come into the sweep of my thinking," said a Waterford businessman. "I went up there once. It didn't seem very Irish."

Foreign Country

Most southern Irishmen have never been "up there" and they seem to have little desire to go, except perhaps to have a look at Giant's Causeway. They doubt that they would be made welcome. If they are unemployed they know that they can freely take a job in England, Wales or Scotland without needing a work permit; they cannot do so in Ulster, which fears an influx of Irish job seekers. It is easier for a Finn to take a job in Denmark than it is for an Irishman from Donegal to work next door in Derry.

Thanks partly to the work of Irish chauvinists in painting the darkest possible picture of life in the "Black North," it is popularly believed by southern Irishmen to be a grim industrial place of little amusement and high unemployment, run by bigoted, Bible-spouting Protestant Orangemen in bowler hats who slander the Pope, oppress the Catholic minority and carry on a nineteenth-century adulation of the Queen and the Union Jack. It is not exactly a true picture of this outwardly calm, beautiful and prosperous corner of Ireland. Nor does it take account of the fact that Ulster, like the Republic, is undergoing dramatic physical and psychological change. But it is uncomfortably close to the truth. There is, without question, a dark and venomous side to Northern Irish life. It casts a long shadow over all the recent efforts of more liberal and open-minded Ulstermen to improve relations with southern Ireland and to bring about religious harmony within Ulster itself.

The cocooned North has long been a breeding ground for bigotry. Protestants and Catholics, now numbering about one million and half a million, have been belaboring each other for centuries because of historic events which made Ulster the ulcer of Ireland. There are few places in Christendom where the humane teachings of Christ have become so perverted. The Irish Republic may have its own collection of fanatics who are beyond the pale of reason, but Northern Ireland excels in its abundance of diseased minds. I have heard it said that Ulster needs nothing so much as a decade of atheism to get itself straightened out.

Not since my days among the Hindus and Moslems of India have I experienced a society where one's religious affiliation is of such paramount importance. A British journalist who wrote an article about Ulster's religious-political sickness felt obliged to begin with these words: "I am not a Roman Catholic. This is a necessary statement before writing about Northern Ireland, which likes to believe in conspiracies—Jesuits in the woodpile, Freemasons under the bed—and does not comprehend neutrality. Are you, people delicately inquire about your name, one of them or one of us?"

Religious distortions mean political distortions. Ulster has all the trappings of parliamentary democracy, but it is, in practice, the least democratic part of the British Isles. The majority rules, all right, but in a way which makes some people more equal than others. Northern Ireland has operated pretty much as a one-party state during the nearly fifty years of its existence, a record excelled in modern times only by the Soviet Union. The fault, however, lies as much with the Catholic Nationalists as it does with the ruling Protestant Unionists, for the Nationalists have not operated as a responsible opposition party determined to improve conditions in Ulster itself; they have been an anti-partition pressure group seeking to unite Ulster with the Irish Republic. But this too is changing. What gives Northern Irish politics ("frozen politics," it has been called) its particularly warped look is the fact that the working-class voters in this highly industrialized state, which consistently has the highest unemployment rate in the United Kingdom, give their support not to a labor or a liberal party but to the ultraconservative Unionist Party, which out-Tories the Tories of England. It has been sufficient for the Unionists to present themselves as the uncompromising champions of Ulster's attachment to Britain.

All of this serves to emphasize to a southern Irishman just how different Ulster is, but the brighter side of the North does so as well. It is a busier, more energetic and more accomplished society than the Republic. The standard of living is distinctly higher. Everything from housing to workers' training centers is superior, thanks greatly to British subsidies of £60 million a year which serve to elevate Ulster conditions to English levels. Industrialization is far more advanced: with half the population, Ulster does twice the trade of southern Ireland. Agriculture, benefiting from subsidies, is more progressive, more mechanized, and accounts for only an eighth of the work force. Although a fair number of people still emigrate (about 9,000 a year), Ulster has increased its population by a quarter of a million since partition. For a number of years it has had the highest birth rate and the lowest death rate in the British Isles. As in the Republic, better times and changing social attitudes have resulted in more and earlier marriages.

Mini-Britain

The border, as Brian Friel has described it, is "a drunken line that reels across the country and stumbles into Lough Foyle at a place aptly called Muff. In its erratic journey the border swims lakes, scrambles over mountains, wades through bogs, leaps streams and rivers and at one point rips clean through a poor man's cottage—or so I've read—thereby making him the subject of Queen Elizabeth when he is in his kitchen and a son of the Republic when he is in bed." It is not a frontier of barbed wire and heavy guns. Considering that as recently as 1956–62 a campaign of I.R.A. terrorism caused six deaths, thirty-four injuries and more than a million pounds' worth of property damage (to use official Ulster figures), it is a most serene and pastoral frontier. It is disquieting, nonetheless, to come upon signs warning motorists away from the "unapproved" roads. Entry must be made on "approved" roads for the customs formalities.

On the Republic side of a typical crossing the customs building is a makeshift structure, a physical demonstration of Dublin's view that the border is only a temporary matter (now completing its first half century). The Irish Constitution and the whole litany of patriotic oratory insist that Ireland is a single national state as well as a geographical entity which is briefly inconvenienced by the supposed existence of a separate northern nation. What may be *de facto* will never be *de jure*, or so the old republicans believe.

On the Northern Irish side there is a comfortable, nicely designed customs building of solid brick construction, testimony to the conviction that Ulster is a valid state which will forever be a self-governing part of the United Kingdom. Crossing the border in either direction is a simple enough business these days in contrast to only a few years ago, when "triptyques" had to be produced and luggage was more likely to be searched. Now there is usually just a quick stamp of a pass and a friendly wave to speed you along.

Once into northern territory the traveler finds that the Irish green of the landscape is no different, but the two-language road signs of the Republic are missing, the roads seem better made, and the postal pillar boxes are painted red instead of green. There are World War II memorials in the towns, and the rest of the public furniture looks unmistakably British. The policemen carry guns, however, as they do not in either Ireland or England. There is an un-Irish neatness about the sturdy farmhouses and the way that farmyards are cleared up and piles of dung and junk are hidden away. There appears to be a greater number of new housing projects, hospitals, schools, churches, factories and motorways than in the Republic. Belfast, with its heavy industry and mixture of Victorian and modern architecture, looks more like an English city than Dublin. The

Union Jack, which in Ulster is as much a political banner as a national flag, can be seen flying from more homes and buildings than in Britain. And the newspapers are more concerned with events in England than in the rest of Ireland, a place which is frequently referred to, by way of highlighting *its* foreignness, by its Gaelic name, Eire.

What seems most foreign of all to the Irish visitor from the south is the way work is taken seriously in the North. Even the Northern Catholics are inclined to look upon Irishmen below the border as a feckless lot of layabouts. For Ulster Protestants, those Calvinistic Irishmen, work is part of the provincial ethic, and much more respectable than pleasure. Not that people mind having a good time. The Ulsterman can be boisterous when he takes time off to relax. But everything in its right time. Sunday, for example, is the Lord's day, suitable for neither work nor pleasure. It is a day when Northern Ireland seems intent on proving how much more pious it is than the "papist" Republic. If there is a gloomier city in all Europe than Belfast on a Sunday, then I have yet to see it. The pubs close, the cinemas close, many playground swings and roundabouts are chained, and morning church is followed by a long, vacuous afternoon. In the meantime, across the border, the Catholic Irish, having gone to Mass, are whooping it up in the pubs and on the playgrounds. They have the notion that the Sabbath is a day to be enjoyed. For Ulster Catholics, the constant struggle is to breathe some life into a day of Presbyterian cheerlessness. People with cars are likely to solve the problem by hastening across the border to the nearest pub. They are joined by a fair number of Protestants who will admit, a little shamefacedly, that they could use a drink themselves.

Unless a visitor arrives in Northern Ireland at Belfast he will discover that the industrial life of the North intrudes very little on the magnificence of the scenery. It is farm country for the most part, and small farms at that, with fine stretches of meadowland, hills rising as abruptly as waves in a storm, snug valleys, and the largest lake in the British Isles. The Mountains of Antrim stand guard along one of the most awesome seacoasts in Europe. Although County Donegal is in the Republic (like Cavan and Monaghan, it used to be part of the old, nine-county Ulster), it is open to Northern Irelanders as a next-door retreat of unrivaled primitive splendor. Belfast is Ulster's only metropolis. There are other cities, but they are hardly more than overgrown towns. Most of Northern Ireland could as well be a quiet corner of northern England or Scotland. It is a small, compact province which, so long as it remains apart from the rest of Ireland, exists as a kind of Britain in miniature. Perhaps it is best thought of as a city-state: Belfast the city, the rest of Ulster a sprawling suburb.

Belfast

Belfast and its immediate surroundings now account for over half a million people, or more than a third of the total population. It is the seat of government, the industrial and commercial capital, the home of such arts as there are in Ulster, and the center of practically everything else in the North. Like Dublin, it has a beautiful setting of green hills and a beckoning sea. By foot or by car, the inhabitants can be out of the city and well into the country within minutes, and it is just such a mass movement back to nature which denotes a Belfast Sunday as much as its eerie, puritanical silence. But Belfast has little of Dublin's style and ease, and I have detected among its inhabitants a certain civic inferiority complex. They seem to realize that Dublin is a more attractive, sociable and cosmopolitan city. Certainly many more young people from Belfast go down to Dublin for amusement than the other way around. But as a Belfast teacher and former Dublin resident told Mary Maher of the *Irish Times*, "Relationships are casual in Dublin. Companionship is free and easy, but not always too meaningful. There's a lot of superficiality in Dublin that you won't find in

Belfast. We don't really tolerate pretention. Here if you meet someone who says he is a painter, he probably is a painter."

Belfast is the Glasgow of Ireland, a vigorous, hard-driving, God-fearing masculine town with few feminine graces. Even so, it has more women than men, just as all Ulster has an excess of females. Women are always in the background: standing in the doorways of their little red-brick homes, wheeling prams, serving behind counters, working at the textile mills, waiting for their husbands, knowing their place. A Belfast news item tells of a woman who was beaten up every Saturday night by her husband, a shipyard worker. When asked by a magistrate why she refused to prefer charges against him, she said, "Ah, no, sir, he's m'husband. I have to give him he's place."

The city is the physical expression of the blunt, rough-and-ready Ulster personality. The friendly Belfast waitress, instead of saying, "Have you given your order?," will snap, "Yi gettin'?" And if she has a load of dishes and finds a customer in her path, there are no meek beg-your-pardons. Instead: "Wud yi min' stannin' out of the road, please?"

Hugh Shearman, in his book *Ulster*, speaks of this as the "curt amiability" of the Belfast citizen.

> The puritan capacity for taking the shortest route from one point to another, for being austerely concentrated, for being intense at the point where intensity is required, has produced from among the people of Belfast, and of Ulster generally, some of the world's best engineers, some of the world's most competent administrators, generals, lawyers and men of learning, and the same directness, the same impatience with roundabout ways, is a part of everyday life in Belfast.

Belfast has grown with the speed of an American city in the two centuries since its population was a mere 8,500. It came late to the Industrial Revolution, thus being saved from having slums as bad as those in comparable British cities, but working-class living conditions were nonetheless pitiful until recent times. Belfast offered manufacturers a pool of cheap, industrious labor, and in time its name became famous for linen and ships, a combination which meant heavy use of female as well as male workers. Many of Britain's greatest ocean liners and warships were made in Belfast. When the *Titanic* was launched a Protestant worker in the shipyard is supposed to have cried, "Even the Pope himself couldn't sink this one!"

Belfast serves God and mammon with equal devotion. It is said of the Ulsterman that he loves the Crown but loves the half crown still more. Brian Moore has described Belfast as "a dull city where men made money the way charwomen wash floors, dully, alone, at a slow methodical pace." To the poet W. R. Rodgers it is an "obstinate city with a built-in intransigence, a hard gaiety, and a voice as aggressive as gravel." He calls it a careful city, too. "I overheard an angry young Belfastman in a chemist's shop complaining about a defective condom he had bought. 'And where,' he asked rhetorically, 'would *I* have been if I hadn't had two of them on?'"

Although some myopic soul once spoke of it as "the Athens of the North," Belfast has rarely been accused of being beautiful. It is a frankly functional metropolis, stolid as the statues of beefy Presbyterian burghers which stand in the parks and squares. In the hustling city center the shops are good enough to lure better-heeled Irishmen from the Republic, but it has little elegance. The city hall which stares down at the main shopping street is a huge, unlovely classical-Renaissance pile of Portland stone. At the edge of the city there is Stormont, the great white Ulster Parliament building which perches on the top of a landscaped hill like a lost palace of the League of Nations. In such an aloof location it is, according to a writer for the *Times*, "somewhat symbolic of the Ulsterman's knack of keeping the reality of politics at arm's length."

In Belfast, politics-as-religion, however, is always at your elbow, and it can hit home like a fist in the face. The graffiti on the walls are unequivocally pro-Protestant or pro-Catholic: "No

Surrender!" "Up the Republic!" "Kick the Pope!" "Up the Rebels!" "Remember 1690!" "Remember 1916!" Hot-eyed young men and aging Gospel preachers come swooping down the avenues bearing signs warning, "FLEE FROM THE WRATH TO COME." On a street corner, a little man with a ravaged face tells a crowd, "I used to be a thirty-cigarette-a-day-man. I was a nervous wreck. I drank like a madman and wallowed in my own filth. And then Jesus Christ came to me in the Wilson Lounge Bar!"

Despite the introduction of lounge bars, and the very recent phenomenon of singing pubs, the old-time Belfast pubs are there in plenty. They are dim and agreeably dingy retreats which sometimes retain their snugs, those confessional-like shelters for private drinking. It is in such pubs that the stranger will come upon as much hearty good talk and natural hospitality as he will find in Dublin. The Ulsterman is supposed to be frugal, but it is hard to see it in the pubs. The measures of whiskey are generous and the drinking is done with a proper reverence. There is no "holy hour" to break up the 10-A.M.-to-10-P.M opening. Brendan Behan, who could claim expertise, found that in the pubs of Sandy Row, the hard core of Protestant Belfast, "you get the best pint of porter in Ireland, except for the Aran Islands, where it's even better, and the reason is that the Sandy Row men don't stand for any nonsense with their beer. They've actually shot publicans there for not having the booze in the best condition."

The conversation flows on about booze, bets, horses, greyhounds, football and the latest bit of political tomfoolery. It is all so friendly and Irish that the visitor can almost feel the border melting away and he wonders why it was ever said that Belfast is a disputatious city. He may even hear some of the innumerable jokes about religious differences which both Catholics and Protestants tell with relish.

A Catholic tourist from the Republic, for example, is said to have muttered, "I'll never come to Belfast again. It's cold

and wet and full of Protestants." To which a Protestant re-
torted, "Take your vacation in hell, then! It's hot and dry and
full of Catholics!"

Then there is the story of the old Orangeman on his death-
bed who telephoned the local Catholic priest and told him to
hurry over so that he could be converted to the religion of
Rome. The priest, who had never in his life had a friendly word
with the Protestant, was happy to oblige. When the old man's
family heard about it they stormed into his bedroom to demand
an explanation. "Don't you see what it means?" he said. "It
means that when I die there'll be one less damned Catholic in
this world!"

But if the banter becomes serious, if a visitor makes naïve
suggestions that Ulster should do this or that about the Protestant-
Catholic relationship, the atmosphere can become icy and the
tone menacing. The unwary stranger will soon learn that he
has come upon a family quarrel of such long standing that it
has become a way of life. The two sides, since they are unable
to unite on anything else, will unite in their aversion to meddlers
who would rob them of the very conflict which puts spice in
their life and makes the city exciting. They seem to need each
other, and harbor a basic respect for each other, like cats and
dogs, cops and robbers, and the embattled husband and wife in
Who's Afraid of Virginia Woolf? They are performers in a
drama written ages ago—still mouthing the same old lines and
making the same ritual gestures.

It is more than innocent play-acting, however. The stage that
is Belfast is also a real-life battleground. It is a peaceful enough
most of the time, of course, and the more genteel neighborhoods
never have trouble, but brawls are frequent and an all-out riot
will come along every few years. Long ago the Protestant "Peep-
o'-Day Boys" and the Catholic "Defenders" carried on nighttime
guerrilla warfare against each other. During the "Troubles" in
the early 1920s passengers on tramcars sometimes had to lie
prone on the floor to escape the bullets coming through the

windows. In the fall of 1964, to take one recent year, a British press report of the latest uproar in Belfast stated: "On the fourth night of the riots Molotov cocktails, iron sewer-grating from the streets, bottles and bricks were thrown at the police. The mob set a trolley-bus on fire and shattered plate-glass windows all around. The casualty list this time included 18 policemen and 15 civilians." Such violence in New York, Capetown, Dublin or practically anywhere else would have commanded the most blazing headlines, but, Belfast being Belfast, they were just noted in passing.

Segregation

The sectarian climate, the automatic sorting out of one from another, is illustrated by a story told by W. R. Rodgers: "During the last census-taking, an English colonel, stationed in Belfast, filled in his census form which was duly collected by a local policeman. Later, the policeman brought it back. 'I'm sorry to be troubling you, sir,' he explained, 'but it's about this class of a question here—religion. Now, you say on this form that you're an agnostic. Would you mind making the answer a wee bit fuller? Could you say whether you're a Protestant or a Catholic agnostic?' "

Roman Catholics make up the largest single religious group (498,000 in 1961), but the combined Protestant denominations have twice as many people. The largest are Presbyterian (413,000), Church of Ireland (345,000) and Methodist (72,000). Few persons claim to be atheists.

The overwhelming majority of Catholics are regular church-goers, as might be expected, and for Protestants the percentage is probably higher than anywhere else in Europe. Because so much of Ulster's social life revolves around the churches and church or semireligious organizations, the pressures to conform are great. Many Protestants never allow themselves to be seen working in their gardens or otherwise amusing themselves on a Sunday. Television and the automobile, however, are having a profound influence on the old rigidities. It is hard for the churches to stop people from laughing in their living rooms at a TV comic, and a family can quickly get to the seashore or a golf course by car. The younger generation, however much it may be indoctrinated to keep the faith and hate other people, is clearly veering away from the old customs and doctrines. It has been powerfully influenced by the permissive manners and morals of Britain in the age of pop and plenty. Belfast and the Ulster resort towns seem to me to have an extraordinary number of dance-mad youngsters, long-haired beatniks, motorcyclists bearing guitars, and pathetic groups of boys and girls just drifting about looking for something to do. Some adults divide the younger generation into the "churchies" and the "rowdies," yet the rowdyism is often inspired by religion.

The most genuine and easygoing mingling of Protestants and Catholics can be seen among better-educated youth. Queen's University in Belfast is the province's greatest example of religious integration. Young people who had been separated on religious grounds all through their school years manage to merge easily at the university level. Intermarriage, however, is still unusual. Many people can claim that "some of my best friends" are Catholics or Protestants, but for the most part the two communities are socially segregated, and separated in many other ways too.

It is not necessary in Ulster to ask a man his religion. It is enough to find out the name of his school or his address or where he works, shops or drinks, for there are clearly defined Protestant and Catholic schools, neighborhoods, offices, factories, shops and pubs. The new foreign-owned plants (where employers are not concerned about a worker's religion) and the new supermarkets and impersonal big stores are helping to break down the barriers, but segregation remains a major fact of Ulster life.

In the days of the Ulster Plantation, the Scots and English

who had forced their way into Ireland had the choice land and the central parts of the towns, while the Catholic Irish were relegated to the outskirts of towns and to the worst land. The pattern of dominance and privilege was set, and it has continued to this day. By and large, the Protestants have the bigger and more prosperous farms, the better homes, the choicer jobs. They occupy most of the places in the government, the civil service, the professions and the skilled trades, while the Catholics are more likely to be small farmers or unskilled workers. Obviously many Catholics have achieved success, but there is just enough of an element of second-class citizenship to diminish their opportunities.

Protestants also have disproportionate political power. Apart from the Catholics' numerical disadvantage, the latter find it difficult to win seats because of blatant gerrymandering and a variety of electoral gimmicks. In recent years the Unionists occupied all twelve of the Northern Ireland seats in the British Parliament. Now they have eleven. The Unionists have held more than two thirds of the places in the provincial Parliament ever since it was created. In some Union strongholds the opposition parties do not even bother to put up candidates. The typical Unionist M.P. is a loyal member of the Orange Order, the militant Protestant fraternal organization, yet he is duty bound, as a member of Parliament, to represent his Catholic as well as his Protestant constituents.

Under the principle that the man who pays the piper is entitled to call the tune, Ulster has had a "business vote" in provincial and local elections, thus giving extra voting power to persons who own firms. A quarter of a million citizens who are entitled to vote in a general election cannot vote in local government elections, because the franchise is limited to householders and their wives, business people and limited companies. At the time of writing, it appears that such plural voting will be modified, but Catholic Nationalists will still have reason to demand "one man, one vote."

Because of gerrymandering and the limited franchise, a num-

ber of towns with Catholic majorities are controlled by Protestants. Londonderry ("Derry"), the second largest city, is two-
thirds Catholic, but Protestants have the majority on the council
and hold the better jobs on the public payroll. This is just a
local version of the national condition. It was revealed early
in 1967 that of 106 public-service positions which paid over
£4,000 a year, only three were held by Catholics. More than
ninety per cent of Ulster's senior civil servants are Protestants.
Some distortion is inevitable, given the province's special history
and tensions. Protestants have always had the edge in educational qualifications, and they are considered better security
risks. It is not surprising to find that the Royal Ulster Constabulary, the provincial police force, is predominantly manned
by Protestants. (When the R. U. C. was created a third of the
places were reserved for Catholics, and still are, but the Catholics
have been reluctant to join.) The Ulster Special Constabulary, a
part-time force which was formed years ago to help combat the
I.R.A. terrorists, is, inevitably, wholly Protestant.

In the west of Ulster and in other parts where Catholics are
more numerous, there are constant complaints that the government is deliberately neglecting them and denying them a fair
share of public improvements and new industry. (Many private
firms, of course, insist on being sited close to Belfast for obvious
business reasons.) Londonderry, for example, is a shabby-look-
ing city which has suffered so long from excessively high unemployment that the *Economist* has called it "the poorest as well
as the most isolated of the British settlements." Many of its
citizens, Protestants as well as Catholics, were incensed when
the small eastern city of Coleraine (population 12,000) was
selected instead of Derry (54,000) as the site of the new University of Ulster. In the allocation of local housing throughout
Ulster the evidence of discrimination against Catholics is strong.
But then it works the other way around when Catholics control
the councils.

Some Protestant employers in their job advertisements will

specify that only Protestants are acceptable—sometimes adding "Christian preferred" to make sure they get the right kind of Protestant. Many Catholic employers will hire only Catholic workers, and priests have been known to instruct their flocks to patronize Catholic shops. It seems only natural to both communities to take care of their own first. One Protestant justification is that the Catholics "are trying to outbreed us and take over." While Catholics do tend to have larger families (with the result that half the primary-school children are Catholic), this has been offset by the higher rate of Catholic emigration. There has been little change in the percentages of Protestants and Catholics in the past half century.

The ghetto mentality of the Catholics shows in their efforts to separate themselves—their religion, their culture—from the surrounding Protestants. They put up their own walls. The tale is told of a Catholic priest from abroad who went to an Ulster village and heard terrible stories from a leading citizen about Protestant intolerance. He asked the man how many Protestants there were in the village. "One, Father," he was told, "and with the help of God we'll have him out by Christmas."

The Catholic attitude is also revealed in a passage in Brian Moore's *The Lonely Passion of Judith Hearne.* Judith and a gentleman friend, Mr. Madden, both of them Catholics, are in a Belfast cinema watching a newsreel:

> The Items. First: The Queen. A few claps. More. The house applauding, louder and louder. Miss Hearne and Mr. Madden sat with their hands in their laps. No handclaps for her, a foreign queen. Let them give back the Six Counties and then we'll clap. Irish people, a disgrace, applauding like that. But Protestants, what can you expect, Scots Protestants, black-hearted all.

There are Catholics who have never been inside a Protestant home and Protestant ministers who have seldom spoken a word to a Catholic priest. A Protestant will hang a photograph of the royal family on his wall, while a Catholic will put up pictures of the Pope and the heroes of the Irish Republic. Some boys play cricket, while other boys play hurling, just as the Orange Order and the Ancient Order of Hibernians go their separate ways. Even where Catholics and Protestants live next door to each other, contact may be minimal. In *The Northern Ireland Problem*, Denis P. Barritt and Charles F. Carter tell of a child who complained to a girl friend that she had no one to play with on the new housing estate. "But," she was asked, "haven't you any neighbors to play with?" She replied, "Yes, there are children next door, but they aren't neighbors, they're Protestants."

Such an iron curtain of the mind comes clanging down as soon as a child is old enough to be hustled off to school. From then on he is, in common with the mass of Ulster children, separated from youngsters of the other religion through the whole of his schooldays. Even on school sporting fields Catholic and Protestant teams rarely play each other.

Two separate educational systems exist side by side. One is managed by local authorities and receives the whole of its building and maintenance funds from the state; the other is managed by the Catholic Church and gets two thirds of such funds from the state. Priests complain of having to spend too much of their time raising money for the schools, but it is the Catholics, not the Protestants, who have resisted integration in education. The government has been urging them to accept the mixed schooling "with safeguards" which does, in fact, exist in a handful of rural places.

History

Separate schooling means that prejudice is reproduced in each new generation. Catholic children are taught about all the wrongs done to Catholic Ireland, while Protestant children hear about the glories of their Ulster forefathers. One school system concentrates on Irish history (and provides Irish-language instruction), while the other dwells on English history. Because historic rivalries are carried on in everyday life it is no wonder that Ulster citizens, young and old, can speak about the Battle of the Boyne of 1690 or the Battle of the Diamond of 1795 as if it had happened yesterday. The annual Orangemen's Day parade is a flamboyant exercise in dedicated remembering. And when Catholic urchins cry, "Remember 1916!," they sound every bit as impassioned as their elders.

An Ulster Catholic's view of history is of ceaseless efforts by English and Scottish Protestants to crush Irish culture and Catholicism, and to Anglicize Ireland beyond all recognition. An Ulster Protestant's account tells how Irish Catholics have attempted to undo the fact of a Protestant presence in Ireland and to destroy freedom of conscience by forcing non-Catholics to accept the rule of a Catholic government. In any event, the long and complex sequence of events after Henry VIII proclaimed himself King of Ireland in 1534 is a poisonous brew of political and religious controversy. "However those events may be interpreted," said Captain Terence O'Neill, the Ulster Prime Minister, "they do demonstrate with absolute clarity the fact that Irish problems are deep-seated and not amenable to facile external solutions, however well-intentioned."

More than one Irishman in the Republic has told me that President Kennedy missed a great opportunity during his 1963 visit to go to the North and "heal the breach between us." I have always remembered this as an exquisite example of Irish pipe-dreaming. Kennedy might have been able to do some good in the North, even as a Catholic, and Prime Minister O'Neill hoped he would come, but healing the breach is something else. Having just flown in from the relative simplicities of divided Berlin and divided Germany, Kennedy was not anxious to hurl himself into the bottomless pit of the divided-Ireland question.

There was a time when Ulster, now the stronghold of Protestantism, was the most Gaelic and Catholic part of the island. It was from the North that the great Hugh O'Neill, Earl of Tyrone, launched the last-ditch struggle against the English, who controlled most of the island and were "planting" Protestants on lands seized from Catholics. When initial successes were follower by shattering defeats, O'Neill gave in to James I in 1603, and four years later he sailed off to the Continent in the Flight of the Earls. Their vast estates went to the Crown, which planted them with Scottish and English Protestants. The dispossessed Catholic tenants struck back with vengeance in the "massacres of 1641" and regained, for a time, much of their land. But Cromwell's forces a few years later avenged the Catholic uprising and put more Protestants on property seized from Catholic owners, who were driven to the barren west. Barritt and Carter write in *The Northern Ireland Problem:*

> It is clear that in the mid-seventeenth century Protestant settlers, at least outside the larger towns, must have felt exceedingly insecure; their very lives depended on the continued protection of English forces. At this time, therefore, the lines of division of the population became more definitely drawn, and drawn in a way which corresponded with the religious division. To the Protestant, the fact that a man was a Catholic was prima facie evidence that he would be disaffected and disloyal to the State: to the Catholic the fact that a man was a Protestant suggested that he was an alien invader maintained by foreign military power.

Although today Northern Ireland, which depends greatly on Britain for its security, is in little danger of being overwhelmed overnight by Catholic Ireland, the fears of three hundred years ago have their echoes. "All down the years of Northern Ireland's existence," said Terence O'Neill, "those who value above else our place in the United Kingdom have seen in a section of their fellow citizens a Trojan Horse ready to betray everything they hold most dear. Perhaps those fears have been exaggerated, perhaps not. But they exist."

Protestant Ulstermen have a siege mentality. They are surrounded by Catholics who threaten to do to them what they do to the Catholics, and they feel only grudgingly supported by Britons who constantly criticize them for going to extremes in their own defense. They show all the stubbornness and unblinking righteousness of a proud people who have sworn to defend an ancient cause. Protestant children soon learn about the thirteen brave apprentices who, on December 7, 1688, slammed the Ferryquay Gate at Londonderry in the faces of the troops sent by James II, the deposed Roman Catholic King, to occupy the city. A few months later James himself arrived with a large army outside the twenty-five-foot-high walls of the city and told the garrison of raw recruits and the Londonderry citizens to surrender. He was given the answer which still ricochets in the minds of loyal Ulstermen: "No surrender!" James, who needed to take Londonderry and subjugate Ulster if he was to succeed in his campaign to restore Catholicism and himself in England, set siege to the city. Lundy, the governor of Londonderry, had already fled and turned traitor, an act which has ever since made his name the Ulster equivalent of Quisling. (To a died-in-the-wool Ulsterman today a Lundy is a Protestant who supports the ecumenical movement.) Command of the city fell to a Protestant clergyman, the prototype of Ulster's militant churchmen.

Londonderry withstood enemy attacks and suffered great privation for 105 days until relief arrived and James II's army marched away. Seven thousand Derrymen died from hunger, disease and enemy fire, but there had been no surrender. Macaulay called it "the most memorable siege in the annals of the British Isles." The garrison at Enniskillen also fought a crucial battle against superior odds, and then the Protestant William of Orange triumphed over James II at the Battle of the Boyne. It led to the downfall of the Stuart dynasty in England and secured Protestantism in Northern Ireland.

In the two centuries which followed, through all the tangled and tragic events in the British-Irish relationship, Ulster remained something of a place apart. While the Irish Catholics formed a huge depressed class, practically a nation of serfs, the Ulster Protestants enjoyed greater security on their land, and they worked their holdings more effectively. They were able, as the Catholics were not, to profit by the improvements they made to their holdings. Even so, Ulstermen too suffered from exploiting landlords. Some of the latter actually chose to replace their Protestant tenants with compliant Catholics who would put up with anything to have a piece of land under their feet.

One historic consequence was the emigration from Ulster in the middle decades of the eighteenth century of about half a million people to England's colonies across the Atlantic. These were the "Scotch-Irish" who provided a number of the leaders of the American Revolution. They blended into American life more easily than did the Catholic Irish who flooded into the United States in the next century.

Northern Ireland's efforts in recent years to attract U.S. industry have spurred Ulster historians in their work of identifying prominent Americans of Scotch-Irish ancestry. The formidable list includes such diverse characters as Davy Crockett, Stephen Foster, Edgar Allan Poe, Stonewall Jackson, Sam Houston, Horace Greeley, Robert R. McCormick, Thomas Mellon and J. Paul Getty. At least ten of the thirty-five men who have been President of the United States had Ulster ancestors: Jackson, Polk, Buchanan, Andrew Johnson, Grant, Arthur, Cleveland, Benjamin Harrison, McKinley and Wilson. It can be appreciated why fist fights broke out at a banquet of Irishmen in Philadelphia a few years ago when Senator Joseph Clark proposed a toast to President Kennedy as "the only Irishman ever elected President of the United States."

Those Ulstermen who remained home in the eighteenth century succeeded in developing important industries in linen and other products despite restrictions imposed by the British. Although Protestants as well as Catholics in Ulster were involved in the efforts to unite Irishmen against the dictates of the English, the growing political strength of the Catholics made many Protestants fearful of losing the connection with Britain. Orange societies were founded to safeguard Protestantism. As early as 1853 a petition demanded a separate Ulster legislature if Home Rule ever came to pass in Ireland.

The agitation against Home Rule (or "Rome Rule") during the second half of the nineteenth century and into the twentieth was a major factor in the worsening of relations between Catholics and Protestants. There were serious riots in Belfast in 1886. Apart from religious feelings, Ulstermen were afraid that Home Rule might be the beginning of a separation from Britain which could result in tariff barriers against Ulster manufactures and other crippling economic changes. In the years just before World War I Ulster's feelings on the matter became so strong that Britain was faced with the strong possibility of armed resistance in the North of Ireland if Home Rule were granted. "Ulster will fight, and Ulster will be right," said Lord Randolph Churchill, father of Sir Winston. An Ulster Volunteer Force was raised to defend "Protestant liberties." Some 220,000 persons signed the Solemn League and Covenant of 1912 to show their determination to oppose an all-Ireland government.

It was World War I which gave Ulstermen the opportunity to demonstrate just how British they could be. Their factories poured out a flow of war materials. They gave their lives by the thousands in trench warfare, especially at the Battle of the Somme in July 1916, and won seventeen Victoria Crosses. In World War II, Ulster went into battle with as much dedication but with perhaps a little less self-abandon. Whereas Ulster had been notable for supplying human cannon fodder, now it excelled in providing topflight British field marshals: Alanbrooke, Alexander, Auchinleck, Dill and Montgomery.

One of the ironies of the post–World War I resolution of the

Irish problem was that the very section of Ireland which had so hotly opposed Home Rule was the one that got it. While the rest of the island was cut loose as the independent Free State, Ulster became the only part of the United Kingdom to have its own regional parliament. It acquired, in short, a degree of autonomy which has so far eluded the nationalists of Wales and Scotland. Moreover, the Ulster M.P.s in the House of Commons in London have a voice and the vote about all manner of British affairs. British M.P.s, however, by longstanding convention, are not permitted to discuss Ulster's "internal affairs." These include practically everything but foreign policy, defense matters and major taxes and tariffs.

The Northern Ireland government operates largely on its own, but in the British manner, in education, housing, social welfare, commerce, labor relations and local government. It has kept in its hands some extraordinary police powers which enable the authorities to deal hard and fast with threats to public order. These stem from the province's early years of violence. To quote Hugh Shearman:

> The new Ulster government, although enjoying strong electoral support, had to establish itself against the efforts of opponents who not only denied it recognition but attempted to frustrate and overthrow it by assassination, bomb outrages, incendiarism and other forms of violence. In 1922 two hundred and thirty-two people, including a member of the new Parliament, were killed, nearly a thousand more were wounded and more than $3,000,000 worth of property was destroyed.

Paisleyism

It was forty-four years after these unhappy events when I went to the North of Ireland for my first close study of life in Ulster. I had been there before, but more casually, spending most of my time in Belfast. Now it was 1966 and I chose to time my visit to coincide with the arrival of Queen Elizabeth II for her first trip to the province in some years. Such a royal occasion would normally have caused only a mild upsurge of British press interest in Ulster, an across-the-water outpost which is usually far to the rear of the thoughts of a London editor. (Northern Irishmen must live with the fact that the British ignore them most of the time. A television program of man-in-the-street interviews revealed that a good many Englishmen scarcely know what Ulster is, much less where it is.)

As it turned out, not only was the British press out in force, but a number of foreign correspondents, photographers and radio-TV journalists flew into Belfast as well. In normal circumstances this would have been an unexpected delight for the Ulster government, which has a unique problem of identification (is it a country or a colony?) and must constantly struggle to gain the favorable attention of bigger nations for trade, tourism and foreign investment. On this occasion, however, the extra press attention was not welcome, because it was inspired by a recent eruption of communal violence and by speculation that the Queen's life would be in danger. Not for years had there been such a revival of the nastier days of Protestant-Catholic, Unionist-Nationalist antagonism.

The journalists came, saw, and were appalled. "JOHN BULL'S POLITICAL SLUM" was the headline on a London *Sunday Times* article which began: "There is a part of Britain where the crude apparatus of political and religious oppression—ballot rigging, job and housing discrimination, and an omnipresent threat of violence—comfortably co-exists with intense loyalty to the Crown." A *Life* magazine report was headlined "IRELAND'S FANATICS FIGHT TO KEEP HATRED GREEN." The London *Observer's* full-page account said:

Belfast this July is the familiar time-honoured powder-keg into which the wearing of the wrong colour, the whistling of the wrong tune, or the waving of the wrong flag in certain areas could throw a match. They are a touchy people. A London socialist who carelessly said something rude about royalty in the city centre this week had to be rescued from the crowd which promptly attacked him.

Bigotry is a casual, unchallenged reflex here: it is difficult to find any institutions, even individuals, it has not tainted. This is a sick, sick country.

As Queen Elizabeth and the Duke of Edinburgh flew into Belfast, the earliest press reports stressed the extraordinarily heavy security which had been laid on; there was a quantity of armed policemen never seen on royal visits anywhere else in the United Kingdom. It was feared that there might be Catholic vengeance on the Queen for the recent outrages committed by Protestant fanatics, and that the Protestants might savagely retaliate. Some time before going to Belfast I had twice flown to Cyprus to report the civil war between the Greek and Turkish communities; now I saw the same pattern of hatred and separation. Why, asked the *Observer*, did the Queen's route "take her past the lavatory-wall patriotism of the fiercely Protestant Sandy Row, with its viciously offensive anti-Catholic slogans?"

It was stretching things too far to see Ulster as another Cyprus, yet the events so far in 1966 were not reassuring. Because it was the fiftieth-anniversary year of the Republic's Easter Rising, the Catholics in Ulster had been flaunting the Republic of Ireland flag more boldly than usual and I.R.A. members had marched somewhat openly in anniversary parades. It was also the fiftieth anniversary of the heroism of the Ulster Volunteer Force at the Battle of the Somme. A new extremist organization calling itself the Ulster Volunteer Force had suddenly raised its head for the defense of Protestant Ulster against Roman Catholics and those who would break bread with Catholics. The hero of the U.V.F. was the Reverend Ian Paisley, a tall, powerfully built evangelist who was easily the loudest and most provocative bigot in Ulster.

Paisley, a forty-year-old fundamentalist and the leader of his own Free Presbyterian Church, had been active for years. He was known for his colorful ranting against the Pope ("old Mr. Red Socks") and for his savage portrayals of Roman Catholicism ("I see here, friends, the Lord's warning against the Whore of Babylon, the Church of Rome, the enemy of freedom down the ages"). He had gathered publicity through such stunts as flying to Rome in an effort to obstruct the meeting of the Archbishop of Canterbury ("a traitor to Protestant Britain") and Pope Paul. Now, as both the instigator and the beneficiary of a new wave of anti-Catholic passions, Paisley had achieved greater prominence than ever before. A master of the McCarthy technique of making ever more sensational charges against the most notable figures in the land, he was on the front pages every day and drawing increasing numbers of people to his mass meetings. Because the Unionist government and the Protestant churches had made some gestures of friendship toward the Irish Republic and the Catholic Church, Paisley was abusing the Presbyterian Establishment, attacking the Prime Minister as an "arch traitor," and sparing not even the Governor of Ulster or the Lord Chief Justice. His private hate sheet, the *Protestant Telegraph*, was being hawked in the streets and prominently displayed by sympathetic newsdealers.

Inevitably, there was physical violence. "A series of thuggish incidents," as one English newspaper put it, swept Belfast. (The countryside remained relatively quiet.) They included terror campaigns which forced several Catholic families out of their homes and threats against an anti-extremist Protestant M.P., who had to be given police protection. Police attended Paisley's meetings with weapons ready and sometimes with helicopters keeping watch in the sky. A religious riot broke out when he led a procession in protest against the "Romanizing tendencies" of the General Assembly of the Presbyterian Church of Ireland. Against the background of these bizarre happenings, a fire bomb which was almost surely intended for the Catholic-owned **pub** next door killed an innocent Protestant widow in her bed. In other Belfast attacks two Catholics were slain and others wounded.

Anxious about the mounting viciousness and the bad name Ulster was getting in the world's press, Prime Minister O'Neill flew back from meetings in Paris and had the Ulster Volunteer Force outlawed. British Prime Minister Harold Wilson in the House of Commons had described it as "a quasi-fascist organization." In the Ulster House of Commons, O'Neill said, "To those of us who remember the Thirties, the pattern is horribly familiar. The contempt for established authority; the crude and unthinking intolerance; the emphasis upon monster processions and rallies; the appeal to a perverted form of patriotism: each and every one of these things has its parallel in the rise of the Nazis to power."

It was not exactly the happiest curtain raiser to the Queen's visit. It also seemed unfortunate that she would be appearing during just that fortnight before Orangemen's Day when such religious tolerance as does exist in the North normally breaks down under the weight of super-Ulsterism. "This is a country," I was told, "where people live side by side for fifty weeks in the year and then hate each other for the other two." Belfast youngsters were already gathering the boxes, old tires, broken furniture and other scrap needed for the great bonfires which would blaze in the city on the night before July 12. Drawings of William III, the much adored Orange king, were being chalked on walls. Strung across the streets of Protestant neighborhoods were banners with such proclamations as "A Strong and Virile Orange Order Remains Ulster's Greatest Bulwark against the Enemies of Our Faith" and "Only by Eternal Vigilance Shall We Overcome the Threat of Papist Rule in Ulster." In the meantime, Belfast's Catholics were lying low.

In such circumstances it was hard not to feel a certain apprehension when the Queen arrived and drove through the fervently loyal or vaguely hostile streets of Belfast. During one important procession I was riding with other correspondents in a press car some distance behind the royal Rolls-Royce. I will not soon forget the electrifying effect of the shouts from the street that the Queen had been attacked. We wanted to leap out to get the news firsthand, but the motorcade had not stopped and did not slow down until arriving at Government House, where there was to be a garden party. We learned that the Queen was all right even though her limousine, which the authorities quickly hid from the photographers, had been damaged. A large block of concrete hurled from an upper story of an office building under construction had crashed on the bonnet of the limousine as it rolled along Great Victoria Street. One second later and it would have struck the transparent plastic roof above the Queen's head. The Ulster government rushed out a statement insisting that there had been no political motive behind the attack. This turned out to be accurate enough. The young Catholic workman who had heaved the concrete at the Queen said he had done it on an impulse, not under orders, and it seemed to be true. He was sent to prison.

It was easy in such days to see Ulster as an incurable; it appeared to be not just the neurotic North but a pathetic self-destroyer. But on reflection I formed a quite different impression. The overall look and mood of Northern Ireland proclaimed that it was actually changing for the better, and that the Paisley phenomenon was a desperate reaction by extremists to the liberalization of Ulster life which had been under way since 1963. Roy Bradford, a thoughtful Unionist politician, has said that "the emotional climate in Ulster today is one of deep disquiet and uncertainty. The sheet-anchors of the past seem to be shifting and drifting. Most of our hitherto accepted ideas are in the melting-pot. In many areas of thought we do not know what has hit us. The reaction is vehement charge and countercharge."

Not as newsworthy as the violence, but just as important, was the fact that the Easter Rising processions by Ulster Catholics had *not* provoked the rioting which would have been inevitable some years ago. There was no reaction to the assault on the

Queen. Orangemen's Day passed without serious incident even though many speakers at open-air gatherings denounced the ecumenical movement. In the Republic there was, throughout the several months of disturbances in Ulster, a most mature silence. In times past there would have been calls for action. Now there was confidence that the Ulster government would deal firmly with the extremists. Paisley, in fact, was imprisoned for three months on conviction for unlawful assembly. (When he emerged from jail he was driven off in a car bearing the sign "Behold the Lamb of God.") Protestant and Catholic leaders in Ulster united in appealing for religious harmony. It was becoming unrespectable to make the old denunciations of the opposing faith.

Terence O'Neill

Just as the awakening of the Republic began when Sean Lemass took over from the aging de Valera, so the cautious liberalization of Ulster commenced when Captain Terence O'Neill, then forty-eight, succeeded Lord Brookeborough, the seventy-three-year-old Prime Minister, in 1963. Brookeborough, who is still an influential voice in Ulster, was a formidable personality: an engaging but autocratic figure who had held the premiership for twenty consecutive years, a record time of unbroken leadership in British parliamentary history. He was a copperplated conservative in the tradition of Ulster's first Premier, Lord Craigavon, who had described Stormont as "a Protestant parliament for a Protestant people." Lord Brookeborough was the patriarch of Ulster's landed gentry, and his estates near the border had been in the thick of the armed clashes between I.R.A. raiders and Ulster police. His son had once been threatened with kidnapping by the I.R.A.

Like de Valera, Brookeborough was primarily concerned with the "orange-and-green issue," but he fought to relieve unemployment and took longer strides in economic improvement. A series of Industrial Development Acts during the first postwar decade encouraged new manufacturers and broadened the base of the economy. As Britain under its early postwar Labour governments installed its welfare-state apparatus, Ulster followed along and was soon benefiting from the very measures—free medicine, family allowances, unemployment assistance—which many Conservatives at Westminster, including the Ulster M.P.s, had opposed. Still, Northern Ireland continued to be Britain's poor relation, and the hostile relationship with the Irish Republic had become one of the longest cold wars in history.

Captain O'Neill, Brookeborough's Finance Minister, was handpicked to succeed him, but he turned out to be a leader with a mind of his own and a quite different set of priorities. He emphasized economic expansion and sought to end "the old cross-border long-distance slanging contest of which all sensible people are sick and tired." He became the first Ulster prime minister ever to visit Catholic schools; he admitted the existence of discrimination; and he made other gestures to improve communal relations in Ulster. He thus offended the diehards in his own party, but his success abroad as a tireless salesman of Ulster has made it difficult for them to pull him down.

During O'Neill's regime dozens of British, American and European firms have been persuaded to set up factories in the province. An array of grants and allowances comparable to those offered by the Republic have been offered manufacturers. They make up for Ulster's disadvantages in lack of raw materials and distance from big markets. Altogether in the postwar period, two hundred sixty new factories, good for sixty-five thousand new jobs, have been built in Ulster. They include such important international names as Du Pont, Goodyear, Standard Telephone, Grundig, Imperial Chemical Industries, Michelin, Courtaulds and Rolls-Royce. They have made up for the decline of the traditional Ulster industries and have absorbed many of the workers moving out of agriculture.

In England, the poor-relation image still persists, and there is insufficient appreciation of how greatly Northern Ireland's economy has been improved. Industrial output has increased far more rapidly than Britain's in recent years. It has become a sophisticated economy which exudes a confidence not seen since the heady days of the last war. The unemployment rate remains high, but the unemployment pay is close to the earnings of unskilled laborers and higher than many a job in the Irish Republic. There are fewer state enterprises to be seen in Ulster than in the south, but there is a new zeal for province-wide planning which is meant to spread out the prosperity like butter on bread. One major effort is the entirely new city of Craigavon, in County Armagh, which is to have 100,000 inhabitants within fifteen years. (But once again the religious issue intrudes: Ulster Catholics say that such a momentous project should be sited in the less prosperous—and more Catholic—west, or that the money should be spent on the rejuvenation of Londonderry.)

With both Lemass and O'Neill stressing economic growth, it made sense for the two premiers to do the impossible and meet each other. It was O'Neill who took the greater political risk. He felt it essential that Lemass come to him within the Ulster borders as an acknowledgment by Dublin that Northern Ireland exists. It is to the eternal credit of Lemass that he agreed to this. The first of the two meetings in 1965 was held in such secrecy that the two premiers did not even tell their wives. "If the news had leaked out," O'Neill has said, "our respective sets of reactionaries would have been out in force with their banners and protests, and these would have been the pictures that would have gone around the world."

Largely because O'Neill's set of reactionaries prevent him from advancing as quickly as he would like, the meetings did not improve north-south cooperation as much as the moderates on both sides had expected, but fresh hopes were raised in December 1967 when Prime Minister Lynch met O'Neill at Stormont for a "summit conference." (The Paisleyites protested by throwing snowballs.) Discussions between Ulster and Republic ministers and officials are now frequent, and the Anglo-Irish Trade Agreement is paving the way toward economic integration. There have long been all-Ireland activities in banking, in sport, in trade unions and in the Catholic and Protestant churches.

It is now widely realized in the Irish Republic that Ulster cannot be coerced into giving up its association with Britain and joining in a united Ireland. "The big mistake," said Sean MacEntee, one of the veteran Fianna Fail leaders, "is to seek political union before we have economic or social union." It seems to me incredible that Catholic Irishmen should have spent nearly half a century misjudging the psychology of the Protestant Ulstermen. Partition is a tragedy, and a unified Ireland is a reasonable aspiration, but everything in Irish history shows that the worst way to achieve unification is to force the issue. The Northern Protestants are Ulstermen first, Irishmen second. In their anxiety to retain their connection with Britain, and as the unfortunates of a perpetual crisis of identity, they insist that they are, above all, British.

According to Captain O'Neill, "We are British or we are nothing," and yet some of his own family roots go back to the ancient kings of Ireland. When I told him that only a few Ulstermen I had met had identified themselves in quite that way, he said, "They are British without realizing it, or knowing what it means. They think England is just like Northern Ireland except that it has a Continental Sunday." Sitting with him then in his comfortable Stormont office (stuffed armchairs drawn close to the cold fireplace, brass fixtures, a photo of himself and President Johnson on the mantel), I marveled at the way he managed to speak with such detachment, and with a measure of superiority, of his predecessors, his political colleagues, and the Northern Irish public. I remembered the Dublin editor who had so accurately compared him to "one of those old-time colonial governors who made sure that the sun never set on the British Empire." O'Neill clearly believed that direct rule from London, perhaps with himself as secretary of state for Northern

Ireland, would be preferable to Home Rule. "It was forced on us," he said, "and we have to make the best of it that we can."

A handsome man with finely chiseled features and a soft, almost silken voice, O'Neill is a courteous, fastidious, carefully groomed, impeccably spoken aristocrat. An old Etonian, in fact. The left-wing weekly *Tribune* of London described him as "a real hoity-toity Tory with an old-school tie" when he became Ulster's prime minister. His father was Britain's first member of Parliament to be killed in World War I and his two brothers died in World War II, while he himself served in the Irish Guards. He became a member of the Ulster Parliament in 1946. O'Neill told me that he now enjoys a cordial relationship with the Catholic leader of the opposition, Edward McAteer, but in the early postwar days "I could not even get a reply from him if we met on the train and I said 'Good morning' or 'Good evening.' I had been out of Ulster for a long time and had not been imbued with the usual hatreds." Even so, O'Neill as an M.P. and later as a minister was by no means a champion of religious harmony in the North or of friendlier relations with the Republic. He deeply resented the Irish Republic's refusal to support the United Kingdom in the war against Hitler, and he says today that "any attempt to improve relationships with the Republic was frozen during the period of the I.R.A. raids in the 1950s." When he became prime minister (a sudden promotion after Lord Brookeborough underwent a serious operation) he "simply had to decide whether to follow the reactionary old policies which perpetuated hatred or strike out on something new."

O'Neill chose the new approach, and he began to chip away at Ulster's "fortress mentality." It would be misleading to suggest that he is a radical reformer, however. He is essentially a more polished version of the rough old Unionists who will not "give an inch" in their struggle to preserve Ulster's special status. He is a defender of the status quo, but because he is a civilized man he is having a civilizing influence on a barbarous and wasting situation. His greatest virtue is that he recognizes what is wrong: "The foundations I have inherited here are foundations of cleavage, hatred and intolerance."

O'Neill, at least, represents change and hope. "In spite of his faults," said a prominent Irishman in the Republic, "he is the only possible man in the breach today, but it would need a succession of five or six Terence O'Neills to straighten out some of the major Northern Ireland problems. I don't think he understands Irish nationalism. It seems to me that he sees it only as either a romantic dream or an excuse for gunplay by people who live in back streets. I don't think he has enough of the qualities which Northern Ireland needs now—that is, enough sympathy, enough knowledge of Irish history, and a sufficient toughness to root out some of the Orange nonsense. But he is so far ahead of anything yet seen on the Unionist front benches that we just have to hope he survives."

O'Neill's most bitter enemies may be found among the "back-woodsmen" of his own Unionist Party and among the more intransigent members of the semi-secret Orange Order. The membership of the Order is usually given as 100,000, or one out of every three or four Protestant men. At least one Belfast editor, however, suspects that this is a highly exaggerated figure. Still, the Order's power is undeniable. The Prime Minister is a member. So are all the ministers of the Ulster government and almost every Unionist M.P. in the provincial Parliament and at Westminster. When the Unionist Party occasionally chooses a non-Orangeman as a candidate for Parliament he is hastily inducted into the Order. Most of the year the members of the Orange lodges work quietly behind the scenes as the local watchdogs of the Ulster way of life, but they spill out into the streets every Twelfth of July to show their strength and fervor. The great parade in Belfast is a fantastic tribal ritual: battalions of stern-faced men in dark suits, each with an orange sash hanging from his neck and many wearing black bowler hats, marching for hours under the colorful banners of Protestant divines and temperance leaders as bands play and giant drums boom. To a casual visitor it must look like a splendid anachronism, a glorious pageant preserved for the benefit of tourism, but if he troubles to trail along on the long march to the meeting grounds at the edge of the city he will find that it is not so innocent a spectacle as it seems.

The Orange Order, its defenders insist, is "a bastion of civil and religious liberty." It is "the guardian of the constitutional system." Irreverently interpreted, this means that the Order exists to preserve the Protestant hegemony and Protestant privileges in Ulster. Despite the efforts of some of its leaders to achieve a new tone of moderation and tolerance, the Twelfth-of-July Orange meetings all over the country have a strong odor of anti-Catholicism about them. In recent years they have been marked by rows brought on by the Paisleyites, who prefer their bigotry undiluted. Although angry shouting is usually as far as things go, there was a nasty scuffle at a meeting in 1967, in which a Unionist M.P. at Westminster, George Forrest, was knocked out. And the moderates were much embarrassed when an Orange procession in Belfast stopped outside a jail and handed in messages of greetings to the Orangemen inside who had been convicted of the murder of a Catholic. Captain O'Neill, who dismisses suggestions that he resign from the Order, has warned that if there is too much crude behavior in Ulster the people of Britain may "feel our conduct not worthy of British citizenship" and abandon Ulster, leaving it "an insignificant body of people lost in the Atlantic and surrounded by enemies."

As a forward-looking prime minister, O'Neill has benefited by several major happenings of the past decade. The Irish Republic has adopted a live-and-let-live attitude to the North. The new age of affluence in Britain has washed over into Ulster. The worldwide ecumenical movement has encouraged religious leaders to meet other churchmen halfway. And the arts have begun to blossom in what was—despite a worthy theatrical tradition and a respectable list of authors, poets and playwrights—a cultural dead end. There has been of late a distinct improvement in the province's intellectual tone. Educational opportunities have greatly expanded and there is a boom in higher education. Queen's University, whose chancellor is Tyrone Guthrie, a world-renowned theatrical director, is in the process of doubling its enrollment. The amount of public money being spent on the encouragement of the arts is impressive. Belfast now has an annual fortnight's cultural festival which produces the kind of joyful experimentation in drama, painting and the other arts which is seldom associated with that hard-bitten city.

Fresh breezes of sanity about the border problem and religious antagonism are blowing. The important new middle class of all denominations finds it advantageous to be broad-minded. Younger-generation leaders are showing their impatience with the old shibboleths. Television is helping to destroy the convenient old image of a priest-ridden, poverty-stricken south, and even the showbands and ballad singers from both parts of the island have a healing influence as they perform on either side of the border. Ulster newspapers are matching the leading papers of the Republic in their more sober reporting of Irish affairs. The *Belfast Telegraph*, once an orthodox Unionist journal, is now outspoken in its demand for a change of heart in Ulster. The Irish Association for Economic and Cultural Relations is composed of leading citizens who are putting the border issue to one side in order to foster an informal all-Ireland alliance for progress.

One great factor in the easing of tensions is the evidence that most Ulster Catholics are convinced that they are better off in Northern Ireland than they would be in the Republic. They may hold to the dream of a united Ireland, but they are not anxious for an abrupt change which might jeopardize their higher wages and greater social benefits. Ironically, it is the welfare state, which the conservative Unionists only grudgingly installed, which has done the most to make the Catholics more content with their lot in Ulster. With their larger families and greater needs, it is the Catholics more than the Protestants who have benefited from health and welfare assistance. The prospects are that they will work more heartily at becoming full members of the Ulster community. They are beginning to play a more constructive role in politics. Only recently the Nationalist M.P.s, who in the early days would not even take their seats in the Ulster Parliament, agreed to become the formal opposition instead of a noisy band of hecklers. The leader of the opposition, Edward McAteer, has even described himself as "setting a hot pace for Captain O'Neill" in his personal efforts to "normalize political relationships in the North."

In December 1967 "the most comprehensive survey of public opinion ever undertaken in Northern Ireland" revealed that attitudes are changing faster than even the most progressive politicians realized. The survey, undertaken by National Opinion Polls for the *Belfast Telegraph*, disclosed that 96 percent of the electorate believe it important that Protestants and Catholics try to get on better with each other. Nearly three quarters of the Unionists approve the efforts to improve Ulster's relationship with the Republic. Most startling was the revelation that 38 percent of Unionists favor a united Ireland so long as it is linked to Britain, while more than half of the Catholic Nationalists prefer a united Ireland attached to Britain rather than an independent all-Ireland republic. A majority of the Northern Irelanders (including 41 percent of Unionists) foresee the disappearance of the border, perhaps within twenty-five years.

As the ramparts of memory crumble and the Irish of both major faiths and of both north and south live in the present, and in greater harmony, the rancorous old question of a united versus a divided Ireland may become beside the point. The whole of the British Isles is already turning into a single free-trade area, and other barriers besides economic ones are coming down. Without predicting whether there will ever be an Irish federation, an all-Ireland government (which probably would be disproportionately influenced by the industrious and talented Ulstermen), or some sort of Irish state within a united Europe, it seems to me inevitable that the estranged inhabitants of the island will draw closely together. I found it moving just a short while ago to sit at lunch with Martin Wallace, the Quaker-educated deputy editor of the *Belfast Telegraph*, and hear him speak of "the real sense of loss" he feels about the divorce of the North from the rest of Ireland. "We are cut off from what is naturally ours," he said, "something that is part of our history and our way of life." It was an echo of what I had heard expressed by thoughtful and openhearted Irishmen on both sides of the border who feel instinctively that the true flowering of modern Ireland must await the binding up of the ancient wound.

Chapter 9

BLOW-UP

It's difficult to write sense about Northern Ireland. While the surrounding scenery was changing out of recognition, including the disappearance of the British Empire, nothing was allowed to change in "Ulster"—not till that tide of indignant humanity swept over Craigavon Bridge, Derry, in October 1968—and by then it was too late.

—Denis Ireland

The Catholics don't want civil rights. They want all of Ireland.

—Belfast Dockworker

Ulster was a time bomb which finally exploded late in 1968. Demonstrators demanding full civil rights for the Roman Catholic minority clashed with Protestant police and Protestant defenders of the status quo. From then on, intermittently for one vicious year, Ulster was convulsed by marches, riots, burnings, bombings, murder and mayhem. Whole neighborhoods in Belfast and Londonderry lived behind barricades in a state of siege. Hundreds of working-class homes were gutted in the worst violence seen in the British Isles since the air raids of World War II. Thousands of British soldiers were rushed in to prevent a massacre. The whole world was watching.

By 1970 it was clear that such an explosion had been inevitable and that this was a classic case of things having to get worse before they could get better. And they did get better, even though it was a commonplace to say that Protestant-Catholic relations had been set back fifty years.

"Virtually nothing was done" about the civil rights issue, as even the most moderate Cardinal Conway admitted, "until the people took to the streets." The bloodshed forced the British government to step in and compel the provincial rulers to speed up reforms and give up some of their police-state instruments. Although Terence O'Neill fell from office, his replacement as prime minister proved no less ready to fend off the Unionist Party's anti-Catholic extremists and try to remedy the most blatant discriminatory practices of the Ulster establishment. The Unionists, of course, remained firmly in charge and the Reverend Ian Paisley had more rabble to rouse than ever, but Northern Ireland would never be the same again. It could no longer carry on as if it were some kind of seventeenth-century Protestant club, with the Catholic help confined to the back stairs and the servants' entrance.

The ugly facts of life in Ulster were exposed as never before to the people of Britain and to the outside world. The Northern Irish authorities had previously been able to override any embarrassing outbreaks of the Ulster sickness. They could match the criticisms of assorted cranks and prying journalists with the effusions of their own propaganda machine. This time, however, the prolonged violence attracted a spotlight that was piercing and unrelenting. Quite apart from the international press, a succession of distinguished investigators, including Members of Parliament and members of official commissions, laid bare the peculiar workings of Northern Ireland. It soon became accepted fact that this was the least democratic and most feudal portion of the British Isles; that Catholics were systematically denied fair representation in local and provincial government; that housing and employment procedures grossly favored the Protestants.

For many ordinary Britons it was their first realization that a part of the United Kingdom, heavily subsidized by themselves, made use of a Special Powers Act whose repressive provisions had even drawn the envy of a South African official. Such perpetual state-emergency powers enabled the authorities to seize and put out of sight anyone judged to be a threat to "law and order." It was also the first time that the British people, who get along so well with their own friendly, unarmed Bobbies, fully appreciated how different things were in Northern Ireland. The black-uniformed men of the Royal Ulster Constabulary, 3,000 strong and nine-tenths Protestant, with guns at their hips and military equipment in their armories, were backed up—in case the I.R.A. or the local Catholics got out of hand—by 8,500 all-Protestant B-Specials, a para-military police reserve whose members kept their weapons handy at home. True enough, Northern Ireland had had to deal with some genuine threats to its very existence from Irish Republican forces, but it was just as true that the typical Catholic had good reason to see the police as the government's blunt instrument to keep him in his place.

We Shall Overcome

Ulster was (and is) controlled by an oligarchy of land-owning Orange Tories, much given to sporting their military titles, however ordinary. They were well practised at dealing with any "disloyal" anti-partition elements in their midst. Now, however, they faced an entirely new political force. As one might expect in Ireland, it was an unruly aggregation of moderates and extremists, liberals and revolutionaries, talkers and doers, but it had vitality and a conviction that history was on its side. In contrast to previous efforts to change conditions in Ulster, the protestors did not emphasize a political solution, such as an end to the border. Their strength lay in their demand for rights, not power—at least in the first place. They concentrated on such everyday matters as votes, jobs and homes. Thus they were able to attract a measure of Protestant support, primarily from the better educated. The majority of working-class Protestants were hostile even though the most militant civil rights leaders called for a new deal for *all* the poor and deprived of Ulster, not just the Catholics. For generations the Orange Tories had successfully exploited the religious emotions of Protestant workers against their own best interests, and they continued to do so.

The Ulster time bomb might have been defused years ago by the Protestant rulers had they been more astute and foresighted, not to say more humane. Or it could have been defused by the Catholics had they been willing to endure all the injustices and indignities of second-class citizenship while proclaiming their loyalty to Northern Ireland. But one might as well have expected the white segregationists in Mississippi or Alabama to encourage racial integration or expected the blacks of the U.S. ghettoes to meekly accept life at the bottom.

Northern Ireland during Terence O'Neill's nearly six years of well-meaning gestures and token reforms had taken on many of the characteristics of the Deep South in the wake of the U.S. Supreme Court's school desegregation decision. Young upstarts of the minority, their expectations aroused, became more vocal and demanding. Eventually, by taking to the streets, they forged their most persuasive leaders and multiplied their following. Outside sympathizers gave at least moral support and outside troops were sent in to protect them from the backlash of majority extremists. And out of confrontation came concessions from a quaking government.

To an American observer of Ulster's agony the drama was painfully familiar. The civil rights demonstrators, many of them idealistic students well to the left in their political beliefs, called for "Freedom Now" and "One Man, One Vote." They sang "We Shall Overcome." The peaceful demonstrations which turned into violent skirmishes with police and right-wing roughnecks drew international journalists and television cameramen like flies to a wound. There were constant accusations of police brutality, and, indeed, the hard-pressed police were often brutal. In turn, there were charges that civil rights was just a smoke-screen for radicals, anarchists, Communists and Irish Republicans to touch off a revolution and destroy the state.

Familiar, yes, but the cast of characters could only have boiled up out of the sulphurous soil of Northern Irish politics. The fastidious captain who served as prime minister gave way to a hyphenated major. The veteran political leaders of Ulster's Catholics, still vainly preaching all-Ireland nationalism but not social action, were suddenly made obsolete by scrappy youngsters talking about "rights," and doing more than just talking. The huge, bellowing evangelist of Cromwellian Protestantism stormed across the land castigating the Pope, Trotsky and cowardly Unionists but he more than met his match in a little urchin girl named Bernadette who whipped up a student revolt, got herself elected to the British Parliament, fought at the barricades of Derry, and became an instant international figure.

The surrealistic character of this semi-country was fully revealed when Irish Catholics cheered the arrival of English troops on the soil of Holy Ireland while diehard Ulstermen, the very first to call themselves British, decried the intrusion of the British. Nicholas Mansergh, the Cambridge historian, once observed that "If the Ulster question were not one of the tragedies of history, it might well be regarded as one of the more remarkable of its curiosities."

People's Democracy

In the summer of 1969, while traveling about the Irish Republic to see how people were reacting to the convulsions in the North, I stopped for a night in a hotel in Dingle, a gray invalid of a town in the Irish West which was enjoying a temporary economic boom. Film director David Lean was shooting a movie on the peninsula and the fallout of American dollars and English pounds could be seen in every pub. Although the hotel was full of movie people I came across an attractive young couple on vacation from their suburban Belfast home. They said they were enjoying the sleepiness of southern Ireland after the feverish tensions in Ulster. When they spoke of the religious antagonisms which had always bedeviled Northern Ireland, I ventured that a decade of atheism might do everyone, Protestant and Catholic alike, a world of good.

"No, you're wrong there," said the lady. "The trouble is, you see, we would all be very *devout* atheists."

And so they would. There was little room in Ulster for the uncommitted, dispassionate individual. The old Irish expression that there are three sides in every argument, "mine, yours, and the hell with it," did not apply to the Six Counties. All of the forces of that schizophrenic society seemed to pull the individual to one side or the other. Northern Ireland was described by its own Agriculture Minister, Phelim O'Neill, as "one of the most fertile breeding grounds for creating trouble and strife in the Western world."

Although the civil rights movement seemed to spring up overnight in 1968, it had been, in fact, several years in the making. It was a convergence of forces which had been working separately, both in Ulster and Britain, to draw attention to conditions in Northern Ireland and to seek solutions outside of the frozen politics of the region. The movement also reflected "an important and new element in the political and social climate of Northern Ireland," according to the Cameron Commission report published in the fall of 1969. (The official commission of inquiry, headed by Lord Cameron, a Scottish judge, sought to unearth the causes of the Ulster disturbances.) "A much larger Catholic middle class has emerged which is less ready to acquiesce in the acceptance of a situation of assumed (or established) inferiority and discrimination than was the case in the past."

In Dungannon, County Tyrone, Dr. Con McCluskey and his wife Patricia were particularly effective in putting together a task force of professional men to investigate and document the extent of anti-Catholic discrimination. Their Campaign for Social Justice in Northern Ireland and the Northern Ireland Civil Rights Association were only the most prominent of a number of organizations which were busy stirring up public opinion and putting pressure on officials and legislators in Belfast and London. Complaints about the Unionist regime were even carried to the European Court of Human Rights in Strasbourg, France.

It took a massive transfusion of liberal and radical youth, however, to convert the civil rights cause into a full-scale movement. A new reform organization called People's Democracy brought together Catholic and Protestant youth to serve in waves of protest demonstrations. Students were turned on, so to speak, by the sight of the police snuffing out a civil rights march to Dungannon in August 1968 and by the violent confrontation of police and protesters in Londonderry on October 5, 1968, a date for the history books.

Londonderry

Londonderry was a fit place for the first great battleground of the civil rights struggle. It was Ulster at its most shameful: the most bedraggled and undemocratically administered city in the British Isles. As the site of the famous Protestant stand against the Catholic siege of 1689, it was, as one British commentator said, "the epitome in Northern Ireland of Protestant triumph and Catholic humiliation." Another observer called it "a totem pole of fanatical Ulster loyalism, as crucial as West Berlin and infinitely more emotional."

The Protestants controlled the municipal council in a city two-thirds Catholic ("It's the Derrymander at work," a local man told me.) They managed to keep the Catholics squeezed into ghettoes where their political power was feeble, for only property owners could vote, and their living conditions execrable. The major Catholic area just outside the old walls of the city was aptly named the Bogside. The occupants of that 40 percent of Derry housing officially described as substandard were living just about as miserably as their forebears of Victorian times. There was, however, the dole to keep body and soul alive. For thousands of Derry Catholics, and many Protestants too, the dole was a way of life. More than 15 percent of the city's working men were permanently unemployed. The numerous shirt factories wanted female instead of male labor. Wearing their shabby black suits and their faces of defeat, the half-men of Derry would stand about in doorways remarking on the weather, waiting for the pubs to open, waiting for something to turn up.

The only predictable excitement in the damp, ghostly city was the annual routine of historico-political parades. On one day the Protestants would fly their flags and bang their drums to celebrate Orange triumphs over Popery. On another day the Catholics would take to the streets with their pipers and folk dancers to show off their green Irishness and their allegiance to Dublin and Rome. Because Protestants would march through their own neighborhoods and Catholics would stick to their own backyard, such events usually transpired without violence. The authorities were therefore understandably concerned in October 1968 when the Belfast-based Civil Rights Association proposed to stage a protest march through Derry's Protestant as well as Catholic neighborhoods. William Craig, the Minister for Home Affairs and a hard-line Unionist, waited until a late hour before banning the proposed route of march: too late for the organizers to rearrange matters. When a crowd of several hundred paraded through the city anyway, in defiance of the ban, they were viciously attacked not by angry Protestant onlookers but by the men of the Royal Ulster Constabulary who waded into them with clubs and scattered them with water cannon.

The debacle turned out to be to the advantage of the civil rights cause. The press and television accounts of the police behavior raised a storm of protest in Britain. Four Labour Members of Parliament who saw the fighting urged the government to hold a public inquiry. Angry students at Queen's University in Belfast, described by the *Economist* as "a previous contender for the world's most docile university," demonstrated against the police and set about organizing People's Democracy. Meantime, a Citizens' Action Committee was formed in Londonderry by a young Protestant businessman and former Unionist, Ivan Cooper, and a young Catholic businessman, John Hume, chairman of the Derry Housing Association. Hume was to become an M.P. and a particularly convincing leader of Northern Ireland's aroused Catholics.

Bernadette Devlin

Cooper, Hume and such other figures as Frank Gogarty, Eamonn McCann and Michael Farrell were exciting new faces on the Ulster scene as the first truly effective assault on the Unionist hierarchy was launched. For sheer drama and glamour, however, they were vastly overshadowed by Bernadette Devlin, a 21-year-old, five-foot slip of a college girl who emerged overnight from obscurity to notoriety as a civil rights wildcat.

Like some of the Black Power champions in the U.S.A., she was entirely a creature of her age. She defined Ulster's condition in stark, simplistic terms and demanded immediate reform. Although portrayed as a champion of oppressed Roman Catholics in Protestant Ulster she insisted that the poor of all faiths were being exploited, and in the capitalist Republic as well as in the capitalist North. Moreover, she denounced her own church as among the "best traitors Ireland has ever had" for failing to fight for the dignity of people. Such extreme views, quite obviously, cost her the support of many Catholics. For others, she was "Ulster's Joan of Arc."

One of six children, Josephine Bernadette Devlin was born in the small market town of Cookstown, County Tyrone. Her father, a carpenter who had to go to England to find work because he was "politically suspect," was (as she has written) "the bottom Cookstown could produce . . . the road sweeper's son."

By marrying him, her rebellious mother, coming from a slightly higher station in life, outraged her family and friends. The Devlins were savagely ostracized. One person who treated them with unusual and sustaining kindness was a Protestant neighbor, but such are the passions of Ulster that this same woman, during Bernadette Devlin's election campaign, howled at her, "You Fenian scum!"

Despite hard times and the death of both parents, she made her way to Queen's to study psychology. Her reputation as a political activist began during the long October night of the formation of People's Democracy in a crowded university hall. After a raging discussion about objectives and tactics it was decided to stage a civil rights parade through Belfast, but there was one snag. Under law, someone would have to sign papers with the police assuming personal responsibility for any violence which might occur. There was an embarrassing silence, and then Miss Devlin spoke up: "I'll sign the papers, Mr. Chairman. I have nothing to lose."

"She's not the size of two turf," it was said. Only passably pretty, she had stringy dark hair and her front teeth were askew. She wore no makeup and, despite being called "a miniskirted Marxist," she was often seen dressed for combat in sweater, blue jeans and low shoes. None of this mattered, for she proved to be clever, quick, well informed, and aflame with conviction. Six months after joining the civil rights struggle, and still a few days shy of her 22nd birthday, Bernadette Devlin was elected to one of the twelve Ulster seats in the House of Commons in London.

As one of the youngest MPs in British history, she went against all tradition by giving a speech on the day of her swearing-in. Moreover, it was an "electrifying" speech, as one member said, which assailed the British for their indifference to the injustices in Ulster, that "society of landlords." The MPs, according to one unsympathetic Conservative, listened to her with "masochistic pleasure." The Unionist regime had to go, she insisted: "Any socialist government worth its guts would have gotten rid of them long ago."

Her activities in England, her well-publicized fund-raising tour of the United States, and her engaging book, *The Price of My Soul*, were all useful exercises in behalf of change in Ulster but she was most effective on her home grounds. She served as an inspiration and a rebuke to the faint-hearted of her faith. Photographs published the world over showed Bernadette Devlin, MP, in the middle of a rubble-strewn Bogside street breaking up paving stones for use against the enemy. She would later be sentenced to six months in jail for this episode in Londonderry.

Running the Gauntlet

The tumult and shouting in Ulster after the opening shots of the civil rights campaign was something like a thirty-three ring circus. The events unfolded with such machine-gun rapidity, and over so broad a canvas, that no individual journalist, politician or fact-finding member of the British Cabinet could take it all in. Over the course of a year it was a rare day when there was not, somewhere in Ulster, a disturbance of major or minor proportions: a demonstration here, a riot there; a water pipeline dynamited or a post office set on fire; a police patrol attacked or a meeting broken up by a Paisleyite mob.

Londonderry and Belfast bore the brunt of the trouble. Their slums became armed camps. Barricades of burned-out buses, sheet metal, telephone poles and old furniture separated Protestant and Catholic streets. Other Ulster towns like Armagh, Dungannon and Newry suffered too, and there were innumerable ugly incidents in every part of the country. One of the most critical clashes of all took place in the countryside in the course of a four-day People's Democracy march from Belfast to Londonderry. At the beginning, on New Year's Day, 1969, there were less than a hundred participants in the 73-mile trek which

Terence O'Neill described as a "foolhardy and irresponsible undertaking." They experienced considerable harassment all the way from the capital. Then, as they came to Burntollet Bridge within seven miles of Derry, their ranks swollen with hundreds of local supporters, they were set upon by a mob of Protestant extremists. Reported the *Irish Times:*

> The major portion of the civil rights procession was cut off and left at the mercy of the attackers. A fusillade of stones and bottles was followed by the full weight of the attack against the young men and women who had pledged themselves to a policy of nonviolence. The attackers showed no mercy. Men were beaten senseless. Girls tore their way through the hedges screaming: "No! No!" Shouting, club-waving men pursued them. They were scattered screaming into the fields near the road. Some of those near the river were grabbed and thrown over the bridge to fall eight feet into icy, knee-deep water. Many were unable to leave the river because of men stoning them from each side.

This running the gauntlet was a turning point. It had a "radicalizing" effect both on the marchers and on many of their sympathizers. Bernadette Devlin recalled later that the students, once they were underway again, began to sing "We Shall Overcome," and then decided it was too tame, "so we resorted to the 'Internationale,' and it was never sung with more fervor than coming away from Burntollet Bridge. That was our strong point: we had faced the attack without fighting back, and we had come out of it singing."

Once the civil rightists reached Londonderry, a number of the policemen, whose protection of the marchers had been half-hearted at best, seemed to go berserk. Bogside residents were terrified as they rampaged through the streets, swinging their batons indiscriminately at everyone in sight. After this "police riot" the Bogsiders raised their barricades for the first time. Later in the year the Cameron Commission scored the "indiscipline and violence" of the police. "There was use of unnecessary and ill-controlled force in the dispersal of the demonstrators, only a minority of whom acted in a disorderly and violent manner."

From then on, civil order in Northern Ireland steadily deteriorated, and each demonstration, outbreak of violence and inflammatory speech had political consequences. Not only was there a contest of wills between the civil rights forces and the government, but the government had to contend with far-right extremists who demanded a crackdown on the demonstrators. Several militant Protestant organizations, organized and inspired by Ian Paisley and his second-in-command, Major Ronald Bunting, made it their business to disrupt civil rights gatherings and terrorize Catholics. Early in the year Paisley and Bunting were sentenced to three months in prison for unlawful assembly but their henchmen carried on.

Terence O'Neill's government was shaky. When his most powerful associates began bailing out he sought popular backing for civil rights reforms in a February general election but did not get it. In April, after yet another serious outbreak of fighting in Derry, he had to ask for British Army units to guard key public installations. Weary and discouraged, O'Neill resigned soon afterwards. Historians would probably give him good marks for making a start at curing Ulster's ills but, for the moment, many Protestants thought he had worsened things by "coddling the Catholics" while many Catholics said he had done little more than "whitewash the pigsty."

Major Chichester-Clark

"O'Neill must go!" the Paisleyites had cried, and now O'Neill had gone, but his successor was something of a carbon copy, and that at least insured that there would be no Unionist attempt to turn back the clock. Major James Dawson Chichester-Clark, 46, was another of Northern Ireland's old-landed family aristocrats: his South Derry seat in the Ulster Parliament had been occupied by his maternal grandmother and by his father and himself ever since it was created in 1921. Like O'Neill, Chichester-Clark went to Eton, served in the Irish Guards and was wounded in World War II. A tall, square-faced, humorless man of impressive military bearing, he had been, as Agriculture Minister, a quiet middleman in the O'Neill cabinet: less of an innovator or rabid Unionist than a pacifier and supporter of modest reforms. Although he said he favored the principle of one man, one vote, he took the view that the Catholics had to show more "responsibility" before they could have full rights. It was routine thinking for a moderate Unionist but the times were anything but routine. As premier, Chichester-Clark was hurtled along by events in a society teetering on the edge of civil war.

Still, he was able to enjoy two and a half months of relative calm after taking office. One of his first acts was to declare a general amnesty. He then promised the Catholics that there would be reforms in housing allocations and in the gerrymandered local government boundaries (Derry's elected council had already been replaced by a special governing commission). At the same time, of course, he assured Protestants that there would be no basic change in Ulster's power structure.

The civil rights campaigners were quieter for a time, largely because of a split between their own moderates and radicals. Summer, however, brought the annual Twelfth-of-July Protestant pageantry. "That's to scare the Catholics away," a Belfast youth explained to a reporter as the big Orange drums boomed in the streets. There were riots in Derry and in the capital, and Ulster braced itself for trouble. The new prime minister hardly improved matters by characterizing the civil rights people as "political streetwalkers" and a "lunatic minority."

Terror in the Streets

The real lunacy began when the government decided not to ban the August 12th parade of the Apprentice Boys of Derry, the super-loyalist association which annually celebrates the siege days of 1689. "It will never change," said one Bogside Catholic as he glumly watched the marching Protestants. "They're arrogant. Every year they push this in our faces and expect us to turn the other cheek."

An innocent visitor to Londonderry might think it incredible that such a tradition could survive in a predominantly Roman Catholic city, but the *Sunday Times* of London provided an explanation:

> The circumstances of the march, in which Protestants parade the walls of the old city looking down on the Catholic slums, amount to an insult against the Catholics. But that, naturally, is the point: the fact that they can insult their fellow-citizens with impunity is the tangible proof that they can survive as a political force.

The Apprentice Boys' march began at ten in the morning. Thousands of Protestants streamed about the city, their Orange banners and Union Jacks flying, their bands playing the usual bloodcurdling tunes, their cannons booming. Although some marchers contemptuously tossed pennies into the Catholic quarter there was no real trouble until mid-afternoon. Someone threw a stone. Soon there was a hail of rocks and bricks. The customary solution for any serious civil disturbance is for the police to drive the Catholics back into the Bogside and clear them off the streets. They began their work with enthusiasm but they were met by barricades and a swarm of Catholics hurling everything they could lay their hands on.

It was a critical moment for Protestant supremacy. Mary Holland of the London *Observer* was told by a cop, "We've got to beat them this time, Miss, or we're done for." When the police finally did break through the barricades and advanced some distance into the Bogside they were attacked with gasoline bombs thrown by youngsters from apartment house rooftops where the illegal flag of the Irish Republic was flying. In many ways it was a children's crusade: little boys and girls making milk-bottle Molotov cocktails for rooftop teenagers whose artillery backed up the youths and men at the front line. It was a standing joke that a housewife told her milkman, "No milk today, thanks; just leave ten bottles."

When the police resorted to tear gas (more precisely, CS gas, used in the Vietnam war) it marked the first time in the British Isles that such a means was employed against a civil disturbance. The Catholics struggled on in "Free Derry" through the night and into the next day and night. Their spirits were greatly lifted by some saber-rattling in Dublin which suggested that Irish troops might soon be at their side.

Both of Ireland's prime ministers were under excrutiating pressure. Jack Lynch had to respond to the demands of the hawks in Eire that something be done to help the beleaguered Catholics of Derry. He called for a United Nations peacekeeping force (and later for a joint British-Irish force) and announced that he was ordering field hospitals set up along the border near Londonderry and was calling up the 2,000 men of the first-line army reserves.

Although actual invasion by Irish troops was extremely remote, Lynch's statements helped convince many Northern Protestants that a conspiracy was at work to bring down Ulster. In Derry, where the police were stymied at the barricades, mobs of Protestant hooligans began to go after any Catholics they could reach, and they seemed to have the blessing of the police. With more than a hundred policemen and some 300 civilians already injured and the situation getting out of hand, Chichester-Clark made the momentous decision to ask for British soldiers. The Bogsiders claimed victory when they arrived, and in a way it was, for now Britain was inextricably involved in the hard business of putting Ulster's house in order.

The Battle of Londonderry set off far more serious violence in Belfast. The grimy Victorian working-class area just to the west of the city center became a savage battleground as the Protestants of the Shankill Road district and the Catholics of Falls

Road and adjoining streets massed against each other and threw up a maze of barricades. In this traditional cauldron of Ulster hatreds guns were used on a large scale for the first time, and not just pistols, rifles and shotguns, but automatic weapons and even machine guns mounted on armored vehicles. Most of the shooting was wild and indiscriminate, and much of it by trigger-happy B-Specials. In one of innumerable tragedies, the nine-year-old son of a Catholic shipyard worker was killed by a stray bullet while standing in his bedroom.

Looters, of course, were busy in the abandoned shops on streets strewn with rubble and broken glass. (Some weeks after the upheaval a shop on Shankill Road, advertising slightly soiled "looted carpets recovered by the R.U.C.," said in a P.S.: "Looters who still have our CARPETS should come in for their FREE FELTS.") The air was thick with the smoke of burning homes, schools and factories. Although both sides were to blame for the damage which reached air-raid proportions, it was obvious that the Catholics were primarily on the receiving end. Most of the barricades were around Catholic streets. Protestant mobs surged repeatedly into Catholic neighborhoods to drive people from their homes and burn down their mean dwellings. The Catholics accounted for most of the eight dead, the more than 500 injured, the hundreds left homeless, and the 5,000 who fled the city in fear of their lives. The government in late August said that more than 400 homes had been destroyed as well as fifteen factories and warehouses, and hundreds of small shops and pubs.

Once again, it was a situation beyond the control of the Ulster police, and the employment of the special force was a little like using gasoline to put out a fire. British troops were called to the rescue. In due course there would be 7,500 on the scene in Ulster. They set up and patrolled a barbed-wire police line more than a mile long between the combating neighborhoods. For the Catholics, the British soldiers were saviors, but the Protestant reaction was one of relief, confusion, frustration and anger. One housewife screamed that "We are not animals who need to be locked in, but they are, down there, the filthy scum, the Papists."

Friendly Persuasion

After those blazing days of August there were other riots and more deaths in Northern Ireland, but the British presence brought a general sense of security, and it bought time to put some changes in motion. Nothing happened fast enough to satisfy the more impatient of the civil rightists, and it would be some time before the Special Powers Act would go, but with London pulling the strings the prospects for a more democratic Northern Ireland were more favorable than ever before.

Significantly, the most immediate and emphatic change was in the police structure. The Royal Ulster Constabulary, which had been placed under the command of Sir Arthur Young, the highly respected Commissioner of the City of London police, was transformed into a wholly civil police force. It was relieved of all duties of a military nature and stripped of its extraordinary equipment. The policemen in their new blue uniforms would no longer carry firearms except in special circumstances. The Protestant B-Specials were replaced by a smaller non-sectarian militia, the Ulster Defense Regiment, which would function as a unit of the British Army. An effort was begun to attract Catholics to the force, but time would tell: calling it the *Ulster* Defense Regiment was a sure way to antagonize many Catholics.

To Ian Paisley, such changes amounted to "a complete and absolute sell-out to Republicans and the so-called civil rights movement." To the Bernadette Devlins of Northern Ireland, however, there could be no real feeling of satisfaction. Nothing truly fundamental had been changed. The same crowd was in charge and almost surely would be for years to come. The economic system was the same as ever. The unemployment rate was still the highest in the United Kingdom and the pay the lowest. Catholics and Protestants still sent their children to separate schools and lived in deep suspicion of each other.

Yet, in such a strange society, it is well to keep things in perspective and to be grateful for small favors. It had been a murderous time, all right, but the riots of 1968–69 did not, all told, come anywhere close to the death toll and property damage of the racial outbursts in such places as Newark and Detroit in 1967. By American standards the violence in Ulster is modest in the worst of times and ridiculously low in normal times. Northern Ireland's ordinary crime rate, in fact, is the lowest in the United Kingdom. One can appreciate why Prime Minister Chichester-Clark says that "Ulster people are fed up to the teeth with being caricatured as a nation of idle and bigoted hooligans." Even during the darkest days of the civil rights campaign the greater part of the country was at peace. Traffic moved, stores opened, factories produced and normal life went on. Most striking of all was the way middle-class Protestants and Catholics in the Belfast suburbs formed joint neighborhood patrols to keep away troublemakers. It is in such behavior, as in the non-sectarian character of the civil rights movement, that one can find clues to the kind of Ulster which might yet emerge, given great good luck and a more wholesome and compassionate Christianity.

What happens in Northern Ireland depends greatly, however, on what happens in southern Ireland. Given the inbred, not-an-inch mentality of the average Ulsterman, I would even say that it depends *primarily* on the good sense and sensitivity of the Irish in the Republic.

It is difficult to imagine any real lessening of the traditional religious tensions in Ulster or any shift to conventional left-right politics so long as the Ulsterman remains convinced that the Catholics within and without the province mean to destroy his hard-won society.

It is easy, however, to imagine such things and even greater changes if the Ulsterman should ever lose his sense of insecurity and then discover that Eire is not such a bad place after all. One of the most salutary consequences of the recent troubles in

Ulster is the heightened sense of reality in the Republic about the North-South relationship. Irishmen thought it neither wise nor desirable to go charging into Ulster with guns blazing, and, on the whole, the Dublin politicians kept their cool. Ernest Blythe, one of the most prominent northerners in the Republic, saw signs that, happily, "official policy in the South will be little influenced in future by the old coercive ideas which have heretofore been so widely prevalent in Nationalist circles."

Before long, not only will Southern bombers and saboteurs, if specimens of such types still linger on, be left without support or sympathy, but so also will all those who entertain old-fashioned notions of forcing the Northern majority into union with the South by means of economic or even military pressure, native or foreign. In future, reliance will be sanely placed on persuasion, on personal and official good relations, and on readiness to operate what must, in the first place, be loose and flexible arrangements for common action, arrangements free from even implied threats of compulsion.

In short, Make Love, Not War. With wooing in mind, some leading Irishmen suggest that it is up to the Republic to make itself more attractive to the northerners, otherwise why should they even consider more intimate relations someday? They stress that there are a number of civil rights and social justice matters which need cleaning up in the Republic as well as in the North. It has suddenly become fashionable to propose ways and means to make the Republic look less like a place where the bishops tell the politicians what to do. Powerful voices, from the Prime Minister to Cardinal Conway, have spoken out in support of a proposal to remove by referendum that part of the Constitution ("The State recognizes the special position of the Holy Catholic Apostolic and Roman Church . . .") which seems to give Roman Catholics special privileges. The debate touches as well on everything from restrictions on divorce and contraceptives to censorship and the heavy role of the Church in education.

There will surely be more talk than action but at least the direction is clear. In both ends of Ireland the curtain is coming down on a long half century of futile feuding. The debris of Irish history is slowly being swept away. Though there will never be an end to the arguments of the Irish and their automatic allegiance to My Side or Your Side, the time may come when it is popular to speak up for the third side: the Hell with it!

EPILOGUE

In Bernard Shaw's play *John Bull's Other Island*, an embittered Irishman named Doyle exclaims:

> Oh, the dreaming! The dreaming! the torturing, heart-scalding, never satisfying dreaming, dreaming, dreaming! No debauchery that ever coarsened and brutalized an Englishman can take the worth and usefulness out of him like that dreaming. An Irishman's imagination never lets him alone, never convinces him, never satisfies him; but it makes him that he can't face reality nor deal with it nor handle it nor conquer it: he can only sneer at them that do, and be 'agreeable to strangers,' like a good-for-nothing woman on the streets.

And Patrick Pearse, the schoolteacher-revolutionary, wrote before the 1916 uprising and his own martyrdom:

> What if the dream comes true? and if
>   millions unborn shall dwell
> In the house that I shaped in my heart,
>   the noble house of my thoughts.

Dreams are what "modern" Ireland has been made of, but if there is any single new characteristic of the Irish Republic today it is the rude air of realism. Anyone who troubles to go through the country and talk to Irish men and women in every sphere of life finds that their thoughts are about money, medicine, work, housing, schools, and a myriad of other practical matters. I suspect that this has always been so for the majority of people, however dreamingly they may have behaved, but they were persuaded to sacrifice their personal requirements for seemingly nobler causes. Now they are less interested in reviving the ancient language or in winning back "the lost six counties" than they are in the reasons why the Republic does not enjoy the same high living standards and welfare services as Northern Ireland. In their more exasperated moments some even question the wisdom of independence itself and admit what is patently true: that, economically at least, Ireland is still very much an appendage of Great Britain. In a conversation I had in Dublin just before writing this book, one of the most important of the new Irish leaders asserted that Home Rule, or self-government within a British framework, would have been the better choice for Ireland. Prolonged exposure to the Irish had made me just native enough to bridle at the very idea, but I was impressed that he was willing to say it. The romantics are going, I thought, and the realists are taking over.

In an *Irish Times* article Dr. Conor Cruise O'Brien said, "The greatest tragedy about the creation of a State on the basis of ideals impossible to attain was the release sought through national fantasy." He spoke of the Republic's desperate game of "let's pretend" which makes Irish the first official language and declares in the Constitution that the national territory consists of the whole island and its territorial seas. "Much of what went wrong was inevitable, like the division of the country. For the rest we are all responsible, in the degree to which we cooperated in nonsense, or failed to expose it, or quietly acquiesced in the injustice being systematically practised against the children of the poor in Ireland."

At last complacency is going. The Irish are facing up to the fact that they have not done well as a free society, or at least not until lately. One scholar told me with emotion, "We have a lot to be ashamed of. We've emphasized the wrong things and neglected the rest. There is a lack of real culture; even our theater is third-rate. There is an unfeeling relationship between teachers and students. We are so content with the mediocre! We have a desperate need to know the harsh truths about ourselves. It is time we judged ourselves by the standards of modern Europe." While the desire for national self-improvement is widespread, the changes which are taking place are more a reaction to external influences than the result of an inner-directed movement toward an agreed-upon national goal. There is a dearth of leadership bold enough or imaginative and persuasive enough to hold out to the Irish public an inspiring vision of the Ireland-that-ought-to-be. As one old revolutionary, S. P. Irwin, said, "We are plagued with the dead hand of a reactionary establishment, and sadly need a goal, a common elevating national purpose spurred by a real patriotism."

Still, for anyone who cares about the Irish, the ferment and the yearning these days make Ireland a quietly exciting country. It is also a lucky country. To say so is to fly in the face of the popular conviction that "this damp place impaled on a corner of the universe" has too many natural handicaps to be a really successful community. But little Iceland, with only a third of Dublin's population, is still more distantly placed in the North Atlantic and lacks practically everything but fish and hot springs, yet it is one of the world's dozen most prosperous nations. Ireland is temperate, beautiful, uncrowded and unscarred by industrial excesses. "Fly away from the hurly-burly," its advertisements say. "Ireland is peaceful." The country's agricultural potential has scarcely been met. An Irish cow still gives only half the milk of cows in other dairy lands, and Irishmen have hardly begun to farm their own surrounding seas. The absurdity and the waste of duplicate governments and economies on a single small island need only common sense and statecraft to repair them.

Coming late to the business of building a modern society, the Irish can profit from the successes and the mistakes of other nations. Ireland need not become just another ulcer-ridden, smogbound steel-and-concrete jungle. It still has time to preserve its natural advantages and its abundance of space and quiet to make a more human existence for human beings. What is encouraging is that the Irish want to be up to date, but want to be themselves as well. For the life of them they will not be West Britons, East Americans, Catholic Swedes, or anyone else. They want their *Irishness*, that ineffable something, and the ambiance of what Yeats described as "this horse-riding, salmon-fishing, cattle-raising country." The Irish one day may have their own shamrock-green spaceships, but they will still remain unmistakably, unforgettably Irish.

ACKNOWLEDGMENTS

Although I have tried to do more than just set down some facts about the Irish, this is essentially a reporter's book, and that means I am indebted to a multitude of people who supplied information, opened doors for me, sat still for questions and spoke their minds most liberally. I do not think reporting in Ireland is quite like reporting in any other country, although Finland, which has its own kind of craziness, comes close. In both nations the danger of making afternoon appointments is that a one-hour lunch may go on for three hours, or until midnight. It is all so pleasant that it is a wonder a book like this ever gets written. Not everyone wants to have his opinions identified in print—"Mind you, I've said nothing!" is an old Irish expression—but just about everyone is willing to meet and talk, and then talk some more. On the rare occasions when an interview proves difficult to arrange, one can always seek out the man in his favorite drinking place. Just by drifting along with the easy flow of Irish life it is possible to informally encounter, sooner or later, everyone who counts. I first met President de Valera in prison. (Specifically, during a ceremony in Kilmainham Jail, where the rebel leaders of 1916 had been executed.) Numerous people were kind enough to give me hours of their time in their offices or homes, but many others I have quoted were never formally interviewed—we just kept meeting in pubs and restaurants or at poetry recitals and after-theater parties. Ireland is like that.

To everyone thus encountered everywhere in Ireland, I am grateful beyond measure. It is impossible to set down all the names, but I should mention several persons who were unduly imposed upon. In Dublin, the veteran Cathal O'Shannon and young Cathal and Patsy Dyke O'Shannon, Ulick O'Connor, Seaghan O'Briain of the Irish Tourist Board, such able government information officers as Charles Whelan, Patrick O'Hanrahan and Martin Sheridan, Basil Clancy of *Hibernia*, Nicholas Leonard of *Business & Finance*, and Caroline Mitchell and Geraldine Ryan, the editors of *Woman's Way*, which I found valuable for its excellent columns on social conditions. At Shannon, Maeve Fitzgibbon and Vincent Tobin. In London, Andrew O'Rourke, First Secretary of the Irish Embassy and Thomas M. Roberts, Chief Information Officer of the Ulster office. My admiration for Sean O'Faolain is evident in this book, and I am grateful for his permission to quote liberally from several of his works. When I asked him if I might use in my introduction his comment about the value of writing a "raging satire" on the Irish, he reminded me that he had never been able to do it. As he explained in his foreword to *The Finest Stories of Sean O'Faolain*, he still has much too soft a corner for the old land. "Some day I may manage to dislike my countrymen sufficiently to satirize them; but I gravely doubt it—curse them!"

I owe much to a number of individual journalists and to such outstanding newspapers as the *Irish Independent* and the *Belfast Telegraph*, but I must say a special word about the *Irish Times*. When one prominent Irishman said to me, "I cannot bear thinking what this country would be like without the *Irish Times*," he was only echoing what I had heard said by at least a dozen other persons. For decades it has been the intelligent and articulate, and often lonely and courageous, voice of Ireland's liberal conscience. It has consistently published information and opinions about some of the most sensitive social, political and religious subjects peculiar to Ireland—material which otherwise might never have seen the light of day. Its concern for Irish education and culture has enhanced the intellectual tone of the Republic. In recent years its social surveys and its sober reporting of Northern Irish affairs have been so illuminating and invaluable that it is possible to assert that, in terms of constructive impact on its particular community of readers, the *Irish Times* is the most influential newspaper in the British Isles. For an outside observer seeking knowledge of contemporary Ireland, it is absolutely indispensable. Douglas Gageby is the editor. The news editor is Donal Foley, and I have mentioned in the course of this book a few, but only a few, of the fine reporters and columnists. I am indebted to them all.

INDEX

311